Jill Hedges is Deputy Director and Senior Analyst for Latin America at Oxford Analytica and was formerly Editorial Manager of business information service Esmerk Argentina. She has a PhD in Latin American Studies from the University of Liverpool and is the author of *Argentina: A Modern History* (I.B.Tauris, 2015).

The myths surrounding Peronism continue to generate misunderstanding about Argentina in the rest of the world. Perhaps the worst of all misconceptions about that complex political phenomenon is the don't-cry-for-me-Argentina vision of Eva Perón that has been so superficially and unfairly implanted in the public's mind by popular culture. Now comes a carefully researched and elegantly written biography by Jill Hedges to separate myth from reality and to help all of us understand Evita more profoundly, as a product of circumstances as well as a tragic but inspiring force for social justice. Jill Hedges does not only demystify and demythologise the iconic personality of Evita; she lays down the facts and she analyses them with keen observation and the emotional detachment necessary to all rigorous social science enterprises. But she also adds to our comprehension of Evita's triumphs as well as defects with a woman's sensibility and empathy. Time has softened the hatred that Evita's enemies in Argentina spewed against her even long after her death. Most Argentines now either love Evita's memory or respect her for her many accomplishments. And yet the caricature of Evita (and that of Peronism) lingers on outside of Argentina. This book will go a long way to dissipate mischaracterisations and lightweight analysis; we can now proceed with our different and reasonable interpretations of history, but we cannot ignore the facts of Evita's life and legacy.

Juan E. Mendez, Professor of Human Rights Law in Residence,
Washington College of Law

Eva Perón's meteoric rise from provincial actress to the most powerful woman in Latin American politics is a story well worth telling. Loved and hated in equal measure, her image and legacy endures to this day, and credit must be given for her considerable achievements in the areas of social policy and women's rights. Jill Hedges has written a sympathetic, remarkably even-handed, and highly readable biography of Eva Perón that cuts through the many myths that surround her life, and adds much to our understanding both of the person and the political phenomenon that became "Evita".

Maxine Molyneux, Professor of Sociology,
UCL Institute of the Americas

This vivid new biography of Evita Perón (arguably the most prominent woman in politics in the mid-twentieth century) is well informed, thoughtful, and perceptive. Jill Hedges portrays both the light and the shade of Evita's spectacular, but brief – and in many ways tragic – life. This is an exercise that includes judiciously sorting through much of the salacious gossip provoked by the spectacular rise of an impoverished young actress. Along the way the study illuminates many fascinating aspects of Argentine social history. Much more accurate than the musical, the true story is almost as gripping.

Laurence Whitehead, Senior Research Fellow,
Nuffield College, Oxford

EVITA

The Life of Eva Perón

JILL HEDGES

I.B. TAURIS
LONDON • NEW YORK • OXFORD • NEW DELHI • SYDNEY

I.B. TAURIS
Bloomsbury Publishing Plc
50 Bedford Square, London, WC1B 3DP, UK
1385 Broadway, New York, NY 10018, USA

BLOOMSBURY, I.B. TAURIS and the I.B. Tauris
logo are trademarks of Bloomsbury Publishing Plc

First published in Great Britain by I. B. Tauris & Co. Ltd in 2016
This edition published in Great Britain by I.B. Tauris in 2021
Reprinted 2021

Cover design by Alice Marwick
Cover image: Eva Perón (1919–52), photographed in 1949.
(© ullstein bild/ullstein bild via Getty Images)

A catalogue record for this book is available from the British Library.

A catalogue record for this book is available from the Library of Congress.

ISBN: HB: 978-1-7845-3327-4
PB: 978-0-7556-0290-2
ePDF: 978-1-7867-3023-7
eBook: 978-1-7867-2023-8

Typeset in Century Old Style Std
Printed and bound in Great Britain

To find out more about our authors and books visit
www.bloomsbury.com and sign up for our newsletters.

For Andrés, with love

 CONTENTS

 LIST OF ILLUSTRATIONS

 PREFACE

*No me llores perdida ni
lejana,
Yo soy parte esencial de tu
existencia.
Todo dolor y amor me fue
previsto.
Cumplí mi humilde
imitación de Cristo.
Quien anduvo en mi senda
que la siga.
Sus discípulos.*

*[Don't weep for me lost or
distant,
I am an essential part of
your existence.
All pain and love was
planned for me.
I fulfilled my humble
imitation of Christ.
Let whoever walked in my
path follow it.
Your disciples.]*

(From a plaque on Evita's tomb)

THE STORY OF Eva Perón is arguably the story of how an ordinary person is capable of extraordinary things. A smart but uncultured woman of 26 when her husband, Juan Domingo Perón, was elected president in 1946, she had little knowledge of or patience with the niceties of diplomacy and ceremony. However, she transformed the role of first lady from a ceremonial one to an activist, powerful one. The way she wielded that power was often arbitrary and provided genuine arguments for critics who decried the fact that an immature, impetuous, often capricious young woman should have untrammelled authority over vast resources and political structures. As her confessor, the Jesuit Hernán Benítez, would later observe, she was responsible for great successes and great errors, some of which might be forgiven in light of her age and inexperience.

Eva María Ibarguren/Duarte, who later metamorphosed into Eva Duarte, María Eva Duarte de Perón, Eva Perón and finally Evita – the affectionate, familiar diminutive of her name that would be universally used by her supporters – did not set out to become what she became when she left Junín for Buenos Aires at the age of 15. However, she not only recognised an opportunity when she saw it, and seized it whenever possible, but she also recognised, or thought she recognised, obligations which she was equally quick to accept. Believing her marriage to Juan Domingo Perón to be not only a personal blessing but a kind of discipleship, she felt it her duty both to transmit to others what she had learned from him, and also to carry out what she believed at least to be his doctrine and his social policy – which would eventually be seen above all as *her* social policy, for good or bad.

Although opponents would claim that Evita merely used the poor or ministered to them because she confused them with herself, there is no doubt that she identified with the poor because she, as she often said, was one of them. However, arguably her great value was that she was never resigned to her fate or that of others, convinced that force of will and political purpose could change it. Despite her observation in her ghostwritten autobiography *La razón de mi vida* that she was 'resigned' to being a victim, in fact she was never resigned to anything, and she was determined that her *descamisados* ('shirtless ones') should not be resigned either.

The fact that a young and volatile woman with no elected office wielded so much untrammelled power, with no limits except those imposed by an indulgent husband who had little interest in curbing activities that brought him political benefits, underscored the legitimate arguments of the opposition that this was not the way to run a country.

However, it is difficult to doubt her idealism, or the idealism of many who have been inspired by her even decades after her death – inspired, like her, to great successes and great errors, some of them bloody. But her insistence that people (notably those in power) had to be responsible for others to improve the lives of everyone has remained resonant, as has the fact that she, without being a feminist, played an enormous role in bringing women into the public sphere as socially responsible actors. Her image as a powerful and committed woman has not been superseded in Argentina; she remains an icon.

Despite the fact that Peronism and Eva herself have been decried as essentially fascist, and both she and her movement had a strong element of authoritarianism, the right is arguably the sector for which Eva has had the least appeal. The Argentine right is inherently conservative, which, in most respects, Eva emphatically was not. Although she preserved a traditionalist valuation of husband, home and hearth, she in no way observed most conventions, had no time for 'good' behaviour and did what she believed she had to do, whether it was appropriate for a woman or not.

While Eva was not a feminist in any normal sense, crediting her husband with granting her (and by extension her people) dignity, she had a resonance for women of her time that the previous feminist movement had lacked. Feminism in Argentina (and elsewhere) had been largely an upper-class, intellectual preserve which paid little attention to the specific woes of working-class women – who in turn had little truck with its proponents or its concepts, however worthy. Eva was a more accessible icon for the working woman, and a suitable one for an image-conscious country like Argentina, young, beautiful and glamorously dressed. However, her constant willingness to subordinate her role to that of her husband, whom she honestly loved and honoured, is difficult to square with a more 'mainstream' feminist line that might have demanded a more independent role. Yet, while she held to a 'traditional' view of the woman's place, she went far beyond it and pushed other women to do the same, sending young women out to organise the Peronist Women's Party across the country, opening nursing schools and pushing some of her early recruits into the first candidate lists to include women, letting them enter elected office for the first time in 1951.

Perón's distinguished biographer Joseph Page defined Evita as:

> a poor, uneducated, instinctive, emotionally volatile woman who put up a valiant struggle against class and gender bias; was artfully manipulated by her husband; yet grew into a political role she performed memorably within the limits of her capabilities and the space allotted to her.[1]

This is a fair and accurate assessment, yet it falls short of explaining her contemporary emotional impact (engendering both passionate love and passionate hatred) and her remarkable post-mortem longevity as a symbol that continues to fascinate and inspire.

 INTRODUCTION

The Personal is Political

I N THE EARLY nineteenth century, the practice of holding a '*Cabildo Abierto*' (literally an 'open council') in Argentina led to a number of key decisions in the independence process. In 1810, a *Cabildo Abierto* held under the slogan '*el pueblo quiere saber de qué se trata*' ('the people want to know what is going on') led to the 25 May revolution that launched the struggle for independence from Spain.

The *Cabildo Abierto* convened in Buenos Aires on 22 August 1951, which consciously harked back to such momentous historical undertakings, was designed to proclaim the candidacy of President Juan Domingo Perón for a second term, from 1952–58, as the candidate of the Peronist Party. All necessary steps were taken to ensure that it would be an historic moment. Hundreds of buses and trains were furnished to bring the Peronist faithful from all over the country, businesses were closed to allow for their attendance, temporary shelter was arranged in car parks and parks across the city of Buenos Aires to accommodate those who could not be housed in overflowing hotels and hostels, and food and entertainment were organised for the participants. A giant stage was set up near the obelisk on the vast Avenida 9 de Julio (the widest avenue in the world), in front of the Public Works Ministry (a building which now features ten-story-high images of Eva Perón on two sides). The organisation proved highly efficient and successful, with estimates of as many as 2 million supporters in attendance on the day in one of the country's largest-ever mass rallies.

However, a major complicating factor intruded. Popular enthusiasm for Eva Perón as the vice-presidential candidate to accompany her husband in a Perón–Perón ticket was overflowing, and the *Cabildo Abierto* was dominated by a huge banner proclaiming 'Perón–Eva Perón, the ticket of the

Fatherland'. Despite huge popular fervour surrounding the candidacy, at least three factors militated against: the resistance of the Catholic Church; the absolute rejection of the armed forces (at least one of the reasons for Perón's own apparent opposition); and the uterine cancer that Evita and those around her had sought to disregard.

Evita's arrival served only to raise the crowd's fervour still further. Looking uncertain, she launched into a speech both evasive and equivocal, pressing home her familiar message – that Perón was the hero and the saviour of the downtrodden.

Her words, however, did nothing to weaken the determination of the hundreds of thousands of her supporters gathered in 9 de Julio, the faces of women and workers, the elderly, illuminated with the thought that she would be vice-president, serving together with Perón. The contention that such demonstrations were purely staged and the affection of the people false and coerced is contradicted by many of the faces in the crowd, transfigured by the thought that they would bring Evita – a woman, an illegitimate and impoverished child from the 'interior', one of their own – to the vice-presidency. They refused to accept her prevarications and her pleas, demanding her acceptance and threatening a general strike. Finally, Evita was heard to say 'I will do what the people say.'

The generalised belief, reflected in the next day's headlines, that Evita would be a candidate, was finally put to rest on 31 August (thereafter known as Renunciation Day), when her 'renunciation' was broadcast on national radio, expressing her 'irrevocable decision to renounce the honour that the workers and the people of my country wanted to confer upon me at the historic *Cabildo Abierto* of 22 August', a decision she called

> totally free and with all the force of my definitive will ... I have ... a single and great personal ambition: that when that marvellous chapter of history that will surely be dedicated to Perón is written, that it says that there was a woman at Perón's side who dedicated herself to bringing to the president the hopes of the people and that the people affectionately called that woman Evita.[1]

* * * * *

Just seven years before the *Cabildo Abierto*, Eva Duarte had been only a reasonably well-known radio actress also known in some circles to be the mistress of Colonel Juan Domingo Perón, vice-president, war minister and, most crucially, secretary of labour in the military government that had taken office in June 1943. Even at the time of his election to the presidency, on 24 February 1946, Eva (who became his wife in October 1945) still had only a relatively limited public role, arousing curiosity among Peronist supporters and contempt among the oligarchic opposition, who considered her an opportunist and, worse, a bastard child, a vulgar former actress and (so they whispered) a prostitute who had used her wiles to take advantage of a string of powerful men. On the whole, not an apparently propitious basis for the first lady to become, in a short space of time, the second most powerful political figure in the country and the most powerful woman in the world at the time – the lady of hope and the standard-bearer of the *descamisados*, as she was known in official propaganda.

In fact, however, Evita would become the logical icon and representative of the Peronist base – the workers, the poor, the dispossessed, whom she credited Perón with lifting to a new level of dignity and empowerment. Symbolically, her own roots were politically potent – an illegitimate child, brought up in poverty, who found fame through hard work and struggle and found love in the man described as 'Argentina's first worker'. But more important was her genuineness and sincerity, coupled with identification with those who remained behind: a beautiful and wealthy young woman, she never forgot her roots and dedicated extraordinary energy and efforts to helping her *descamisados*, with whom she acknowledged a 'sacred debt' that she never felt able to repay. 'Eva's social passion was composed of both an authentic sensibility and narcissism'[2] – an irresistible combination.

That sacred debt, beyond any doubt, sprang from the events of 17 October 1945, described extensively elsewhere and in more detail in Chapter 6. Perón's temporary ouster from power prompted hundreds of thousands of workers to converge on the scandalised capital on 17 October, concentrating in the Plaza de Mayo in front of the Casa Rosada (Government House) to demand Perón's return. The government was forced to capitulate, reinstating Perón to all posts and calling elections for the following February, easily won by the briefly ousted colonel.

Evita was an insecure woman, whose entire life until that point had been one of insecurity and extreme precariousness. With no father and no protector, she grew up depending on her mother's income as a seamstress to avoid hunger; as an actress she suffered long periods of unemployment and uncertain income. Her relationship with Perón and her increasing success as a radio actress had given her the first emotional and financial security she had known, and with his arrest and uncertain prospects even that security had been threatened. The actions of those who marched on 17 October saved Perón and, by extension, Evita and her *descamisados*. It was a debt she never forgot. Nor did she fail to understand the insecurity and precariousness faced by those *descamisados*, always one wage packet or one illness away from deprivation.

As first lady, Evita pursued a course far different from those of the retiring and upper-class women who had occupied the post until then, attracting both fervent loyalty from the poor and boundless contempt from much of middle- and upper-class society, which poured scorn on the unconventional origins and supposed moral turpitude of 'that woman' who had ideas above her station and appeared to be at least the equal of her husband in political power.

Saving the vast differences in their origins, the most obvious previous example was that of Eleanor Roosevelt, whose political commitment to the underprivileged, activist public role and apparent desire for political power had generated widespread criticism and even hatred a decade earlier. (Eleanor Roosevelt, from one of the most prominent families in the United States, was far removed from Eva's deprived origins although she was attracted early to social activism. However, she also suffered numerous tragedies, losing her parents and a brother when young and an infant son after her marriage, which may have contributed to her sensitivity on humanitarian issues.) While Eleanor was derided for her awkwardness and unattractiveness, Evita was sneered at for her 'glamour' and ostentation. Nevertheless, both women, having little example to guide them, were forced to learn and to make their mistakes in public from a highly visible position. Eva learned quickly and the mistakes she made, at least in her own political terms, were quickly overcome and not repeated.

John Nance Garner, Franklin Roosevelt's first vice-president, reputedly defined the office of vice-president of the United States as 'not worth a bucket of warm spit' (or words to that effect); the vice-presidency of Argentina is arguably worth even less. Why, then, would Evita, whose power was not limited by any such institution, have desired such a position? Some argued that she did not, saying that she had flatly rejected the proposal of the General Confederation of Labour (Confederación General del Trabajo, CGT) that she stand, or that, given the extent of her power, 'the vice-presidency was too small for Evita'.[3] Others argue that she herself had orchestrated the move and saw it as the culmination of her meteoric career, an institutional recognition of her position. The short answer, indeed, is that she must have wanted it, or at least the offer, whether as recognition or political leverage: she was the president of the Women's Peronist Party and a driving force behind the CGT, and the two organisations would not have pushed her candidacy without her backing. Her inability to accept was one of her few political defeats.

Certainly there can be little doubt that the symbolic value of the post meant a great deal to Eva's followers, who in some measure would also have been lifted by the designation – she would have been both the first person of such humble origin and the first woman to hold such a post. Women had only received the vote in 1947 – an event largely and somewhat unfairly credited to Evita – and the elections of 1951 were to be their first opportunity to exercise that right.

Moreover, Evita was the undisputed defender of the poor and defenceless at the centre of power, and the officialisation of her position in government would have had had at least symbolic significance in that respect. Through the Eva Perón Foundation, she met and personally helped literally thousands of individuals, offered hope to hundreds of thousands more by extension and, in more concrete terms, oversaw the construction of hundreds of schools, hospitals, working women's residences and nursing schools. Her own personal experience, as someone who could expect little help from institutions or authorities and was forced to rely on family networks and other personal relationships to survive and prosper, led her to understand the importance of this personal element and the role of protector (to whom loyalty is owed in exchange for protection) very well. As Zanatta has noted, she came from 'a society in which individuals often lacked protection or rights, but which was endowed with strong and vast social forces'[4].

The downside to this remarkable record was the contribution it made to the concept of working outside of institutions, often through coercion, and with disdain for the law, as well as to the exclusion of those branded as 'anti'. This arbitrary and partisan exercise of power gave weight to opposition criticisms, although these were often based primarily on far more questionable issues such as her sexual history and supposedly unfeminine thirst for power. Nevertheless, the opposition to Evita had very real reasons for objecting to her arbitrary and polarising methods of exercising power, and for rejecting the increasingly heavy-handed government efforts to impose Perón and Evita as the undisputed saviours and rulers of Argentina. These included the imposition of her autobiography as obligatory reading in schools and other early reading lessons designed for indoctrination rather than pedagogy ('Evita loves me. Mama is good. Mama is beautiful. Evita is good and beautiful. Viva Mama! Viva Evita!' 'My little sister and I love mama, papa, Perón and Evita.'[5])

In addition to her glamour, her charisma and the unique personal touch she brought to Peronism, however, Evita was a political leader in her own right. Perón often claimed that she was his creation, and in some respects he was right: a woman of little formal education and no previous political activism, Evita learned the fundamentals of politics and leadership from her husband. However, her talent, her energy and her tenacity were her own. Perón as a political figure and Peronism could have existed without Eva (albeit with differences in content and style); indeed, he was well on his way to becoming president before she became a public figure, and her political role only took shape after the 1946 elections. By contrast, in her time, Evita could not have existed as a political leader without Perón, who, unusually for a man of his time (and a military man at that), gave his wife great freedom and scope to take on that role.

Within less than a year of the *Cabildo Abierto*, Eva Perón was dead at the age of 33, killed by the cancer that was already advanced at the time of her 'renunciation'. Her tragic early death did not create her legend or her wild popularity, which was already more than evident in 1951 and earlier. Like Carlos Gardel, the great tango singer and popular idol whose untimely death in a plane crash in 1935 launched a wave of popular grief (and a massive funeral unparalleled until that of Eva nearly two decades later), her place in history was already secure. However, in both cases, early death may have helped to cement them as the personification of a period considered a 'golden age' by many – the 1920s, in the case of Gardel; the 1940s, the period of Peronist largesse and promise, in the case of Evita. Moreover, both were saved from the inevitable decline that would have come with age and over-exposure. It is said of Gardel that 'he sings better every day'. In Eva's case, even her charisma, beauty, political intelligence and the genuine popular adulation of her could not have sustained her position indefinitely as the political and economic climate deteriorated, and even her astonishing energy could not have sustained the rhythm of work that she maintained against all odds for several years before her death.

Much of the myth surrounding Evita – notably the contrasting 'black myth' of the opposition and the mirror-image 'white myth' constructed by the Peronists – tends to obscure the realities of a remarkable career and a life that was both inspiring and polarising, and a person far more interesting than the stereotypes created. As J. M. Taylor has rightly noted,[6] much of the quasi-religious aura conferred on 'Santa Evita' after her death was the product of the government propaganda machine (and elements of the government and party hoping to curry favour and gain influence) rather than the belief of her fanatical supporters that it was purported to be. Like Eva herself, most of her supporters were culturally Catholic, if not necessarily fervently devout or well versed in Church dogma. Their attitude towards Evita was closer to that of a family relationship rather than a belief in her sainthood – in other words, the presence of her photo in many working-class homes and the candles lit before it did not reflect a superstitious notion of her divinity, but the fact that similar candles were often lit before similar photos of dead loved ones, both to demonstrate that they were remembered and because of the perception that those already in heaven might help to intercede to seek protection for those still on earth. Evita had protected her *descamisados* when alive and might be expected to continue to do so in an abstract way.

The contrast to this vision, the 'black myth', held by the upper and a significant part of the middle classes, defined Eva as wholly evil, a debased woman driven by power and revenge who dominated both those around her and the masses through a sexual hold.

Despite the evident justification for disquiet among many non-Peronists over the drift of the government and the eventual mythic status of Evita, the other obvious characteristic of the narrative constructed following her death – whether the 'white' or 'black' myth – was its extremely *machista* nature. The notion of either the pure and suffering mother or the promiscuous and scheming whore was entirely in line with *machista* stereotypes of women and what their role should be (and it should be noted that women were frequently at least as *machista* in their views as men). It is hardly necessary to note that neither Evita nor anyone else fitted comfortably into these one-dimensional stereotypes. The reality – even allowing for the fact that it can be interpreted in line with the eye of the beholder – is far more complex, and more interesting. Eva was an exceptional character, with exceptional virtues and defects, both an example of what an individual is capable of, and a warning of the risks of almost uncontrolled personal power.

While many criticisms of Evita and of the Peronist government more generally are valid and well-founded, the persistent perception (reinforced by a string of sensationalist biographies) of Eva as nothing more than a cynical, mendacious and power-crazed woman at the front of a fascist regime is one-dimensional and unfair. Indeed, this version has tended to portray her millions of admirers as ignorant dupes mindlessly following a false prophet or shiftless vagrants offering devotion in return for handouts. This is an insulting and untruthful vision that denigrates both Evita and a large segment of the Argentine population and popular culture, more willing to trust in personal relationships (even when clientelistic) than inefficient and corrupt institutions with a poor record of serving the underprivileged. On the contrary, offsetting her defects, one of Evita's great values was her ability to generate affection and loyalty among ordinary people who never forgot her, and who admired her in practical and personal ways rather than as a semi-deity (or even a political 'maximum leader').

Evita was right in believing that she would endure. Indeed, her image remains ubiquitous – on the 100-peso note, on the Public Works building, in a statue outside the National Library where the presidential residence formerly stood. However, her life and legacy are currently somewhat easier to revisit, given a fall in the degree of controversy surrounding her. Her private life is no longer a focus of attention (although she may have become, for many, increasingly a figure on a T-shirt, like Che Guevara, rather than what she originally stood for). The Evita Museum in Buenos Aires now has a research centre and offers seminars and courses on Evita's political legacy. Nevertheless, the greater focus on her political image does not mean that that image is no longer co-opted for others' political ends. For example, Evita's image – either smiling or combative, depending on the context – was constantly used as a background to former President Cristina Fernandez de Kirchner's speeches.

There is almost unlimited public material on the brief life and career of Eva Perón, in the form of endless newspaper coverage (both hagiographic and slanderous), photos, newsreel footage, published speeches, lectures and (ghostwritten) memoirs, and a vast array of books, articles and memoirs of those who knew or purported to know her. However, the primary material that might throw new light on her private life is relatively scant. Official documents relating to the early life of poor people are few and not carefully maintained; those recording the births, marriages and deaths of average fellow citizens of Chivilcoy or Los Toldos would not have felt it necessary to preserve them zealously as documents of future historical importance. Some documents were deliberately destroyed by Eva and her family themselves during her lifetime in a bid to conceal her illegitimacy. Poor people write few letters to friends and relatives; if Eva and her family in Junín corresponded during her years as an actress in Buenos Aires, as seems probable, those letters have not survived or have, understandably, been kept private by a family plagued for decades by public attention (often highly negative and unwanted). The post-1955 dictatorship (the 'Liberating Revolution'), took extraordinary pains to try to eliminate any record of her (and Peronism's) existence, destroying documents, records, photos and souvenirs of the Perón government – even the presidential residence. Moreover, Eva's public career and her reign at the Eva Perón Foundation were famously improvised, non-institutional and marked by verbal orders rather than written communications. As a result, different sources often present entirely contradictory versions of the same events, all of them set out as incontrovertible truth. Nevertheless, much can be pieced together from the records that remain, including those that deliberately distort or conceal facts, while different versions of events may dispute names and dates but their significance remains largely the same.

Despite having died at only 33 (astonishing considering the amount she crammed into that short life), Eva Perón had a long-lasting impact perhaps second to no one else in Argentine history. Although that impact has both positive and negative sides, it emerged from her drive and her genuineness, and from her real experience as someone who had climbed from the bottom and never lost touch with her origins, despite her need to overcome them. This is perhaps one of her many paradoxes: though Peronism has been accused, with justice, of creating a handout-dependent client base, in practice Evita was strongly ambitious both for herself and for others – she wanted others to want progress and to demand betterment. That Peronism became dependent on the patron-client structure, thus limiting the real gains of working-class independence, was an irony that she perhaps failed to see.

A more contemporary parallel could be found in the late Venezuelan president, Hugo Chávez, a 'populist' figure marked by both narcissism and a sincere desire to improve the lot of his people, albeit on his own terms. While also tempted by the lack of institutional channels to seek improvised solutions bypassing institutions, his failure to create sustainable institutions and his creation of a system heavily dependent on his own personality cult have generated longer-term difficulties not dissimilar to those already experienced in Argentina. In the cases of both Chávez and Evita, that contempt for institutions had the effect of further degrading already weak institutional systems (although their disregard for the need to build effective institutions can also be understood in the light of their need to feel 'indispensible'). However, while Chávez alone played the roles of Perón the statesman and Evita the defender of the people, Evita's more informal role has allowed her to transcend many ideological barriers over the course of time, while the figure of Perón himself has (unfairly) been reduced to almost a supporting role.

Despite the contrasting and unreal images attached to Evita after her death and the difficulty in reconstructing some private aspects of a very public life, in fact she was in many ways transparent, an ordinary person who demonstrated both the extraordinary things of which an ordinary person is capable, and also the extraordinary errors. She was rightly accused of being rancorous and resentful, yet these feelings were no more than the (entirely justifiable) sentiments of significant and long-excluded sectors of the population, victims of intractable social injustice and contempt. However, whereas many of her compatriots were dominated by a feeling of impotence, Eva rebelled against that injustice, becoming in the process an icon for other generations who felt similarly moved to rebel against injustice, whether personal or social. Faced with an unpromising life that began in poverty in a small and hidebound provincial town, and with death from cancer at 33, she played the cards she was dealt, refusing to accept fate and tackling both life and death bravely, albeit with increasing radicalisation and violence as her anger, physical pain and frustration increased towards the end. As her illness advanced, she became increasingly obsessed with the Foundation, her 'mission in life' and the scant time she was given to realise it – obsessions that doubtless helped to sustain her in the terminal phase of cancer, despite her fear that the *descamisados*' gains could disappear with her. She suffered injustice and illness, but she was not a victim. She was the embodiment of the phrase 'the personal is political'.

 CHAPTER 1

Los Toldos

Y pienso en la vida,	*[And I think of life,*
Las madres que sufren,	*The mothers who suffer*
Los chicos que vagan	*The children who wander*
sin techo y sin pan,	*With no roof and no bread,*
Vendiendo La Prensa,	*Selling the newspaper,*
Ganando dos guitas…	*Earning two cents...*
Qué triste es todo esto,	*How sad it all is,*
Quisiera llorar!	*I feel like crying!]*

(Acquaforte; tango, Marambio Catán and Horacio Pettorossi, recorded by Agustín Magaldi in 1932)

THE TOWN OF Los Toldos ('the tents'), some 300 kilometres from the city of Buenos Aires, was originally settled in 1862 by a Mapuche tribe led by Don Ignacio Coliqueo, an ally of newly elected President Bartolomé Mitre, who as a general had succeeded in uniting the Argentine Republic following the 1860 Battle of Pavón. The current town, with a population of close to 15,000 in 2010, was re-founded in 1892, and its official name was changed to General Viamonte after it became the seat of the newly created county of that name. The town now boasts two attractions for visitors: the house that is the purported 'birthplace' (and now the museum) of Eva Perón, and a monument to its most famous native daughter, inaugurated in 2011. This in a town that held her and her family in contempt and that she never visited after 'escaping' to the city of Junín in 1930.

While Los Toldos, like most small towns isolated across the Pampas, has limited public entertainments, the options on offer in the early years of the twentieth century were even more reduced, and focused on the church and gossip about the neighbours. The famous tango singer Carlos Gardel, then a little-known folkloric artist, appeared in Los Toldos in September 1913 with his then singing partner, José Razzano, described in the local press as 'a delightful and agreeable evening'.[1] Other struggling troupes crossing the Pampas undoubtedly also visited Los Toldos, but such delightful and agreeable evenings must have been the exception rather than the norm. The Pampas itself, a vast, flat, unvarying expanse that stretches for miles, with an infinite horizon, represented a virtual barrier to the world: small towns like Los Toldos sat in the middle of that vastness, with roads often cut off by flooding, no electric light and nothing but the vast sky at night. Life in such a place was nothing if not a reminder of one's insignificance; even today, with electricity and paved roads, the sense of isolation is remarkable.

Even more isolated than Los Toldos was the nearby *estancia* (ranch) of La Unión, administered for the Malcolm family by Juan Duarte (who according to some reports in fact bought the property), a solid citizen of the larger town of Chivilcoy some 150 kilometres distant. Duarte (originally Duhart, of French Basque descent) was born in 1858 and married to the respectable Adela Uhart, with whom he had eight surviving children: María, Adelina, Catalina, Juan, Pedro, Magdalena, Eloísa and Susana Elvira. Duarte, a local political operator who gained influence through relations with local conservative politicians (becoming a justice of the peace in 1908), would take with him to La Unión, in 1908, an 18-year-old girl from Los Toldos, Juana Ibarguren, to act as cook there, while his wife remained in Chivilcoy with his legitimate family. This was far from an unusual arrangement at the time and, whether she was aware of her husband's parallel family or not, Adela would most likely not have been shocked, or prepared to make a scene, over the existence of a mistress as long as she was kept at a distance and out of sight, away from the legitimate family and social circle. However, while the contemporary understanding of 'men's needs' meant that the situation was not uncommon, social norms were harsh for those second families, who were regarded largely as non-persons to be shunned by 'decent' people. This despite the fact that around a third of all children born in Argentina at the time were illegitimate.

Juana (later to be known invariably as 'Doña Juana') was the daughter of a Basque carter, Joaquín Ibarguren, and the local woman Petrona Núñez (herself also apparently an illegitimate child). Despite being 'white', and therefore socially less marginal than the Indians of the village, the Núñez family reportedly lived on the edge of Los Toldos and were not considered acceptable to even poor polite society. According to some later accounts, Juana's mother 'sold' her to Duarte in exchange for a horse and buggy.[2] If true, this would seem to be an extremely high price for a young woman of marginal family in those times, although the story would later be used to humiliate her offspring. According to her nephew many years later, Juana was the only young woman brave enough to take up the offer of work at La Unión, alone with the overseer and the workmen.[3]

Whatever the case, Juana and Juan would soon form a closer relationship, which would lead to the birth of five children: Blanca (born in 1908), Elisa (1909), Juan (1914), Erminda (1916) and Eva María (1919). Whether the decision to form such a relationship with her boss was due to genuine affection, necessity or the protection it provided against the attentions of his workforce, it was an enduring one and lasted until around 1922. Juana's nephew later attributed the prolific nature of the relationship loosely to the fact that 'there was no television in those days'. Although amusing, the comment does contain considerable truth: with perhaps no electricity, no radio, no near neighbours, life at La Unión must have consisted largely of work, food and sleep, doubtless punctuated by drink, cards and perhaps cock-fighting for the ranch workers. In keeping with Duarte's political ambitions, convivial nature and pretentions of importance, he appears to have opened La Unión to offer food and drink to the local *gauchos* and other residents, creating further work for his cook and mother of his numerous children.

Although no birth certificate is extant (first Eva herself and then the dictatorship that overthrew Perón in 1955 would destroy documents and historical records), Eva María was born on 7 May 1919 at La Unión, where her mother was attended by an Indian midwife. Eva would be the last of their five children, and there are rumours that Duarte questioned her paternity, as he recognised the first four children but not Eva. Whether the paternity issue is the case or not, it can only be said that she bore a strong resemblance to her siblings and to Duarte himself. Eva was registered as Eva María Ibarguren and, like Erminda, baptised on 21 November of that year in Los Toldos. However, documentation would later be removed; at the time of her marriage to Perón in 1945 a forged birth certificate appeared, stating that María Eva (not Eva María) Duarte had been born on 5 July 1922, daughter of the married couple Juan Duarte and Juana Ibarguren de Duarte – an attempt to conceal the fact of her illegitimacy and demonstrate that her parents had been legally wed. The date would appear to coincide with the birth certificate of a child who had died as a baby and whose birth certificate was 'replaced' by the false record of Eva's birth. However, the year reflects the fact that Duarte was by 1922 a widower, Adela having died in 1919, and could plausibly have remarried.

Within a short time, Duarte would return to Chivilcoy, leaving his second family behind. Again, the reasons are disputed: some say that La Unión was no longer profitable, or even that Duarte was dismissed by the Malcolm family, while others attribute the return to Chivilcoy to the fact that Duarte had lost political influence with the decline of the conservative powerbrokers to whom he was attached following the rise of the Radical Party and the election of President Hipólito Yrigoyen in 1916. Most likely, the return related to the death of Adela.

With the loss of both her protector and her employment, Doña Juana returned to Los Toldos with her 'tribe' of five, where they faced not only poverty but the stigma of their illegitimacy. A small and isolated, and hidebound, community of around 3,000, Los Toldos and its residents were largely poor, as Eva would note years later ('in the place where I spent my childhood the poor were much more numerous than the rich'[4]). Few had electricity or a radio, although the state Radio Nacional began broadcasting in 1924 and it was common in those years for companies to send trucks with loudspeakers to broadcast in the plazas of such places as Los Toldos, offering an interval of entertainment beyond that of local gossip. 'Small town, large hell' is still a common Argentine phrase today. The means of stratifying society included seeking to define oneself as 'better' than one's neighbours (whose business was one of the few sources of interest beyond the home), despite having no evident economic, cultural or ethnic 'advantages'.

The Duarte/Ibarguren children provided a convenient target, although their poverty and living conditions were no worse than those of most of their neighbours. Not only illegitimate (or 'natural') children in the sense that their parents were not married, they were also 'children of adultery' (or bastards), the lowest rung. This distinction would persist for years to come. 'Natural' children were common among the poor, who often did not marry; those who aspired to the middle class sought to imitate the mores of the aristocracy (or oligarchy, in the Peronist vocabulary) and normally contracted respectable matrimony, even if in other respects their lives may have differed relatively little from their 'social inferiors'.

The indomitable Doña Juana, still eye-catching and proud, was widely rumoured to have found herself other 'protectors' in short order (who purportedly provided useful but somewhat undignified services like supplying the family with chickens). Whether or not this is true, she would appear to have used the connections to gain work, rather than to live as a 'kept woman'. After taking a course in dressmaking at the local technical school, Juana began to earn her living by sewing, gaining the concession to provide the smocks worn by all schoolchildren. Although the long hours at her sewing machine left Doña Juana exhausted and with varicose veins, she would refuse to rest even on the doctor's advice, insisting that she 'did not have time' given the family that depended on her – a phrase that would be repeated endlessly by Eva later in her life as she struggled to work at a frenzied pace despite her advancing illness.

The sewing machine allowed Doña Juana to rent a two-room house (literally) on the wrong side of the tracks and to keep her children fed and clothed – indeed, they were said to be better and more cleanly dressed than their schoolmates, although they wore canvas, rope-soled *alpargatas* rather than leather shoes, and clothes handed down from older siblings. The house was small and mean, but made of brick rather than the metal sheets and cardboard that would become common in shantytowns later, and food was sufficiently cheap to ensure that the family did not actually suffer hunger. Having worked as a cook for over a decade at La Unión, Juana unquestionably knew how to prepare fairly abundant meals for large numbers from cheap raw materials, and stews and meat pies (*puchero* and *empanadas*) would have sufficed for basic needs. As late as 1938, a report by the director of the Labour Department would note that children in the north of Argentina 'who do not die in their first months, begin their development in deficient conditions [...] when the mother cannot feed them and receives no assistance from the state.'[5] Doña Juana's children were not in that situation.

Significantly, Juana made sure to provide for her children herself, rather than seeking charity from the 'beneficent societies' of the better-off, which would have implied accepting humiliation together with alms – something that would underlie Eva's later obsession with 'social justice' ('alms for me were always a pleasure of the rich: the soulless pleasure of exciting the desire of the poor without ever satisfying it [...] For me alms and charity are the ostentation of wealth and power to humiliate the poor.'[6]). Nor was the 'welfare state' even a distant dream at the time; state institutions were not in place for the benefit of the poor, who were left to their own devices and to their own family networks for support.

However, luxuries were not the order of the day: Erminda, writing many years later, recalled that little Eva had yearned for a doll for Christmas, and that the only doll her mother could buy was cheap because its leg was broken. Juana explained that the doll had fallen from the camel of one of the Three Kings and hurt herself, and that they had left her for Eva to look after. According to Erminda, Eva loved the doll to desperation and looked after her like an invalid.[7] On another occasion, when she was four, Eva overturned the pan of hot oil with which her mother was cooking onto herself, burning her face black until the scab fell away to reveal the ivory skin she retained.[8] Her bravery on this occasion, like her love for the mutilated doll, are cited as giving an insight into her future obsession with helping the afflicted and her courage in the face of her final illness. While too much can be read into this, there is no doubting her courage or the empathy she gained for the poor in the course of her difficult and sometimes harsh childhood. In her ghostwritten autobiography, years later Eva would refer to her 'indignation when faced with injustice':

> I remember very well that I was sad for days when I discovered that in the world there were poor people and rich people; and the odd thing is it was not the existence of the poor that hurt me so much, but rather knowing that at the same time there were rich people.[9]

On 6 January 1926, Juan Duarte suffered an automobile accident in Chivilcoy (supposedly on his return from taking Epiphany gifts to Los Toldos), and died two days later. The funeral on 9 January possibly provided a key opportunity – one of many – for Eva to experience injustice at first hand, although the circumstances of the event have been over-dramatised. Determined that her children should have the opportunity to see their father for the last time, and perhaps to prove that their existence was as important as that of the lawful family, Doña Juana hired a car and driver and took her five children off to Chivilcoy, a not inconsiderable journey considering the state of both roads and vehicles at that time. As noted above, Duarte's wife had predeceased him and the famous versions that have her ejecting her rival from the funeral are thus inaccurate. Indeed, some sources claim that the two families were acquainted and maintained 'cordial relations', although this seems somewhat unlikely given the circumstances and the geographical and social distance between them.[10] However, the appearance of the mistress and the illegitimate offspring was not in line with the norms of social behaviour. Upon the intercession of a relative, the Ibargurens were allowed to kiss their father's forehead for the last time, and allowed to walk behind the funeral cortege.

Whether, as has been claimed, this incident was the source of Eva's later 'indignation when faced with injustice' (or rancour, as others would describe it), and whether she may have resented the unpleasant moment she was forced to endure, it probably drove home further the gulf that separated the Ibarguren tribe from the respectable members of society. As Erminda noted later, from that moment 'we silently formed a pact of solid unity around her [Doña Juana]'.[11] (Erminda's memories on another point at least are unreliable: she refers to the affectionate embrace at the funeral with their half-siblings, who had now lost both parents, and repeatedly refers back to a loving co-habitation between Duarte and Juana – married, according to her version – and the goodnight kisses from both parents that marked their childhood.[12])

In 1927 Eva began primary school in Los Toldos, which she attended with Erminda, known within the family as Chicha. The target of jibes from schoolmates, whose mothers discouraged them from playing with the illegitimate Ibarguren tribe, she was apparently a relatively poor student (apart from comportment) and missed many days' attendance, although teachers remembered her early interest in music and reciting poetry. The schooling received can only have been difficult to relate to the realities of Los Toldos, with its emphasis on Argentina as a great, prosperous and important nation. With only a few playmates outside the family – she and her sisters were subjected to insults and, literally, mud-slinging in the street – Eva's closest playmates were Erminda, the nearest in age of her siblings, and their dog León. According to Erminda much later, Eva loved to climb trees and to escape to the fields outside the muddy streets of Los Toldos, as well as to stage playlets and games of statues, to read and to look after baby birds and other small animals she discovered (as well as her crippled doll).

Erminda's memoirs, published in 1972, are clearly designed to nourish a particular image of her sister, then already dead for 20 years, but her insistence on Eva's bravery, whether in climbing trees or in facing adversity, illness and death later in life, rings true. It is also hardly surprising that she would have been particularly addicted to climbing trees and venturing into the fields outside the village – given the dreary reality of her life, the freedom and escape provided by both tree-climbing and games of imagination must have been a welcome relief. Eva was also close to her only brother, Juan (Juancito), who made toys for his younger sisters and whom she always loved and protected in later life, despite his playboy aspirations and tendency to get into trouble.

The insular, family-focused life thrust on the tribe by the conventions of Los Toldos cemented the distrust of broader society and dependence on family; the need to both depend on and rally round Doña Juana, the only parent and breadwinner, accentuated this clannishness which would remain throughout Eva's life (spilling over into nepotism as her influence rose). It also partly explains the fact that surviving residents of Los Toldos had relatively few memories of Eva and her siblings: a few friends remembered that they were marginalised, teachers recalled that Eva was very quiet and liked to read, and their cousin Raúl Suárez remembered that the girls were pretty and rather conceited and that Juancito played football with him in the fields near the house, on the other side of the tracks from 'respectable' Los Toldos, where the school, church, general store and central plaza (and not much else) were lodged. The few photos of the time show Eva to have been a somewhat sullen-looking little girl (unsurprisingly) with large and intense dark eyes.

The suggestion that the girls were 'conceited' also rings true: Doña Juana clearly did not want her daughters to experience a repeat of the hardships that had marred her life, but rather to put their good looks to better account and find a more respectable future. She was strict with her daughters, ensuring that their clothes were spotless and their comportment unimpeachable – at least in public, although Eva was reported to have uncontrollable tantrums from time to time, a characteristic that did not leave her as she grew up. Even in the few photos of her earlier in life, Juana was attractive and plump but severe-looking behind large glasses. Later photos of Doña Juana show a heavy but well-turned-out woman, carefully coiffed, unsmiling, with a bitter expression and a somewhat calculating eye – a dependable head of household, but not someone to be trifled with. Given her history, a degree of bitterness might be understandable. Eva would inherit that resilience and sense of responsibility, as well as the determination that those she saw as her responsibility (her *descamisados*) should aspire, and feel entitled, to something better.

Eva was also said even as a child to be both headstrong and highly emotional, supposedly throwing herself on the floor in an uncontrollable fit of weeping when her grandmother died, although even this story is open to question – according to some sources, her maternal grandmother Petrona Núñez outlived her famous granddaughter, dying in 1953. At the same time, obviously she had no paternal grandmother to mourn – even had Juan Duarte's mother been alive (which seems unlikely given his own years), she would scarcely have had any kind of relationship with his illegitimate offspring in Los Toldos.

Whether or not through the intervention of new lovers (as was widely rumoured) or through other means of wangling favours, by the late 1920s Juana had been successful in securing a job for her older daughter, Elisa, in the post office as well as a job as a messenger boy for Juancito. These positions, which helped put the family on a slightly less precarious financial footing, were gained through connections with the Conservative mayor, connections emanating either from Duarte or from another local landowner, Carlos Rosset, who was purportedly Doña Juana's lover and possibly landlord. By this time also, Blanca, the eldest, had finished school and with the help of an Ibarguren relative had gone to the larger town of Bragado to the teacher training school, one of relatively few respectable career options for women at the time (and a significant achievement for a woman of her family background).

However, the old Conservative Party had fallen on hard times throughout the country by the late 1920s, and with the return to the presidency of the Radical Hipólito Yrigoyen in 1928 it suffered wide electoral losses (a key factor in the *coup d'état* that would remove Yrigoyen in September 1930). Doña Juana and her acquaintances lacked the same contacts with the new Radical mayor, who proposed to dismiss Elisa (whose appointment and dismissal both reflect the degree to which connections and patronage extended even to the most modest levels). Anticipating such a move, Doña Juana reportedly went to see the new mayor and burst into histrionic and public tears upon receiving confirmation that Elisa would lose her job. Disconcerted, the mayor suggested that Elisa might be transferred to another branch of the post office – seemingly precisely the outcome Doña Juana sought. She suggested Junín, a much larger city some 50 kilometres distant, which offered better prospects for the family. Their notoriety was a greater burden in Los Toldos than in unknown territory, and the city, with a railway line, municipal offices and courts, and a military base, offered far greater opportunities for an entrepreneurial woman experienced in cooking and sewing for a living, and seeking employment (and marriage) prospects for five children. Other versions suggest that Elisa's transfer was arranged by another family friend and post office employee, Oscar Nicolini, who would return to play a significant role in Eva's life and political career later.

Having successfully gained Elisa's transfer, in August 1930 Doña Juana hired a truck and packed her family and meagre belongings off to Junín for a new start. This was a difficult time for a new start: the Depression was beginning to make inroads into the Argentine economy, which had enjoyed a buoyant decade since the end of World War I. Not only the Duarte/Ibarguren family were migrating from the countryside: thousands moved during the 1930s from towns and villages to cities, including Junín and, in particular, the overcrowded and impoverished industrial suburbs around Buenos Aires. With the economic focus shifting from agriculture to import-substitution industrialisation, the mass migration broadened economic opportunities for some, and merely displaced others into an urban poverty where their roots and social networks were lost.

Political changes were also coming to a head, with the September coup that would usher in the 'Infamous Decade' and political resistance to economic shifts coming from anarchists and socialists, in Junín as well as elsewhere. These political and socio-economic shifts would give rise to key elements of the Peronist movement in the 1940s, and Eva's life experience would give her the resonance for the dispossessed that made her an icon. In the meantime, however, Doña Juana was a survivor, and she would not be a casualty of change.

 CHAPTER 2

Junín

J UNÍN, LOCATED ON Route 7 some 260 kilometres from the city of Buenos
Aires and the municipal capital of Junín district, had a population of
some 85,000 at the time of the 2010 census. However, by 1930 it was
already an important provincial city. Founded in 1827 (although it was officially a fort until 1864), its name was formally changed in 1829 from Fuerte
Federación to Fuerte Junín, a derivation of the Quechua word for 'plains', in
honour of the Battle of Junín that formed a key event in the independence
of Peru from Spanish rule. Despite suffering frequent Indian attacks the
settlement continued to grow, and in the 1895 census Junín already had a
population of around 12,000, many of them employed by the railways.[1]

As Argentina became a major agricultural exporter in the 1880s, with
Junín in a strategic location in the fertile Pampas region, the railways
expanded across the province of Buenos Aires. Both the Central Argentine
and the Buenos Aires and Pacific Railways reached the city by 1885, followed by the Argentine National Bank, and the Buenos Aires and Pacific
(which, like Route 7, linked Junín with the western province of Mendoza
and Chile) had important railway workshops there that became Junín's
chief employers. The effect of the railways also led to the creation of three
rapidly expanding but almost separate sections of the town, divided by the
tracks. Thanks to that rapid expansion, Junín was declared a city in 1906.
In more recent years, the city has also been a tourist destination thanks
to the Salado river and a number of nearby lakes, as well as a focus of the
booming agricultural sector.

The city has continued to expand since, thanks to the concentration
of municipal offices, courts and other health and social services and to
the buoyant agricultural sector, though not to the railways, which were

virtually closed down following privatisation in the 1990s and have only operated a limited cargo service since. However, even in 1930 it enjoyed a social, economic and cultural dynamism unimaginable in Los Toldos. Junín in the 1930s also had many poor people (most of them living near the railway lines), but it also had a significant foreign-born population – British railway employees, Italian and Spanish merchants – who had their own social clubs and distractions, as well as the lawyers and public officials employed in the municipality and tribunals who constituted, together with the officers stationed at the army base, a local middle class. Already in the 1930s the city had bars, cafes, a theatre, a cinema (and doubtless less respectable places of entertainment), as well as electricity, radio and local newspapers of some repute. Carlos Gardel, already the most famous tango singer of his time (indeed, of all time), sang in Junín in January 1930 and again in August 1933,[2] and the city was a frequent stop for other well-known entertainers and touring theatre companies.

According to school records, Eva María Duarte (no longer referred to as Ibarguren) transferred from her primary school in Los Toldos to the Catalina Larralt de Estragamou School No. 1 in Junín on 11 August 1930, having completed third grade in Los Toldos.[3] This gives an approximate idea of the date when Doña Juana (thereafter to be referred to as the 'widow Duarte') moved her family to the city. Having finished her studies in Bragado, Blanca rejoined the family in Junín and found work as a teacher, while Elisa took up her place in the post office and Juancito again found work as a messenger boy (later a soap salesman). With only Erminda and Eva still in school and three incomes (however minimal) entering the household, the family's position was thus less precarious than in the early years in Los Toldos, although its economic prospects were still modest. The family moved several times in Junín to houses that were larger and more centrally located but not much more luxurious than that of Francia Street in Los Toldos, finally settling in Winter Street on the main Plaza San Martín in the old section of Junín; the house was typical of old houses in this part of Buenos Aires province, with a living/dining room, patio and three bedrooms.

Doña Juana initially continued to work as a seamstress; despite the greater employment opportunities in Junín, her gender, lack of education and lack of investment capital by and large limited her own options to more of the same. However, at some point early in their tenure in Junín she returned to her earlier experience as a cook, beginning to offer meals for the single gentlemen who abounded in the city thanks to municipal bureaucracy, railways, the barracks and flows of travellers who visited Junín for business. Junín in 1930 was largely innocent of restaurants or other respectable eating places, and single men were not customarily used to doing their own cooking. Among her regular clientele were three reputable members of the local bourgeoisie: Major Alfredo Arrieta, head of the local garrison; José Alvarez Rodríguez, a widely respected educator who was head of the state high school (*Colegio Nacional*); and his younger brother, the lawyer Justo Alvarez Rodríguez. They were sometimes joined by Moisés Lebensohn, a young socialist journalist and later a prominent Radical politician, who founded the local newspaper *Democracia*. (Lebensohn would later become a prominent opponent of Perón, leading a Radical boycott of the constituent convention charged with drafting the 1949 'Peronist' constitution. He was several times imprisoned for his harsh criticisms of Peronist 'totalitarianism', although unlike most of his Radical counterparts he defended Perón's social policies.)

Doña Juana's new enterprise, and the presence of single men in the household, would later lead the anti-Peronist rumour mill to claim that in fact she had operated a brothel in Junín, with the implication that she had exploited her daughters as prostitutes. The famous writer Jorge Luis Borges would later claim that Eva had been a 'common prostitute', while other sources claimed that her mother had run a 'house of prostitution'[4] and that 'a great deal of flirtatious giggling, horseplay, and some pretty little scenes of affection [were] put on by the mother and daughters for the benefit of the men'.[5] In the latter case, at least, it is not difficult to believe that such 'pretty little scenes' might have been put on to attract the attention of an eligible bachelor. In middle- and upper-class families, too, suitors might be treated to such scenes; the novels of Jane Austen and the plays of Tennessee Williams are rife with them.

However, the notion that prostitution was exercised in the house of Doña Juana is demonstrably absurd: with her stringent insistence on 'correct' behaviour, Doña Juana had exerted herself to ensure that her daughters' own beauty would help them gain a respectable position in society rather than the sort of life she had faced as a discarded mistress with five children to feed. Her elder daughters had entered decent jobs, not without sacrifice. Moreover, most obviously, in the conservative society of the time, respectable men such as the garrison leader and the prominent director of the secondary school would not publicly have frequented a 'house of ill repute'. Much less would they have married women they had met in a brothel: Justo Alvarez Rodríguez would eventually marry Blanca, and Alfredo Arrieta would become Elisa's husband. This is a measure of Doña Juana's considerable success in pushing her daughters up towards the middle classes, something that could never have been realised through channels of dubious morality. The Radical intellectual Arturo Jauretche, who would later claim that one of Doña Juana's brothers had been affiliated to the Radical faction FORJA and had subsequently become a senator, would note years later that 'they were not low-class people or anything of the kind. I can demonstrate that with two facts: one of the girls married an officer, Major Arrieta; the other married Alvarez Rodríguez, a lawyer.' In somewhat less flattering terms, in the latter case Jauretche described the bridegroom as an alcoholic and noted that 'if it had been considered a humiliation, the Alvarez Rodríguez family would not have let him get married, and he didn't have the character to stand up to his brother'.[6]

However, Erminda and Eva remained at school with no immediate prospect of change. Eva remained by all accounts an average student with few friends and relatively few activities for a pre-adolescent girl. The only subject in which she appears to have stood out was in recital, and she would recite 'poesies' to her fellow students when it was too wet to play outside; her sixth-grade teacher Palmira Repetti later claimed to have recognised her talent and encouraged her to pursue it. Social life in Junín, like much of Argentina's 'interior' (as Buenos Aires tends to refer to the rest of Argentina's provinces), was largely limited to school, church, social clubs for the more privileged and the '*vuelta del perro*' (literally 'walking the dog'), the stroll round and round the plaza on Sunday afternoon arm-in-arm with friends or relatives, greeting other friends and receiving time-worn compliments from loitering young men. In this respect, Junín differed relatively little from Los Toldos, especially for those with little money to spend. According to one contemporary, whose sister was Juancito's girlfriend,

> I never knew Eva to have any boyfriend [...] It was sad! Here in Junín there was nowhere to go to dance or have fun [...] A girl in the town couldn't do anything. Eva didn't have a happy childhood: she always aspired to something more than this.[7]

Surviving photos show a day out with family friends at a nearby lake with her sisters, suggesting that at least some social life was possible, and pleasant. (It also suggests, again, that although their lives contained privations, in many respects their situation was no more dramatic than that of many other Argentines of the time – life was hard, but they did their best, worked hard and enjoyed personal pleasures as well as darker times.) They were carefully watched over by Juancito, who as the only man of the family was protective of his sisters' honour – perhaps in part because of his own incipient fame as a 'ladies' man'.

Nevertheless, Junín did have a cinema, which offered three films for a bargain price on Tuesdays, and by this time it had become clear that Eva's real passion was acting, and the possibility of becoming a star one day. (The family, by this time, also had a radio and could listen to the singers and soap operas – *radioteatros* or *novelas*.) All biographers note that her favourite actress was Norma Shearer, at the peak of her fame in the early 1930s, who had come from an impoverished background in Canada and had triumphed in Hollywood, becoming one of its biggest stars and marrying Irving Thalberg, the 'boy wonder' who became head of production at MGM at the age of only 26. Eva would take Erminda's turns at washing the dinner dishes in exchange for photos of favourite stars from film magazines, and would stand in front of a mirror at home, imitating the poses in those photos – not, it must be said, an unusual pastime for a girl of her age. Indeed, Erminda also collected film star photos, and fan magazines have been a staple genre in Argentina and elsewhere for generations. However, her apparent shyness and lack of friends seem to have encouraged her imagination and her desire to be 'someone' – or 'someone else'.

Eva's vocation for acting was fuelled by her participation in 1933 in a stage play called *Arriba estudiantes* (Students Arise), put on by a student cultural group at the National College where José Alvarez Rodríguez was director and where Erminda now studied. Thereafter, she often frequented Junín's only music store, whose owner had set up loudspeakers and from time to time allowed members of the public to use them to perform. Eva became a frequent 'customer' and became ever more convinced of her destiny to leave Junín and triumph in Buenos Aires. This desire increased after she finished primary school in early 1934, aged 14. The decision not to continue studying was not uncommon at the time, and even many middle-class women did not go on to secondary school. However, she had few options in Junín at the age of nearly 15: stay at home, help her mother and wait for another respectable bachelor to offer the prospect of a decent marriage.

Eva lacked the more conventional aspirations of her older sisters and, as she made clear at the end of her life, could not tolerate the thought of a lifetime as a provincial housewife. Just before her death she told her maid:

> I was never satisfied with that life, that's why I left home. My mother would have married me to someone in town, and I could never have stood it, Irma: a decent woman has to carry the world before her.[8]

Doña Juana's middle-class aspirations were respectable but mediocre from this point of view, while Eva's grander dreams of fame and fortune were more dubious and harder to achieve, but far more inspiring. Moreover, her beloved brother Juancito went to Buenos Aires to perform his military service, leaving her more alone than ever.

Eva's apparent lack of interest in a conventional life does not seem to have prevented a few early and mild flirtations (possibly taking advantage of the watchful Juancito's absence), including with a young man of some means whose family did not approve of her. Another early experience reported by some authors highlights a far less innocent incident, although one that sadly does not seem at all improbable. According to these versions, Eva and a friend were invited by two young men 'of good family' to make a day trip by car to the seaside resort of Mar del Plata, an invitation that was accepted innocently (though it could hardly have been made in good faith, given that Mar del Plata is nearly 400 miles from Junín – a drive of some seven hours even now). Knowing that her mother would not allow the trip, Eva sneaked out of the house and met her friend and the two gallants, with the girls hoping to make their first visit to the seaside. The car turned off the road some distance from Junín and the hosts attempted to rape the girls before leaving them at the side of the road, where they were found and returned to Junín by a trucker some time later.[9] The notion that young girls of 'their class' were fair game for such an escapade was far from uncommon, and even had they attempted to denounce their attackers, the girls would have received worse treatment from the police than would the sons of landowners.

On a happier note, it is also claimed that Eva may have been exposed to politics (albeit through romance) for the first time at around this time. Some four years after the 1930 coup against Yrigoyen (in which a young and unknown Captain Juan Domingo Perón had played a peripheral role), Argentina was well into the 'Infamous Decade', with the military government of General José Félix Uriburu having given way in early 1932 to the fraudulently elected one of President Agustín P. Justo. Uriburu had sought to cut government spending by slashing public sector jobs, adding to the economic distress already felt as a result of the Depression and mass migration to the cities. Moreover, the so-called Concordancia, an alliance between the conservatives, elements of the Radical Party and other smaller rightist groups, sought to return Argentina to the elitist, agro-export structure of the pre-Yrigoyen era, and deteriorating economic conditions exacerbated tensions with labour. Anarchist activities peaked following the trial and execution of Sacco and Vanzetti in the United States in 1927; the Italian anarchist Severino di Giovanni, who emigrated to Argentina following the rise of Mussolini in 1922, led a campaign of 'direct action', including bombings that targeted US interests in Argentina in particular. Di Giovanni himself was tried and executed in 1931. (Like Eva years later, his burial place was supposed to be secret, but flowers began to appear at his anonymous grave within a day of his burial.)

Junín was not isolated from these events, and in fact political and union agitation focused on a specific local issue – the dismissal of railway workers at a time when the Central Argentine and Buenos Aires and Pacific railways were to be merged. That eventual merger was delayed until 1938 by a series of strikes, organised by a small group of anarchists apparently including a young man called Damián Gómez. According to some versions Eva was smitten with Gómez, and any romance may have brought with it some grounding in anarchist views on labour–capital relations and class conflict, an early 'political romance' that may have informed her future. (In point of fact, the Argentine anarchist view – that women's chief role was to lend emotional support to the exploited male head of household, rather than act as a member of the workforce who served primarily to reduce wages – was not a million miles from the position Eva would advocate in later political speeches and writings, although she was certainly more aware of and sensitive to the exigencies requiring women to work.) Whether this is true or not, her own experience might have provided fertile ground for such education, as would her later relationship with Perón.

At the beginning of January 1935, at the age of 15, Eva would leave Junín forever in pursuit of her dream of stardom. Although very young, the age of 15 was not at the time a scandalously early age for a girl to leave home. The Argentine custom of holding a 'coming out' birthday party for 15-year-old girls, which remains standard, reflects the fact that it was considered the age at which girls were eligible to be married. For young women of more modest means, it was certainly an age at which it was considered normal to seek work, either near home or in the capital, where countless young women like Eva would find themselves alone, working as maids or in factories. Nevertheless, the fact that she went driven not by necessity, but rather by ambition, is remarkable. The circumstances of her departure remain unclear, although the most widely reported version – that she was taken to Buenos Aires by the tango singer Agustín Magaldi – is plagued with doubts.

The most malicious version of the Magaldi story, often taken as gospel by anti-Peronist gossips in later years, suggests that Eva, as a pretty but relatively nondescript 15-year-old, snuck into Magaldi's dressing room when he visited Junín, seduced him and convinced him to take her to Buenos Aires with him. A more circumspect version of this story suggests that she returned to Buenos Aires with him and his wife, although in what capacity remains unclear. Either of these stories is open to question: there are no definite records of Magaldi having sung in Junín at around this time – and, as noted earlier, the newspapers of provincial towns with few entertainments tended to report enthusiastically on such things – and he was already separated from his wife. Nor is it obvious that he would have fallen helplessly under the spell of a thin, flat-chested, moderately pretty provincial teenager. According to Vera Pichel (herself from Junín), it was Juancito who managed to get Eva close to Magaldi when he visited Junín, and she and the family persuaded him and his wife to take her to Buenos Aires and help her.[10]

Whatever the truth, there is evidence that the two were acquainted at some point at least after Eva reached Buenos Aires, and that Magaldi may have helped her at a later date. Another alternative that has been mooted, and is possibly true, is that Magaldi was passing through Junín at around this time (perhaps returning to Buenos Aires from his native Santa Fe) and somehow ended up dining at Doña Juana's establishment, where either Eva herself or Doña Juana, worn down by Eva's insistence, asked him to take her to Buenos Aires and provide her with some introductions. This would leave open the possibility either that she accompanied him back to the city (where Magaldi shared a house with his mother and could not reasonably have been expected to provide accommodation for a 15-year-old girl on whatever terms) or that she contacted him upon arriving there herself and he provided her with some contacts. However, like many other aspects of Eva's life, it has never been demonstrated with any certainty what the relationship with Magaldi was – if indeed it went beyond a minimal acquaintance and a few theatrical contacts. During Eva's lifetime, once she became first lady, many things about her past were not talked about – and many others were, in secret, but often falsely, spreading unsubstantiated rumours that 'everybody knows'.

Despite the suggestion in the rock opera *Evita* that Magaldi was a third-rate singer who would 'never be remembered for [his] voice', in fact he was one of the most popular tango singers of his time, arguably second only to Carlos Gardel, and is still remembered for his voice decades after his death. Known as 'the sentimental voice of Buenos Aires', Magaldi had a fine light tenor voice (unlike Gardel, a baritone) and had studied opera after hearing Enrico Caruso sing. After attempting a classical repertoire, he began singing popular music in the early 1920s and in 1925 formed a successful duo with Pedro Noda which would last for a decade, although he also successfully performed alone and recorded a number of solo albums. His repertoire focused more on social ills than on the romantic misadventures that were standard fare in tango lyrics, and might be described almost as 'pre-Peronist' in the themes of exploitation and misery it touched upon.[11]

Born in Casilda, Santa Fe province, in 1898, Magaldi was, like Eva, a product of Argentina's interior and lacked Gardel's good looks or his air of debonair man-about-town. His radio success never matched his recording career – reportedly because his known socialist sympathies did not endear him to the conservative government in place from 1930. Indeed, during the 1930s his political sympathies reportedly cost him work and most likely reduced the influence that he could have brought to bear in favour of a young protégée in the best of cases. Nonetheless, generally known for his generosity to others, Magaldi may well have helped put the young Eva in contact with people able to offer her work or mention her in the press. Whether or not any 'romance' was involved, his social sensitivity (like that of Damián Gómez) might both have represented a basis for mutual attraction and left an influence over her later thinking. In practice his usefulness in the anti-Evita myth most likely stems more from the fact that he died of peritonitis in 1938 and was thus no longer able to confirm or deny the relationship by the time she became famous.

It would appear that Eva had already visited Buenos Aires once or twice in 1934, accompanied by her mother, and that she had obtained one or two small radio jobs before returning to Junín. However, her determination to

remain there increased with time (and indeed, if she had already participated in two radio broadcasts, however briefly, it would be logical for her
to believe in her chances of success, and that 'conquering Buenos Aires'
would be far less difficult than it was in practice). Erminda was adamant
that Eva, despite her determination, would not have dared to go to Buenos
Aires without Doña Juana's permission, and that permission was stubbornly
withheld, leading to arguments that her other daughters would never have
opposed. However, the likeliest version of her eventual departure is that
Doña Juana was persuaded either to accompany her to Buenos Aires to participate in an audition for a small radio contract, or to let her go alone. (The
existence of a letter, purportedly from Eva to Doña Juana, saying how much
she had yearned for this trip and how far away she felt from her family,
'although I have only just left', suggests the latter.[12]) Eva also found an ally
in José Alvarez Rodríguez, Blanca's brother-in-law, who warned Doña Juana
of the dangers in stifling her daughter's incipient vocation. Doña Juana may
also have been swayed by the fact that Juancito was still in Buenos Aires, so
that Eva would not be entirely alone – and indeed, perhaps, by the fact that
Eva's prospects in Junín were limited at best. With or without her mother,
Eva left for Buenos Aires in January 1935 and, despite the difficulties she
would face, as a young, poor woman from the province with no contacts, no
money and no training, she remained there.

 CHAPTER 3

Buenos Aires

U P UNTIL THIS point only the main outlines of Eva Duarte's life can be traced, while some of the actual facts are elusive and likely to remain so. Nor can substantial interpretations be made based on the limited experiences of a young girl whose life at that point had differed little from that of many of her contemporaries, beyond the fact that the difficulties she faced gave her an understanding of those contemporaries and an empathy for their circumstances. As noted earlier, her background, though undoubtedly unorthodox for a future first lady, was not significantly different from that of many members of the poorer classes – many of whom, with or without Peronism, managed a degree of social mobility and entered the lower middle classes, as Doña Juana and her daughters had done (although far more did not). On the contrary, she was more unusual for her force of character, which allowed her to get out of Junín and achieve not inconsiderable success in a difficult profession such as acting.

However, at this stage in her life it is unrealistic to read into her early experiences the kind of 'ideological content' that is tempting both to detractors (who paint her simply as resentful and vengeful) and admirers (who now seek to turn that more superficial version on its head, rendering her as a nascent political animal and ideologue). Despite her drive and accurate instincts, however, there is nothing substantive to suggest that Eva at 15 was a latent political thinker or even that her ambitions tended in the direction of politics. On the contrary, her clear ambition, like that of many girls, was to be an actress, a film star, and her confidence in her ability to achieve that aim (out of proportion to any genuine thespian gifts) was strong and did not admit failure. That confidence and self-belief, in a girl of 15, is both striking and poignant, which may partially explain why she

found a number of friends willing to help her – and not only for the preda-
tory sexual motives highlighted by her detractors.

At the same time, Eva would never again refer to her past as an 'artist'
once she became first lady, except in the briefest and vaguest of terms,
and thus few reflections remain apart from a few comments to friends published by those sources later. As such, there is little material on which
to base an analysis of her experience as an actress or its effects on her
later consciousness. Interviews years later with both friends and enemies
give some insights, although these are often contradictory and probably
deformed by the passage of time. Almost without exception, those sources
speak of a young woman of limited education and culture but considerable
natural intelligence, and an outstanding will to succeed at whatever cost.
The 'cost' is often in the eye of the beholder, depending on whether the
source viewed her as a victim or a manipulator, a target of sexual harassment or an enthusiastic accomplice. Eva's own perspective comes largely
in the third person, and even the wildly bowdlerised memoirs common to
many other former performers are absent.

Like other big cities, the Buenos Aires where Eva arrived in January
1935 was at once an imposing and intimidating place, offering great
promise but at great cost. One of the most modern cities in the world at the
time, Buenos Aires, a port city, had become rich on agricultural exports
and expanded rapidly to around 1.5 million people at the time of the 1914
census, of whom around a third were foreign-born. By the time of Eva's
arrival there were around 2 million people in the city itself, and a similar
number in the industrial suburbs that made up the Greater Buenos Aires
area. The city had gas lighting and then electricity, trams and elegant,
European-style architecture from an early date; in 1908 the Teatro Colón,
considered second only to La Scala among opera houses, was opened with
a performance of *Aida* conducted by Toscanini. By 1935 it had a wealth
of theatres, cinemas, cabarets, revues and restaurants; a contemporary
described it as an imperial capital lacking an empire. Its residents, the *porteños*, had become accustomed to national wealth and power in the 1920s,
when Argentina was the world's eighth largest economy, and the rising
middle class since the early part of the century had ensured the election
of three governments led by the Unión Cívica Radical: those of President
Hipólito Yrigoyen in 1916 and 1928, and those of the 'anti-personalist' (i.e.
anti-Yrigoyen) Marcelo T. de Alvear in 1922. In 1929, José Ortega y Gasset
noted that Argentines 'do not content themselves with being one nation

among others: they hunger for an overarching destiny, they demand of themselves a proud future'.[1]

However, while 'the Paris of the Americas' was a comfortable and welcoming place for the well-to-do, it was far less so for the working classes, whose employment in the dirty factories and slaughterhouses in the industrial suburbs kept the city and country prosperous but whose presence in the city centre was unwelcome. That Argentina, and Buenos Aires in particular, still offered the prospect of upward mobility is evident in the number of immigrants still attracted to the city – most of them poor migrants from southern Europe – many of whom were able to gain a place for their children in the expanding middle class (if not in oligarchic high society). For anyone wanting to break into acting, Buenos Aires was the focal point for the whole of the region. However, then as now, it was a city that was expensive and difficult to negotiate, which promised much more than it gave to most of those incomers – not least for a young girl with no family connections and no money.

Nor was the mid-1930s an especially propitious time for a young actor aiming for success. Although Argentine cinema had a significant history in the early part of the twentieth century, during the silent era, it began to decline drastically in the 1920s, due in part to competition from imported films, mainly from the United States, but also to the expansion of radio and the practice of offering live performances by tango orchestras at cinemas. The latter two factors did much to bolster the tango as a popular entertainment but did little for interest in films, often secondary to the live entertainment offered.[2] Although tango star Carlos Gardel appeared in an early silent film in Buenos Aires, *Flor de durazno* (1917), and in a number of shorts in which he sang tangos in the early 1930s, he made his film career elsewhere, convinced that he could not gain international fame in local productions. The film industry would begin to recover in the late 1930s (and would gain international significance from the 1950s) but scarcely represented a passport to fame.

The theatre was faring little better in the 1930s. After a period of glory in the 1920s, the effects of the Depression and the political crisis took their toll post-1930, although a number of theatres continued to operate in Buenos Aires, offering revues, productions of often dubious quality (and often short-lived) and cabaret. Although actors' unions had made some gains in terms of guaranteeing one day's rest per week and a minimum wage, these, like other labour norms, were routinely flouted, with lower-level actors required to provide their own costumes, work as many as two performances a day and four on Sundays, and receiving no payment during rehearsals – and often none thereafter, if the play was unsuccessful. All this for a salary of some 60–100 pesos a month for minor players like Eva (around 17–29 dollars at the then exchange rate), although leading actors obviously earned far more. Only the radio was beginning to offer greater opportunities for actors with the rise of radio soap operas (*radioteatros*), culturally despised but widely followed by the middle and lower classes.

Eva arrived in Buenos Aires at Retiro station on 3 January 1935, with or without her mother (who may or may not have given her money), and with or without Juancito waiting for her at the station, although he would be a permanent and comforting presence during her early years in the city. Her earliest accommodation was a room in the district near the Congress. Purportedly, Magaldi provided her with contacts with some people connected with the theatre.[3] Eva lost no time in beginning what would become almost a permanent occupation in the coming years: a constant round of theatres and producers' offices, asking what plays were due to be produced and whether actors were required, and a round of film and theatre magazines in the hope of getting a photo or a note published. The rooming houses (*pensiones*) would change often, frequently for the worse as money was extremely tight; at one point, the young Eva lived at the end of the tramline in the rough working-class area of La Boca, where she learned to protect herself against the less-than-romantic advances of the local toughs as she walked home along late at night, and acquired (or expanded) a salty vocabulary for which she would later become famous.

Somewhat incredibly, within three months of her arrival she had already gained her first stage role, albeit a small one: on 28 March 1935 the play *La señora de Pérez* opened at the Teatro Comedia on 9 de Julio. She played a maid and had only one line – 'dinner is served' – but was rewarded with a mention in a review in the newspaper *Crítica* by the well-known journalist Edmundo Guibourg (according to some sources, the contact who helped her gain the role), who noted that 'Eva Duarte was very correct in her brief intervention', and a longer mention in the local newspaper of Junín, *El Pueblo*.[4] Even such a small mention was invaluable to an actress starting out, and it is suggested that Magaldi may have commended Eva to Guibourg. (Guibourg and his wife, the actress Paulina Singerman, took it upon themselves to look after Eva, who came often to have tea with them, and he gave her a speaking role in a play some years later.[5]) Also of significance was the fact that she was hired by the company of Eva Franco, a member of a distinguished theatrical family and, at the age of 29, already one of Argentina's most acclaimed actresses. Despite the small size of both the role and the salary, this would seem an auspicious start for any young girl newly arrived from the interior, and can only have encouraged Eva to believe in her destiny.

Although she would not appear in all the plays presented by Eva Franco's company (and would not be paid during the periods in which she was not performing), Eva remained with the company until early 1936, despite rumours of tensions between the two actresses after an incident in which the star found in her dressing room a number of huge bouquets from admirers, which on closer inspection proved to be for her younger colleague. Franco would later dismiss the rumours and call the affair 'an amusing incident', although she expressed astonishment that 'a young girl just starting out in the theatre already had so many admirers'.[6] Despite lapses in employment, Eva worked with the company in *Cada casa es un mundo* (Every Home is a World), which opened on 19 June, and later in *Madame Sans Gene*, which opened in November and in which she played several (largely silent) walk-on roles. According to rumour, her continuity with Eva Franco's company was due to the less-than-avuncular interest in her shown by the star's father, José Franco, a famous actor in his own right then working with his daughter's company.

Eva was appearing in *Cada casa es un mundo* in the role of the maid when, on 25 June, all Buenos Aires theatres closed their doors on the shocking news that the great Carlos Gardel had been killed the day before in an air crash in Medellín, Colombia, during a concert tour. Gardel, born Charles Gardes in Toulouse, France in 1890 and brought to Buenos Aires by his unwed mother at the age of two, had become Argentina's first international star and the image of what *porteños* liked to imagine themselves to be. Having come from a poor background, Gardel became famous and spent his money lavishly, on horse racing, clothes, cabarets, travelling, and looking after his mother and old friends generously. The tour of the Caribbean, Venezuela and Colombia, which was to have continued to other countries for another month, was designed to promote his US-made films, but his existing fame made the concert tour a delirious success; the plane crash cut short an already illustrious career that appeared set to achieve even greater things.

When Gardel's body was returned to Buenos Aires on 5 February 1936, in a funeral evocative of Evita's death years later, some 30,000 were waiting at the dock to meet the coffin. Tens of thousands lined the streets to pay tribute to their idol, whose coffin was displayed in the recently inaugurated Luna Park stadium before being transported the following day some six kilometres up Corrientes Avenue (the theatre and cinema district) to Chacarita Cemetery. The statute of Gardel in Chacarita (known as 'the bronze that smiles') still often has a lit cigarette placed in its hand, and it is still said that 'he sings better every day' (although recent overly computerised re-recordings of his voice might undermine this claim).

Although Eva Franco retired temporarily from the stage in early 1936, her theatrical company continued into that year, producing among other works the play *La dama, el caballero y el ladrón* (The Lady, the Gentlemen and the Thief), in which Eva Duarte had a small speaking role as a secretary. Potentially more important, Eva reportedly had begun her radio career in December 1935 at Radio París with a small role in a *radioteatro*. She also joined Radio Excelsior on trial as part of an amateur company, where she supposedly formed an acquaintance with the well-known radio scriptwriter Héctor Pedro Blomberg, with whom she would have a significant professional relationship some years later (and possibly a more personal one in the interim).

In May 1936 Eva joined a new company headed by José Franco and Pepita Muñoz, which began a tour of Rosario (Santa Fe province), Mendoza and Córdoba lasting until September. Although the repertoire included several plays, in which Eva had largely silent roles, the success of the tour was the luridly named *El beso mortal* (The Kiss of Death), an internationally acclaimed play by Lois Le Gouradiec that warned of the risks of venereal disease and played to packed houses throughout the tour. In Rosario, a local newspaper published the first photo of Eva to appear in the press (albeit in the second row of a cast photo). As was customary, the leading actors stayed in decent hotels while the bit players were relegated to fleapits of the type that their salaries could provide. Eva shared a room with Josefina Bustamante, an older actress who would remain a close friend and protector for some time. A possibly apocryphal anecdote relating this tour also throws interesting light on Eva's character and later fragile health. One member of the company became ill and was hospitalised, presumably with a venereal disease. The others were forbidden to visit but Eva did so out of solidarity and may have contracted the disease, possibly with far-reaching future consequences.

In Mendoza, matters apparently came to a head with José Franco, who had not lost his none-too-avuncular interest in Eva. According to various versions, in Mendoza he confronted the young actress and informed her that she would be left behind there if she refused to sleep with him. The fact that she returned with the company to Córdoba and Rosario would suggest that she complied, but the relationship appears to have gone beyond a simple one-night stand. By the time they arrived in Rosario, other members of the company had seen their complicit looks and had seen Franco leaving her hotel; before long 'a friend' contacted Franco's wife in Buenos Aires, who immediately took a train to Rosario and ensured that Eva was dismissed. According to Eva Franco years later, her mother later told her that her father (a well-known Lothario) 'had fallen in love with Eva Duarte […] I told him that if he did not separate her from the company he would never see us again.'[7] By all accounts, Eva herself appears to have imagined herself in love, and the forced break-up – with the attendant consequences for her employment and income – must have been a blow.

As noted earlier, Eva's sexual experiences during her period as an actress (both real and imagined) would become a significant element of her 'black myth', and, in later times, even grounds for arguing that she was a 'liberated woman' ahead of her time who chose her sexual partners as she wished. In her vitriolic contemporary biography *The Woman with the Whip*, Mary Main asserts that Eva:

> had a phenomenal gift for attracting the attention of influential men and making use of them […] And once she had gained that attention she did not really let go of her victim but pursued him in person and by mail until the last drop of usefulness had been squeezed out of him.[8]

All of these versions are exaggerated and unrealistic. Despite the salacious (and unhealthily prurient) stories circulated by the 'decent people' after her ascent, there is no evidence that Eva was a prostitute or a sexual predator. (The view that she was sexually insatiable sits uncomfortably with the equally anti-Peronist claim that she was sexless and frigid, only interested in power.) Eva wanted to be an actress and would not be deterred from that purpose. Like most other actresses (and some actors) of her time, acquiescence to demands for sexual favours was in many cases the only path to gaining work. Thus, this was a hazard that had to be accepted, and the advice to 'put up with an unpleasant moment and then forget about it' was probably widely followed. At the same time, the notion that any woman who rose from obscurity to a position of power could only have done so through dubious means was widespread. Years later in an interview, Eva's former radio and theatre colleague Pablo Raccioppi would say 'I couldn't say that Eva Duarte was a prostitute. But, among women who succeed, there is always a part of their life that remains obscure.'[9] As disconcerting as this statement might seem, the sentiment was widely shared.

This was not only the case for actresses; many socially disadvantaged working women such as domestic servants were expected to 'put out', and even women in more middle-class occupations such as office work faced harassment as a regular feature. (Even years later, the then Archbishop Jorge Bergoglio, later Pope Francis, would note that he recalled good Catholic ladies insisting that their maids must be free from disease, 'because I have sons and I want the maid to be healthy so my sons won't look elsewhere'.[10] This suggests that virtual prostitution was still seen as part of the domestic servant's duties. Nor did this attitude stop respectable ladies from blaming their servants for these relations and any possible consequences, treating them as the predators rather than those that used them.) The nascent feminist movement of the 1930s had done little to change these prejudices, not least because most feminists were socialists (or in a few cases anarchists), usually middle- or upper-class and often professionals, and thus had little traction with the bulk of either society ladies or working-class factory and domestic staff. Moreover, 'most feminists at the time subordinated women's interests to socialist ideology',[11] and focused many of their efforts on women's suffrage, envisaged primarily for the educated and of limited interest for many women of the time.

At the same time, despite the job insecurity that plagued actors and actresses (across the world) and the consequently poor food and lodging – all testimonies of the time refer to Eva's fragile health, thinness and minimal food intake – it could be argued that Eva and the friends like Fina Bustamante and Anita Jordán with whom she shared rooms and experiences did not lead a uniquely deprived or squalid life, certainly no worse than that of many members of the working class (to say nothing of the rural poor). As noted, the sexual pressures they faced were no more acute than those of many other working women, while in fact they did enjoy the possibility of seeking out relationships with men they fancied – something socially forbidden for 'decent' women at the time – and were not forced to live in the household of their harassers. Moreover, they were doing something that they presumably enjoyed (which for Eva was her driving passion, until she found an even greater one), and could be said to be living a moderately exciting and sophisticated life, certainly in comparison with the small towns from which many of them came, where walks round the plaza and marriage to a local boy were the most exciting prospects available. Considering the domineering personality of Doña Juana, it seems likely that being alone in Buenos Aires, even living on tea and biscuits in a cheap *pensión*, represented a degree of freedom for Eva that she could never have enjoyed at home. While it was a life that defied the repressive sexual mores of the day, the value of chastity and arriving a virgin at the altar may have been seen as questionable or even risible by Eva and other poor young women trying to make their way – a point of view that would become increasingly widespread among later generations – although for people brought up with the morals of the time the thought that the first lady might have had such experience was genuinely shocking.

Another frequent, and related, criticism is that Eva was a bad actress – something that she herself admitted to a degree, telling her confessor that she was 'bad in the cinema, mediocre in the theatre and passable on the radio'.[12] No recordings of her radio programmes or registers of her fleeting stage performances remain, but watching her films makes it impossible to argue the point. However, this also does not set her apart from the vast majority of her contemporaries. Although the Argentine theatre and cinema have reached outstanding levels of quality and the country has produced many distinguished artists, few of them were in evidence in the cinema or theatres during the 1930s. Most plays during this period were put together hastily, on the cheap, and with little regard for quality (in particular among the secondary players).

Even in films – and Argentina has produced many films of great quality – the quality of acting was by and large remarkably bad during this period, and in this respect Eva does not stand out. Only a few, like Mecha Ortiz, the tango singer and actress Tita Merello ('Tita of Buenos Aires') and the comedienne Niní Marshall, stood out for their talent and expressiveness. There was relatively little acting training available in these years, and even fewer actors who took advantage of what there was. This lack of distinction among players was also a factor in the widespread use of the 'casting couch', given that actors were seldom chosen for their histrionic gifts.

It is true that Eva, like many other young women before and since who dreamed of stardom, imagined this as a glamorous and magical future, rather than the result of hard work at the craft of acting. Although in fact Eva was known for being hard-working and dependable, she seemingly made little effort at this time either to learn greater acting skills or to correct her deficient diction, despite being sneered at for her 'provincial' speech and tendency to mispronounce words. Although a National Conservatory of Recitation and Stage Art was founded in 1935, the critic Edmundo Guibourg noted that aspiring actors rarely took advantage of the possibility of training but rather 'jumped from the street to the stage, without any prior preparation,' in an environment that tended to stifle any ambition of genuine artistic achievement.[13] In Eva's case, Pablo Raccioppi noted that when he suggested to her during her radio days that she study to improve her pronunciation and thespian skills, she replied simply that 'to succeed in life […] you have to make friends with the one in charge. Afterward […] success comes by itself.'[14]

Nonetheless, the fact that Eva worked fairly constantly, and that she found a number of genuine protectors, indicates that she had qualities that stood out, over and above any sexual availability that would not have marked her out from most of her contemporaries. This is particularly true given the number of women who would take it upon themselves to look out for her, including Singerman, Bustamante, Jordán and Pierina Dealessi, a well-known actress who hired Eva for her company in 1938. Dealessi would later note that she hired her for only 180 pesos per month, the normal wage for actors of her level, but that she often gave her milk and *mate* (a popular Argentine infusion) and took her home to sleep at the flat where she lived with her mother.[15] Another friend, Edmundo Guibourg, noted that 'we had an immense friendship because she felt protected, in a circle that not only shunned her but offended her because she had had a complicated life for which they did not forgive her.'[16]

Discounting later motives of enlightened self-interest, many of those who knew her stressed that she was quiet, modest, sensitive, a nice girl who sent money home to her mother from her scant wages and 'when she earned a peso she would spend it buying presents for all her friends'. At the same time, 'she was a good friend and a bad enemy, but she had a facility for making friends with important people'.[17] She herself would be reported as saying 'only my enemies have defects – I never see them in my friends.'[18] Added to this were the persistence and absolute conviction she demonstrated throughout her life; Eva had a willpower and drive that set her apart from most people, and certainly from most young actresses who might readily have succumbed to the temptation to give up and opt for an easier life when success proved elusive.

Nor, as she would later stress herself, did she forget the kindnesses she received – her memory for kindnesses was as prodigious as her memory for insults, and she seldom lost a chance to repay either. One case in point is that of the retired journalist Miguel Brunetti, who passed the nights of his retirement in a bar in the city centre. Noticing a young woman who entered to ask for a glass of water, he invited her to sit down and have coffee with *medias lunas* (croissants) and urged her to return at any time. For many months he bought her coffee and *medias lunas* until she gained more regular work and gradually disappeared from his orbit. Some years later, the first lady stepped out of her chauffeur-driven car in front of the bar and sat down with Brunetti, purely, she said, to ask what she could do to help him. Although Brunetti refused her offers of a house or a car, the example has been widely cited, and is far from being the only one.[19]

After her abrupt return from Rosario and the end of her personal and professional relationship with José Franco, Eva was unemployed for several months before joining, in December 1936, the company of Pablo Suero, who was producing his own translation of Lillian Hellman's *The Children's Hour*, *Los inocentes*. Eva played the small role of a student, Catalina, and the role allowed her to take her first trip outside the country when the company took the play to Montevideo in early January. Suero, a small fat man known as 'the toad', was a Spanish immigrant known as an important figure among the Buenos Aires intelligentsia. Suero too would become Eva's lover during the successful run of *Los inocentes*, although when it was over he famously and publicly humiliated her when some time later she went to his office seeking work: after waiting for several hours in his crowded office and repeatedly asking the secretary to announce her, she was treated to Suero bounding out of his office and shouting at her 'do you think that because I slept with you I'm always obliged to give you work?'[20] Red-faced, Eva stammered an apology to his closed door and withdrew from the office, undoubtedly feeling a bit more of the 'rancour' that she would later be accused of displaying. (Suero would be run over and killed by a car in 1943.)

Following *Los inocentes*, Eva had little work for several months, apart from a brief role in the Luigi Pirandello play *La nueva colonia* (The New Colony), directed by the distinguished writer and director Enrique Santos Discépolo, a prolific author of tangos, many of them absolute classics. The play was unsuccessful and ran for less than two weeks in March 1937, and Eva would not work again in the theatre until November. However, in mid-year she was hired for a brief appearance in the film *Segundos afuera* (Seconds Out), a boxing story starring Pedro Quartucci and Pablo Palitos that was savaged by the critics (though Quartucci would resurface a few years later in Eva's life). The film was premiered in August, just as Eva was working in a new *radioteatro*, *Oro blanco* (White Gold) at Radio Belgrano, where a few years later she would become the station's highest paid actress. In November she gained a (wordless) small part in a highly successful comedy, *No hay suegra como la mía* (There's No Mother-in-Law Like Mine) which would continue for several months, until March 1938. This would be the beginning of a period of far steadier and increasingly visible work – still poorly paid and small roles, but roles nevertheless.

On 1 March 1938 Eva participated in a radio talent contest sponsored by the fan magazine *Sintonía*, in which she presented the advertisements dispersed throughout the broadcast. The contest was to choose a singer to participate in the new play *La gruta de la fortuna* (The Grotto of Fortune) scheduled to open later that month, presented by the company of Pierina Dealessi. Thanks to her growing friendship with Dealessi, Eva would form part of the cast of the play. At least as importantly, the job allowed her to meet the editor of *Sintonía*, the handsome and dashing Chilean journalist, racing driver and somewhat stereotypical man-about-town Emilio Kartulowicz, whom she impressed by telling him that she had gone to see him race when he visited Junín. Eva fell seriously in love with Kartulowicz, in the 'no half measures' style that would characterise her throughout her life, though the relationship also helped promote her still fledgling career, opening the way to an occasional photo or brief article in the widely read *Sintonía*. According to later testimonies, Eva would sit for hours in the magazine's reception area waiting for Kartulowicz, who seemingly wearied of her tenacity and the inconvenience it implied for his pursuit of other young women. Nonetheless, he appears to have been genuinely fond of her and continued to help her after the relationship ended, publishing photos and recommending her to producers able to offer employment.

For whatever reason, 1938 marked the end of Eva's most difficult period and the start of a largely upward trajectory in both employment and salary. After *La gruta de la fortuna* ended, Eva remained with Dealessi's company in other small roles for the remainder of the year, often staying with the older actress to avoid going home alone late at night. She also had at least a brief romance with the company's producer, Rafael Firtuoso, which may have reinforced the support she received from Dealessi. (On their break-up, Firtuoso is supposed to have said to her, 'you weren't born to go hungry'.[21]) The other plays in the repertoire were poorly received and got negative reviews, although Eva received a few brief and relatively favourable mentions; in one of them she played a maid who 'falls from grace' and becomes pregnant, and is later seen singing a tango to her baby. In September, despite the relationship with Kartulowicz having ended, Eva was also the subject of a brief 'interview' in *Sintonía*, in which she purportedly expressed her views on love, to the effect that 'true love comes only once in a lifetime' and that her 'ideal man should be affectionate, very affectionate. He should be a combination of lover and husband.'[22] While the interview is redacted in a syntax that scarcely suggests the natural conversational style of a young woman and represents the sort of boilerplate article published interchangeably about any young actress being promoted, it was Eva's first real mention in a fan magazine (one of those she had avidly followed herself in Junín) and represented a boost for a hitherto modest career. Also during this period, Eva began to find some modelling work, participating in several advertising campaigns for the agency Linter Publicidad – arguably a better choice of employment for a pretty girl generally agreed to be a static and inexpressive actress.

In January 1939 Eva joined Camila Quiroga's company for another successful play, *Mercado de amor en Argelia* (Market of Love in Algeria), directed by Guibourg, which was considered 'not suitable for younger viewers' and in which Eva played an odalisque, the largest speaking part she had had thus far. More importantly, however, 1939 saw a rapid shift in the focus of Eva's career from the stage, where she never advanced beyond marginal supporting roles, to the radio. In May the newly formed Compañia de Teatro del Aire (Theatre of the Air Company), headed by 'Evita Duarte and Pascual Pelliciotta', joined Radio Mitre to begin broadcasting a series of *radioteatros* by the well-known writer Héctor Pedro Blomberg, whom Eva had encountered earlier and who was rumoured, correctly or not, to be another of her well-placed lovers. The magazine *Antena* published

Eva's photo and the start of her first starring radio role, in *Los jazmines del 80* (The Jasmines of 1880), coincided with her 20th birthday; later in May *Antena* gave her her first magazine cover, and occasional (largely fictional) interviews and articles began to be published. Eva had come a long way in the little more than four years since she had left Junín, finally climbing out of the poverty and complete insecurity of the starving bit player.

Not everything in 1939 went Eva's way. Some reports indicate that she had come close to marriage with a young actor with whom she was living, and that he suddenly and without explanation abandoned her, clearing out the flat they shared. Also around this period, her name was linked to an industrialist with whom, according to an interview at the time, she intended to marry and settle down, leaving her artistic career behind. The businessman, apparently Juan Llauró, supposedly broke off the relationship after his chauffeur implied that she had made a pass at him.[23] More concretely, her brother Juancito would prove a source of worry, not for the only time. Juancito had stayed in Buenos Aires after completing his military service, and had remained a frequent companion and source of emotional support for Eva, separated from the rest of her family and, at least in her early days, a timid and fragile figure. The two siblings would remain very close, looking out for each other in good times and bad – the two most rebellious members of the Duarte/Ibarguren tribe, they stood together and her brother would remain closer to Eva than the rest of her family. However, in 1939 Juancito, who had not given up his sometimes dubious practices, was accused of embezzling money from the savings bank where he had found work after conscription. In order to prevent him from going to jail, Eva sold what little she had accumulated and paid off his debts, giving up the flat she had finally attained and returning to a cheap *pensión* for the time being.

Nonetheless, before much longer Juancito would return the favour: after his precipitous departure from the savings bank, he found work as a salesman with Guereño, the company that produced Radical soap (the 'king and lord of soaps', later renamed Federal soap), a major sponsor of *radioteatros*. Ever charming, Juancito also became a close friend and confidant of the Guereño family, which would later boost Eva's career as a radio actress further still. On a rare visit to Junín in 1936, when Erminda was ill with pleurisy, Eva had rejected Doña Juana's demands that she return home permanently, saying that she would come back only when she had 'conquered' Buenos Aires. While that conquest seemed a faint possibility in 1936, by 1939 it increasingly appeared to be drawing near.

 CHAPTER 4

Radiolandia[1]

F ROM THE TIME of its first broadcast on 27 August 1920, the radio
in Argentina had expanded rapidly and had gone from strength to
strength, with the number of radio stations increasing at a similar fast pace. Much of the content was culturally highbrow, at least originally: that debut airing involved a full version of Wagner's *Parsifal*. President
Marcelo T. de Alvear, the 'anti-personalist' Radical who took office in 1922,
became the first president to address the nation by radio. By 1923 there
were four other important radio stations, and around 150,000 radio sets in
the country, with radios becoming a rapidly increasing consumer item.[2]
News broadcasts were also gaining space, although these initially involved
an announcer reading the daily newspaper, while from 1923 sportscasting
was also introduced, with the boxing match between Jack Dempsey and
the Argentine Angel Firpo, the 'wild bull of the Pampas', born in Junín;
football began to be broadcast the following year.

However, the popularity of tango was perhaps the key to the rapid
rise of radio as a form of entertainment. Radio stations promoted tango
orchestras and singers who, like Carlos Gardel and Agustín Magaldi, and
the conductors Julio de Caro and Francisco Canaro, became household
names. As the number of radio sets and radio stations proliferated, the
medium became an increasingly attractive one for advertising, while the
amount of air time available required a rising amount of content. By the
end of the 1920s, much of this had become more formalised, with news
broadcasts taking place in the key 8.00–9.00 morning slot and musical and
theatrical offerings going out in the evening. However, popular enthusiasm
and extensive air time would rapidly begin to require content produced
specifically for the radio in the form of both informative programmes and

radioteatros. The more culturally sophisticated of these were reserved primarily for the night slots, around 10.30 pm, but the early evening slots at 5.00 pm were often given over to the sort of romantic stories designed to appeal to women preparing dinner and, not least, domestic servants who listened to the radio while cleaning and ironing.

It was to this audience that Eva's early radio broadcasts were largely directed. While elite anti-Peronist ladies would later scoff, claiming that they had tuned in to howl with laughter at her poor diction and provincial accent, this was the sort of romantic, rose-coloured story that Eva and millions like her could relate to, and it made a name for her among working women of often humble origin long before she became known for her political activities. In addition, this was a key audience for producers of household products such as soap, so someone like Eva who had contacts in the industry had an immediate advantage. Added to that advantage was the fact that she sounded – and was – young and somewhat wistful, and that she was a pretty girl who looked the part in the advertising and fan magazine photos that accompanied the productions. Her roles were those of young, poor but honest women who, after suffering for several instalments, finish in the arms of the handsome hero. With her (later obvious) capacity to attract interest and sympathy, and her ability to convey sincerity, these qualities made her virtually ideal for the type of programme that would see her star rise in a way that it had never done 'on the boards'.

In a 'secret account' of Eva sent from the British Embassy to the Foreign Office on 7 March 1947, the author defines Eva as an unsuccessful actress,

> despite her many friendships with directors, impresarios and actors. In 1940, with the help of a wealthy soap manufacturer she got employment in broadcasting, in which she was equally unsuccessful, though she was able to hold her position as the result of the favours she bestowed on successive directors.

The note also describes her as 'common, almost completely illiterate but physically attractive. She was also extremely foul-mouthed.'[3] This would appear to be a fair reflection of the sort of comment that circulated among the wealthier classes (likelier to have contacts with the Embassy) once Eva became first lady, although it is a partial picture of her career; indeed, a later communication from British Ambassador John Balfour (hardly an uncritical admirer) would observe that 'incidentally, the stories of her earlier life are highly exaggerated'.[4]

Following her success in *Los jazmines del 80*, in August 1939 Eva starred in another well-received romantic *novela* by Blomberg at Radio Prieto, *Las rosas de Caseros* (The Roses of Caseros), in which she received good reviews, although her subsequent programme, *La estrella del pirata* (The Pirate's Star) did poorly and she faced another brief period without work. Worse, as the nominal head of her own production company, she was forced to cover its debts. Nevertheless, her photo appeared on two magazine covers in the latter part of 1939: in *Sintonía* in October and *Damas y Damitas* in December. According to the later reminiscences of Vera Pichel, then editorial manager at *Damas y Damitas*, Eva came to see her to ask for her help, as one working woman to another, saying that she needed the magazine cover to bolster her career; Pichel lent her a costume for the occasion and the resulting photo duly appeared on the cover.[5]

Despite a certain hiatus in her radio work in late 1939 and early 1940, the new year was a professionally active one for Eva. In August she would appear for the last time on the stage in small roles in two plays, *Corazón de manteca* (Heart of Butter) and the prophetically named *La plata hay que repartirla* (Money Should be Spread Around), neither of which did well and both of which closed relatively promptly. However, Eva also returned to work in films in that year, starting in early 1940 with *La carga de los valientes* (The Charge of the Brave), set during the 1827 war with Brazil and premiered in May, and later *El más infeliz del pueblo* (The Unhappiest Man in Town), starring the popular comic actor Luis Sandrini and released in 1941. Although largely unnoticed in the latter, Eva received a good notice, in the Junín press at least, for her work in *La carga de los valientes*, and in an interview with the local newspaper *La Verdad* the director, Adelqui Millar, praised her work and predicted a successful career.

In truth, Eva's relative success in films during 1940 may have been due in some significant part to her romance with the owner of the company Pampa Film, Olegario Ferrando, which would prove short-lived. Reports in the magazine *Antena* in June 1941 claimed that 'she represented Paradise for him, she is not called Eva in vain'.[6] In mid-1940 Eva had purportedly told the magazine *Guión* that she would marry an industrialist and retire by the end of the year; whether she was referring to Ferrando, or to the earlier-mentioned businessman (possibly Llauró) is not clear, nor is it certain that the interview was real (nor for that matter the fiancé).

However, by later in 1940 she was back on the radio and there was no further sign of retirement or of marriage.

Eva's busy round of public activities in 1940 points up the unlikelihood of another rumour surrounding her life in this period. Eva was said to have had an affair with Pedro Quartucci, either during or after the filming of *Segundos afuera* in 1937. (According to María Sucarrat, Quartucci paid for a flat for Eva for several months in 1940 and the two enjoyed a lengthy relationship, although other sources are silent on this.[7]) Quartucci, already a well-known actor in the 1930s (and frequently the subject of rumoured romances, although he was married), himself said little of Eva thereafter, noting that he had met her while filming *Segundos afuera* and had subsequently worked with her again in *Una novia en apuros* (A Bride In Trouble) in 1941. Quartucci said only that 'the filming of [*Una novia en apuros*] took 70 days, and no one paid much attention to Eva, because she was a fairly timid, quiet and submissive girl. She didn't mix with anyone and didn't socialise with the stars.'[8]

In 1999 Quartucci's daughter Nilda, born in October 1940, brought a court case in which she claimed to be Eva's daughter, citing as evidence that blood tests showed she was not the daughter of Quartucci's wife Felisa Bonorino. Although versions of the supposed event differ, Nilda claimed to have been taken away by Quartucci as soon as she was born and taken to his wife to be raised as part of his legitimate family. It must be assumed that Bonorino believed the baby to be the child of her husband and Eva Duarte, either because she suspected a relationship or because he or a third party told her so. Supposedly on Quartucci's orders, Eva had been told that the baby had died – an act of monstrous cruelty if it were so (but a not-uncommon practice in cases of the kind, given that 'fallen' women were considered to be unsuitable mothers, though the married men who fathered their illegitimate offspring apparently could be seen as appropriate role models).

Although Eva's surviving relatives rejected demands to perform DNA tests on her body and the Supreme Court rejected a petition to this effect, in 2006 a court dismissed the case on the grounds that DNA tests showed that Nilda was not Quartucci's biological daughter and thus not the offspring of his relationship with Eva Duarte.[9] While this conclusion raises the obvious question of whether she could have been the child of Eva Duarte with another man, since the biological relationship with the mother was never proved or disproved, at first sight the suggestion that Eva had a child appears extremely implausible. Given that she worked in two films and two plays during the period of her purported pregnancy (the two plays only a couple of months before Nilda was born), it is difficult to believe that this would have gone unnoticed throughout the nine months.

Moreover, the 'Liberating Revolution' that overthrew Perón in 1955 obsessively searched for facts, rumours or outright falsehoods which could have served to blacken the reputation of Perón or Evita, and the possibility that they could have overlooked a bombshell as large as an illegitimate child seems remote. In particular, in 1955 only 15 years had passed since the supposed birth, memories were still relatively fresh and among the people who had known Eva in her early years in Buenos Aires were many anti-Peronists who would doubtless have been pleased to revive any contemporary rumours.

Nilda Quartucci claimed that Eva subsequently learned that her daughter had lived and was in fact the daughter of the Quartucci family, but by that time was first lady of Argentina and could say nothing about the issue. One of the so-called 'proofs' cited of Eva's motherhood is a letter sent to her sisters by her confessor, Father Hernán Benítez, 33 years after her death, in which he refers to her 'secret suffering', which was the true key to her greatness and which none but he and her sisters knew. According to the letter, that suffering, worse than the cancer that killed her, followed her to her grave, and she frequently told him that she could not bear it and was disposed to take 'extreme measures'.[10] Benítez himself would note years later that as a rising young priest he had gained considerable repute among some of Buenos Aires's wealthier congregations and frequently preached at Radio Belgrano during the 1940s, during the same period that Eva worked there. He admitted that, during Holy Week of 1944, the apparently distraught young actress had asked to speak with him but that he subsequently forgot the appointment he gave her and did not turn up. Some time later, when Perón introduced him to Eva, she pointed out to him that he had stood her up when she was seeking his assistance, presumably because she was a poor radio actress and not the bearer of one of the Argentine aristocracy's illustrious surnames.[11]

However, while this would be a deeply tragic possibility, it nonetheless remains highly unlikely. On all evidence, Eva liked children and at least in the early years was hopeful of having a child with Perón. (According to the Peronist historian Fermín Chávez, from early in her life she suffered from uterine problems that eventually developed into her terminal cancer, and miscarried after her marriage as a result, although this story may have been designed to counter the usual assumption that Perón was sterile.) This may have been the 'secret suffering' to which Benítez referred.

Entering into pure speculation, it is not impossible that Eva could have had a child that she was forced to give up or could have had an illegal abortion during her early years that could have resulted in the problems Chávez spoke of – had she become pregnant as an impoverished young actress alone in Buenos Aires, this could have appeared the only option. Other rumours have suggested that she could have had a child before leaving Junín, possibly arising from the relationship with the anarchist Damián Gómez; some even suggest that she could have given birth to a seriously disabled child and that this was an element of permanent suffering. (Two fictional versions of her life that incorporate substantial real-life testimonies as well as imagination, Tomás Eloy Martínez's *Santa Evita* and Abel Posse's *La pasión según Eva*, both refer to her having secretly looked after a group of seriously disabled children before meeting Perón, and to her anguish when they were to be removed to a care home and supposedly 'lost' en route.) It is also speculated that Eva's hope of having a child and the intolerable symbolism of losing her uterus may have been a factor that led her to reject surgery that might have saved her life, although her refusal to accept the need for cancer surgery may equally have sprung from understandable fear (Vera Pichel cites her repeated fear that doctors were 'sons of the oligarchy' who would wish to do her harm[12]), or the nefarious but not uncommon practice of the time of not telling patients that they had cancer.

After a hiatus in her radio work after the failure of *La estrella del pirata* (almost certainly due to professional rather than maternal reasons), Eva returned to Radio Prieto later in 1940 with her company in the novela *Los amores de Schubert*, by Alejandro Casona and sponsored by Llauró. She also participated in a talent contest at Radio Argentina sponsored by the magazine *Guión*. By early 1941 her programme was sponsored by Guereño, Juancito's employer, with which she signed a five-year exclusive contract, beginning with the programme *La hora de las sorpresas* (The Hour of Surprises) at Radio Argentina. Also around this time, she began filming *Una novia en apuros*. Again she had a small role and critics largely overlooked her participation in favour of the film's stars, but her five-year contract with Guereño gave her an economic and professional security she had not previously enjoyed.

The following year she became the leading actress of the Candilejas company and moved to Radio Mundo (and later Radio Belgrano) for a series of *radioteatros* that allowed her to move to a flat (or, according to some sources, a room at the Savoy Hotel in Callao Street, near the Congress building) and begin to enjoy a more settled life. Later, she would move to a flat at 1567 Posadas Street, in the upmarket Recoleta neighbourhood, where she and Perón would later cohabit until he assumed the presidency in 1946. Directors and fellow actors continued to disparage her histrionic talents but recognised both her intelligence and professionalism. The *novelas* continued the usual predictable themes and had forgettable names such as *Una promesa de amor* (A Promise of Love), *El rostro del lobo* (The Face of the Wolf), *Mi amor nace en tí* (My Love is Born in You) and *La otra cara de la máscara* (The Other Side of the Mask). Film and radio magazines published an increasing number of articles and photos of the rising young actress. Many also speculated as to romances with her leading men, such as Marcos Zucker and Pablo Raccioppi, although the latter was married and the former widely assumed to be gay.

This type of gossip, typically attributing love affairs to film starlets and young actors (both to boost their profile and, in some cases, to conceal non-heterosexual tendencies), was common around the world at the time and often fictional, but in public perceptions it added to Eva's already not inconsiderable romantic resume. While this may have mattered little to her during this phase of her life, it would fuel anti-Peronist rhetoric and doubtless influenced her decision to virtually erase her previous career after her marriage to Perón. In fact, with the exception of the more evident relationships with José Franco, Emilio Kartulowicz, Pablo Suero and the like, many of Eva's supposed affairs are likely to have been apocryphal; after her death, no supposed former lovers came forward either to brag of the relationship or to complain of having been used/abused, and the frequent references to her numerous affairs do not mention names. To a degree, this appears to be a case of the phrase frequently used in Latin America: 'everybody knows it', which more often than not is a euphemism for 'lots of people think it, but nobody actually knows it'.

Early in 1943, on medical advice (and supposedly because she had been offered no new roles worthy of her status), Eva took a lengthy break from work, between January and July, staying part of this time with a friend in La Plata, the capital of Buenos Aires province. According to Vera Pichel, she was hospitalised in the Otamendi y Miroli clinic in

Buenos Aires for at least part of this time.[13] This obscure period has also given rise to rumours either that Eva was already dogged by the serious ill health that would become evident only a few years later, or that in fact she had either a clandestine birth or a clandestine abortion that could have caused irreparable damage and possibly even presaged the uterine cancer that would kill her. Whether or not this is true, or whether a key factor was lack of work as opposed to health concerns, professional photos from around this time show a different look to Eva. While her earlier photos (even those intended to be risqué) showed a somewhat ingenuous, candid and rather shy-looking young woman, later professional photos show a harder and more veiled expression, and a veneer that was previously lacking, whether due to greater age and experience or to the effects of many years of ill-treatment. However, beyond the personal level, her absence from the radio waves (or the 'ether', as it was usually described) in early 1943 was of limited wider importance in a context of dramatic political upheaval.

Although the effects of the Depression had largely subsided by 1943, the post-1929 shift towards import-substitution industrialisation and the crisis of agricultural exports had brought with them a process of mass internal migration from the countryside and from smaller cities to the industrial suburbs of Buenos Aires and other large cities. For the first time, native-born migrants outnumbered European immigrants in the cities, but those migrants had little access to the wealth and diversions of Buenos Aires. Wages remained low and trade union organisation limited, not least because unions had hitherto had little effect on labour practices – a vicious circle in which low levels of unionisation limited the effectiveness of unions, which in turn limited the attractiveness of joining. The governments of the 'Infamous Decade', both military and fraudulently elected civilians, maintained a repressive stance towards labour, and the post-1930 shift back towards the political dominance of the traditional conservative elites ensured that the working classes remained politically marginal. Nevertheless, the fall in unemployment as the economy began to recover after 1935 led to greater union militancy, and the number of strikes increased, reaching 113 in 1942 (of which only 45 obtained pay demands).[14]

At the same time, by 1943 the political vacuum at the centre of government was increasing, with the Radical Party still in disarray after the death of Yrigoyen in 1933, and the governments of the so-called Concordancia alliance increasingly discredited by corruption, fraud and illegitimacy.

Moreover, sectors of the military became increasingly concerned over foreign policy as World War II progressed, with some elements supporting the Allies and others openly pro-Axis. President Ramón Castillo (who had assumed office when the previous incumbent, Roberto Ortiz, was forced to step down in 1940 on the grounds of ill health), a conservative member of the elite from the impoverished northern province of Catamarca, quashed any plans for economic reforms designed to shift benefits from agriculture to manufacturing, despite the fact that both agricultural exports and imports of manufactures had been disrupted again by the war. Castillo's neutrality in the war angered both factions within the armed forces (not least given that neutrality cost Argentina military aid from the United States, which was lavished on rival Brazil). Matters finally came to a head when Castillo insisted on putting forward Robustiano Patrón Costas as the official presidential candidate in 1943. Patrón Costas, a member of the landed elite from Salta province, adjoining Catamarca, was anathema to much of the military, due to his pro-Allied position, the 'feudal' conditions in which his Salta workforce lived, and the continued electoral fraud that would be required to bring him to the presidency.

On 4 June 1943 a *coup d' état* overthrew Castillo and put General Arturo Rawson briefly in charge. However, the coup (which would come to be known as the '4 June revolution') was engineered not by Rawson or any other senior officer, but by a group of junior officers who had formed a secret *loggia* known as the GOU (Grupo de Oficiales Unidos, although other supposed titles were *Gobierno! Orden! Unidad!* or the Grupo de Obra Unificación). While the GOU's supposed aims were no clearer than its title, two of its leading creators and ideological influences were Colonel Juan Domingo Perón and his close ally Colonel Domingo Mercante. Although its actual aims were nebulous and probably not universally agreed among its participants, at the first GOU meeting to which other officers were invited, in May 1943, Perón's 'tongue ran away with him and he said: "we are going to make a revolution",' an announcement that apparently took those present by surprise.[15] Despite this general lack of clarity, surviving GOU documents (many probably authored by Perón) highlight issues such as nationalism, political and economic independence and the need to attend to the demands of the poor and dispossessed, ideas that would be central to Peronism. Nor was it clear whether the GOU proposed to remain in government or to seek, alternatively, a military dictatorship or a return to clean elections.

In the event, Rawson lasted only briefly in the presidency, rapidly replaced by General Pedro Ramírez, with General Edelmiro Farrell as vice-president and war minister. Farrell himself, in turn, was significant primarily due to his friendship with Colonel Perón, whose influence over his superior was widely remarked. Perón himself became secretary at the War Ministry and, in October, asked for and received the job of running the National Labour Department (DNT), a hitherto marginal organ that had focused largely on collecting labour statistics; its powers to implement labour legislation that was on the books but dormant were negligible. Once in situ, Perón (abetted by Mercante) rapidly raised the DNT's profile and his own, opening the office to trade unionists and promising to work for the welfare of the working class – albeit through a balance between the needs of labour and factories, not through class conflict. The DNT became the Secretariat of Labour and Social Welfare a month later, giving Perón a cabinet post, and would rapidly become a hive of activity. Within two years it brought legislation establishing professional and technical training courses, minimum wages, sick pay and annual leave, pensions and a system of labour courts; it also enforced existing legislation for the first time. Moreover, the Secretariat actively encouraged union organisation, and the number of both trade unions and union members virtually tripled between 1941 and 1945. However, this came at a cost for union independence: unions led by Peronist sympathisers won benefits that others did not, and new decree legislation established that only one union would be recognised in any given field. With control over the Secretariat and influence in the War Ministry, Perón was rapidly consolidated as the strongman of the new government.

However, the military government did not confine itself to labour reform, but among other things also aimed to elevate cultural norms and, in particular, bring them into line with the Catholic, Hispanic heritage of 'Argentineness' (*argentinidad*). This was not a novel approach for the armed forces: the official version of Argentine history thus far had been based on the alliance between 'the Cross and the Sword' that had conquered and civilised (sic) the territory. Moreover, Perón's overtures to the workers found an echo in the Catholic social action of the 1930s: based on the 1891 Papal encyclical *Rerum Novarum*, elements of the Church had been active in labour rights and the Juventud Obrera Católica, founded in 1939, was especially active among the urban working classes.

The government's (largely successful) efforts to keep the Catholic Church onside also included the imposition of compulsory religious education in December 1943, the banning of slang and vulgar language in tango lyrics, and censorship and prior approval of film and radio scripts to ensure that they were morally uplifting, or at least did not clash with the norms of good taste and decency. As a result, from mid-June all actors and writers aiming to broadcast on the radio had to pass first through the Office of Post and Telecommunications, headed by Colonel Aníbal Imbert, to get his seal of approval on all scripts before they could be produced. Imbert also ruled on how long *novelas* could be, how many chapters they could include and whether they were guilty of including 'sensationalist narratives or unedifying stories, the use of expressions that bastardise the language, etc.'[16] Returning to work, Eva was one of the many who had to wait long hours to see Imbert in order to get their projects off the ground. In addition, in August 1943 Eva was one of the founders of the Argentine Radio Association (ARA), an organisation aimed at defending the rights of workers in the medium. While waiting endlessly to see Imbert, Eva would encounter his secretary, Oscar Nicolini.

According to most versions, Nicolini was already known to Eva, an acquaintance from Junín, although others suggest that he befriended her in Imbert's office. Nicolini was a career employee of the postal service, and some versions indicate that during his tenure in Junín he had been responsible for investigating a complaint brought by Eva's sister Elisa against a co-worker; more highly coloured versions suggest that he was also one of Doña Juana's lovers and benefactors. In any case, he and Eva established or re-established a friendship in the Central Post Office building in Buenos Aires. By her own admission, Eva at this stage of her career had little interest in or understanding of politics, but she did understand the importance of what would now be called 'networking'. Just as Doña Juana had used even tenuous political contacts (and shifted them as political power shifted) and relations to gain employment and better opportunities, Eva had long since showed that she was effective at playing this game, both with her theatre and radio contacts and with Juancito and his links with Guereño and the king and lord of soaps. Nicolini represented an 'in' with Imbert that would prove useful – in particular given her months-long absence from the radio circuit, which can only have been damaging to the career of an only moderately well-known young actress.

Opinions are also divided as to whether Imbert was to become one of Eva's lovers, and indeed as to whether they liked each other at all. According to some, she rapidly became his mistress after Nicolini made the requisite introductions, while according to others, Eva's friend Dorita Norvi was Imbert's mistress and Imbert actively loathed Eva and her strong character.[17] The question becomes more confused by the fact that Eva's former co-star Pablo Raccioppi would much later claim that the central flat she moved to in 1942 was rumoured to be Imbert's 'love nest',[18] despite the fact that there is no other suggestion that she and Imbert would have met before the coup and his move to Post and Telecommunications. (Even more confusingly, other versions suggest that in fact Eva was already involved with Perón at this stage and that the figure of Imbert was used as 'camouflage', despite the fact that there is no evidence that she and Perón had ever met at the time – nor any obvious reason why they would have kept the relationship secret in 1943, only to begin flaunting it quite flagrantly only months later.)

In practice, as usual the truth is probably less extreme than painted. Given Eva's skills at 'making friends with the judge' (to quote the epic gaucho poem *Martín Fierro*), it is unlikely that she would have maintained an actively hostile relationship with Imbert, whose position allowed him considerable leeway in promoting or prohibiting radio performers. At the same time, Eva was a reasonably well-known radio actress but not significant enough a figure to loom large on Imbert's radar, assuming that they were not in fact lovers. Following the rise of Perón and Eva, it became *de rigeur* to claim that all men who crossed her professional path had been her lovers. Whatever the relationship with Imbert, he would prove useful to Eva's career at least by approving a series of duly edifying scripts that would give her greater dramatic possibilities than ever before. Her ability to establish relationships of whatever kind at this level startled her colleagues; Marcos Zucker, who appeared with her both on stage in *La gruta de la fortuna* and on the radio in *Los jazmines del 80*, would later say that 'when we saw that she was linked to military and political personalities it surprised us all; we couldn't imagine that a colleague of ours was involved with those people'.[19]

Whether thanks to Imbert, Guereño or other intervention, it was announced in September that Eva would star in a series of programmes for Radio Belgrano dramatising the lives of famous women in history, including Queen Elizabeth I, Catherine the Great, Sarah Bernhardt, Isadora

Duncan, Lady Hamilton and Madame Chiang Kai Shek. Whatever inter-pretation can be made of the foreshadowing this series implied for Eva's own future career as a famous woman in history, the series, which began broadcasting in October 1943 and continued through 1944, would mark the apex of Eva's acting career. It brought her a well-remunerated con-tract, the opportunity to move to a flat in a fashionable area of Buenos Aires, and national recognition (of her name if not her talent). Perhaps most importantly, it marked the first time that a group of important writers would create scripts specifically for her; one of those writers, Francisco Muñoz Aspiri, would later become one of her speechwriters. Despite the difficulties that marked the start of the year, with frail health and a possible broken romance, Eva was ending 1943 at a level of success that she had never before experienced. No longer an inexperienced 15-year-old, at 24 she had learned how to make use of networks and gain advantages from her personal and professional contacts of whatever type. However, her radio career would soon take a back seat to other concerns and, within two years, be terminated altogether. On 15 January 1944 an earthquake would devastate the city of San Juan, in western Argentina, and would start a pro-cess that would transform Eva Duarte the radio actress into Eva Perón, Evita, the Lady of Hope – or 'that woman'.

 CHAPTER 5

Perón

MUCH OF THE political career of Juan Domingo Perón contained a hefty dose of providence, and of being in the right place at the right time. His meeting with Eva was no exception, and would leave a mark on Argentine politics that endures more than 70 years later. That chance meeting, in the context of a catastrophic earthquake, would generate a political earthquake as well, altering the social and political landscape and the course of the nation's life, not just that of the couple and their immediate associates. Without Eva, Perón would still have been Perón, albeit within different parameters, and Peronism would have become a major political movement. By contrast, without Perón, it is difficult to see how Eva could have become Evita or left her stamp on society, despite her remarkable qualities. Nevertheless, those remarkable qualities would arguably let her outshine her husband (whose own remarkable qualities were not neglible) and make her a force to be reckoned with long after both were gone.

At the time of the San Juan earthquake, Colonel Juan Domingo Perón was 48 years old (or 50, depending on the version accepted) and, with less than a year's practical political experience, was already on the road to becoming the most important figure in Argentina. Like Eva, Perón came from Buenos Aires province, and like Eva, his was an illegitimate birth (though unlike her, he could be classed as 'natural' rather than as a 'bastard', as neither of his parents was married to anyone else, and they eventually wed in 1901). Officially, he was born in the town of Lobos on 8 October 1895. However, some sources indicate that Perón was in fact born a day or two earlier, just outside Lobos, while others place his birth in nearby in Roque Pérez on 7 October 1893, with his birth only registered two years later when his father decided to recognise his illegitimate son.[1] According to this version, sustained by Perón himself later in life, the birth was registered in Lobos because it housed the Registry Office nearest to Roque Pérez.

Perón was the second son of Mario Tomás Perón and Juana Sosa Toledo; their older son, Mario Avelino, was born in 1891. Perón's paternal grandfather, Tomás Perón, had been a distinguished doctor and later a senator, but Mario was to have a less impressive career. After his father died in 1889, Mario abandoned his medical studies and became a public employee in Lobos, forming a relationship with Juana Sosa, a young country girl of Indian ancestry. Argentines of European origin sought to distinguish themselves from their darker-skinned compatriots of possible indigenous ancestry, and the fact that Perón's parents were not married and were socially unequal represented a social stigma, albeit not one that appears to have affected Perón deeply.

When Perón was five years old, Mario moved the family to the remote southern region of Patagonia, in the territory of Santa Cruz. His isolated childhood seems to have informed Perón's adult character and thinking, which was independent and somewhat aloof, but acutely aware of the miserable social conditions in which rural workers lived. In 1904, the family moved slightly to the north, to the territory of Chubut, although Perón remained largely isolated. Like Doña Juana, Juana Sosa appears to have been indomitable, iron-willed and ready to face whatever came.[2]

Also in 1904, Perón and his brother Mario returned to Buenos Aires to study, although shortly thereafter Mario fell ill and returned permanently to Chubut. Perón remained in Buenos Aires in the home of his paternal aunts, increasing his independent nature and, according to his schoolmates, the tendency to be bossy (a term also used to describe Eva). Although he began studying to enter medical school, he abandoned the idea after being accepted by the military academy (Colegio Militar). There he acquired a life-long admiration for German military discipline and for authoritarian attitudes (which was widespread not only within the military, but among society more widely), although as British Ambassador Sir David Kelly would later note astutely, he was 'not in the least interested in Nazi or other ideology'[3]. The lack of ideological commitment would remain a constant throughout his life.

Perón entered the Colegio Militar in 1911, where he was more notable as an athlete than as a student, and on graduating in 1913 he entered the infantry as a sub-lieutenant. After a stint in Paraná, Entre Ríos province, he was said to have been among the troops sent to quell protests in what became the *Semana Trágica* (Tragic Week) in Buenos Aires in 1919, although he would later claim that he had 'only read about it in the newspapers', since at the time he was involved in 'containing' another worker protest. This one was at the British-owned La Forestal plantation in San Cristóbal, in the north of Santa Fe province, where he purportedly succeeded in negotiating a peaceful settlement by acceding to worker demands. Commenting later on the *Semana Trágica*, he would remark that 'they said they were pro-Russian communists; I'm inclined to think they were just poor Argentines scourged by physiological and social misery'.[4] In 1920 he transferred to the non-commissioned officers' school at Campo de Mayo, near Buenos Aires. Here he became highly respected as an instructor, showing a natural gift for teaching as well as rapport with and care for the men under his command. Many who came from poor families were unschooled in even relatively basic matters, and Perón was given to teaching them personal hygiene and basic etiquette in addition to military matters.

In 1926, Perón was sent to the Superior War School, founded to train middle-ranking officers for higher command posts, and graduated in 1929, shortly before the start of the Great Depression. A year later, Captain Perón would become involved, if only in relatively marginal fashion, in the military plots to overthrow the aging President Hipólito Yrigoyen. Perón joined the officers backing General José Félix Uriburu, although a few days before the 6 September 1930 coup he withdrew from Uriburu's camp and joined that of his military rival, General Agustín P. Justo, whose supporters favoured a joint military-civilian government. While the sudden shift from one side to another was typical of Perón, he played a very minimal role in the coup, and one that he later regretted, noting the nefarious precedent it set in public life, the ending of the hopes of greater social progress and the strengthening of the most conservative sectors of the oligarchy.[5]

With Uriburu the eventual winner in the power struggle with Justo, Perón and other Justo supporters were rapidly marginalised, and he was sent to patrol the Argentine–Bolivian border for two months, before assuming his new post as professor of military history at the Superior War School in 1931. However, after Justo was elected president in fraudulent elections in 1931, Perón was promoted to the rank of major, and also served as aide de camp to the defence minister. However, at this stage of his career Perón was still far more devoted to his military and academic pursuits than to politics, honing his talents as a writer, teacher and communicator. The post of military history professor helped to develop his teaching vocation, and during his tenure he also wrote three books on military history, as well as a history of Patagonian place names. At the same time he remained a talented athlete, and was army champion of both boxing and fencing; he was also a good horseman and an accomplished skier, which would bring him further professional opportunities some years later. Throughout his life Perón remained enthusiastic about sports as both participant and spectator, also including auto racing, although unlike most of his countrymen he had only passing interest in football. (Perón's aptitude and enthusiasm for individual sporting disciplines and indifference to team sports makes for an interesting if unsurprising psychological footnote.)

During this period, Perón had also taken another step common to ambitious young military officers. In January 1929 he married 20-year-old Aurelia Tizón, known as 'Potota'. Aurelia, a music teacher, was the daughter of a middle-class Buenos Aires merchant with good connections in the Radical Party that would later be of service to his son-in-law. She was 13 years younger than Perón (or 15, if the unofficial birthdate of 1893 is accepted) and deferential as befitted contemporary customs, always referring to him as 'Perón' when speaking to others. The marriage would have been considered a beneficial one for both sides, given Potota's respectable and well-connected family and Perón's ascending career, good status and good looks. Both were largely conventional in their habits and customs: entering the military (or the priesthood) was a traditional means of advancement for upwardly mobile or academically minded young men of respectable but not wealthy family, while Aurelia's fondness for music and painting and her good upbringing made her an excellent wife for an army officer. Their ten-year marriage was generally regarded as successful and happy, and they were a popular couple among their contemporaries. However, the formalities of the time and of their relationship (as well as Perón's frequent coldness with respect to other people) are reflected in the fact that virtually his only public comment on Aurelia, made in a 1970 interview more than 30 years after her death, was: 'In '28 I married Aurelia Tizón. She was a very nice girl, a concert guitarist. She played very well. Unfortunately she died young.'[6]

Despite their apparently contented decade-long relationship, the Perón-Tizón marriage produced no children. The question of Perón's infertility, which according to some sources was confirmed by a family doctor during this first marriage, was a thorny one for his followers in a *machista* society. It has been disputed by rumours that both Eva and his third wife, Isabel, had been pregnant by him and had suffered miscarriages (although Peronist historian Fermín Chávez in particular contended that Eva's health problems began far earlier than recognised, and that she was unable to conceive). Perón himself later claimed that he had fathered a child by an Italian actress during his stay in Europe in the late 1930s, although his subsequent attempts to locate her never bore fruit.

Subsequently, well after his death, a lady named Martha Holgado persistently claimed to be his illegitimate daughter, even purporting to have maintained a close relationship with him during his term as president and to have been present, Zelig-like, at many significant historical events – at which, oddly, her presence seems to have passed unnoticed by the participants. This version was cited by the author Horacio Vázquez-Rial, who claims that Perón had an affair with Martha's mother, Cecilia Demarchi, when he was still married to Aurelia and Cecilia was separated from her husband, Eugenio Holgado, and that Holgado subsequently pressured his wife to return and recognised the child as his own.[7] According to this version, Perón himself subsequently told this story to Martha after Eva's death (although if this is so, it is difficult to see how he could have known with certainty that the child was his and not Holgado's). A 2003 DNA test indicated that Martha was not Perón's child, and that she was almost certainly the full blood relative of her brother, Eugenio Holgado, who was never claimed to have been Perón's offspring.[8] In any case, other testimonies, as well as the fact that none of Perón's three marriages produced children, would tend to suggest that he was in fact infertile.[9] Moreover, other versions reject this story entirely, on the grounds that Perón was an attentive husband who might become overly involved in his work but not with other women. Indeed, although in his roughly 80 years of life Perón had a number of relationships (including three marriages, two of them cut short by the early death of a young wife), he seems to have been given to 'serial monogamy' and never had a reputation as a womaniser despite his good looks and attractive personality. (In fact, Perón's three marriages added up to a total of only 30 years of holy matrimony; he was technically single or a widower for around half a century.)

Early in 1936, Perón was named military attaché in the Argentine Embassy in Santiago, Chile, a country with which Argentina maintained frequently tense relations. Perón and Aurelia remained in Chile until

March 1938, during which time he was promoted to lieutenant colonel, although he was also accused of spying for Argentina and was rumored to have been expelled by the Chilean government. Perón was later known to have formed a group of informers for the purpose of obtaining information on Chilean military plans, an activity common for military attachés – in fact their main function. (Supposedly Aurelia made various trips to Buenos Aires for health reasons when in fact Perón was using her as an agent to pass information to Army intelligence.[10]) However, his successor, Major Eduardo Lonardi, with whom Perón and Aurelia had apparently had a warm relationship, was eventually caught and deported, purportedly leading to a grudge that influenced Lonardi to lead the coup against Perón in 1955.[11] Nevertheless, Lonardi's widow, many years later, spoke warmly of Aurelia and indicated both that Perón was an attentive and caring husband and that the two were an 'exemplary couple'.[12]

In September 1938, Perón became a widower when Aurelia died of uterine cancer at the age of only 30 (although in surviving photos she already looks to be well into middle age). She had suffered from vaginal haemorrhaging and frequent hospitalisations for some time, even before they left Chile, and the experience would be one that Perón would be condemned to repeat, leading to frequent claims that he did too little to force Eva to receive treatment despite recognising her symptoms and knowing what lay ahead. At a loose end for several months after Aurelia's death, in February 1939 he was sent to Europe to receive training at a regiment in the Italian Alps, an assignment he would later inflate to suggest a more significant intelligence role in the run-up to World War II. In 1939 and 1940 he served at various Alpine outposts (scarcely the centre of military strategy), and reportedly also visited Germany and Vichy France.

While Perón was, by his own account, impressed with the use of mass organisation and mass spectacle in both Italy and Germany and with the apparent benefits of military discipline for society as a whole, the experience helped to inspire his fear of the 'inorganic mass' and his faith in the relationship between a leader and masses, rather than any ideological commitment. Perón was not a convinced fascist, as many anti-Peronists have automatically supposed. An admirer of vertical power structures, and unscrupulous enough (and superficial enough) to ignore many aspects of fascism, Perón abhorred large-scale violence. Like many others, he was naive enough to believe that the corporate structure of the military, which he had found congenial and effective in his military career, could make civil society more harmonious and efficient. Moreover, the fact that his eyewitness experience was largely confined to fascist countries then able to claim some significant successes must also have coloured his views. However, his inherent dislike of violence was greatly increased by his visit to Spain on his way back to Argentina in 1940, where he was appalled by the still-recent destruction caused by the Civil War and its ongoing effects; he would later cite this as his reason for stepping down and avoiding a potential civil war at the time of the 1955 coup.

Perón returned to Argentina in late 1940 and was almost immediately transferred to a mountain regiment in Mendoza province, a position where his Alpine training as a ski and mountain warfare instructor could be put to good use. A year later he was promoted to the rank of colonel and put in command of a mountain regiment, also helping young officers to prepare to enter the Superior War School. In 1942, Perón was assigned to the Inspectorate of Mountain Troops, and placed under the orders of General Edelmiro Farrell, a complaisant superior officer whose relationship with Perón would help Farrell to the (de facto) presidency and Perón to the position of power behind the throne a short time later. Returning to Buenos Aires in March 1942, Perón quickly became involved in the political undercurrents of the army's younger officers (many of whom had been his pupils and with whom he had a good relationship). He also became close for the first time to another young officer with whom he hitherto had only a passing acquaintance, and who was also a protégé of Farrell, and assigned to the Inspectorate.

Lieutenant Colonel Domingo Mercante, born in 1898, was the son of a railway engineer and leading member of the railway union *La Fraternidad*. Like Perón, Mercante was a product of the Colegio Militar and the Superior War School and, like Perón, he joined the infantry, a less aristocratic branch than the cavalry. After being assigned to the Campo de Mayo base just outside Buenos Aires from 1924 to 1940, Mercante was reassigned to a distant base in Neuquén (then a territory) in the south of the country following a falling-out with a superior officer, returning to Buenos Aires only at the end of 1941. With a working-class and trade union background, Mercante had greater first-hand knowledge than Perón of social conditions in that area, but both shared concerns regarding corruption in the military, the electoral fraud that had perpetuated undemocratic and unrepresentative governments since 1930, alienating much of the population, and the poverty that affected many sectors of society. Perón increasingly believed that fraud and repression were strengthening the position of the Communist Party, a party that Mercante viewed as 'anti-Argentina'. The two rapidly became close and would remain so for years to come, with Mercante not only a friend but an efficient collaborator. Though Mercante recognised himself that he lacked charisma and fluidity as a public speaker, he was convinced that Perón had the qualities to lead, whereas he himself had the skills to organise and implement.

Perón was also involved at this time in another, more clandestine and dubious relationship: on his return from Mendoza in early 1942, Perón brought with him a teenaged mistress, María Cecilia Yurbel, known as 'Piraña' (a nickname given to her by Perón supposedly due to her formidable appetite). Born in 1924, María Cecilia lived with Perón in his flat in the Palermo district of Buenos Aires, kept in the background, and introduced as his daughter when it was necessary for her to appear. She accompanied him on a visit to Radio Belgrano in December 1943 (when their paths apparently did not cross with Eva's) and her photo was published, identifying her as the teenaged daughter of the widowed colonel, then secretary of labour.

In the run-up to the 1943 elections, developments favouring a *coup d'état* were furthered by the death of former President Agustín P. Justo, the preferred candidate of some sectors of the military, in January of that year. With the only serious military contender out of the running and the risk of Robustiano Patrón Costas being elected on the rise, the stage was set for the 4 June coup and for Perón's rapid insertion into the political life of the country. Despite his hitherto conventional military career, the experience in Europe would appear to have awakened Perón's taste for both politics and conspiracy. From this time, his career would take a turn which would have surprised most who knew him as a dedicated career officer and teacher, despite their frequent appraisal of him as a charismatic officer with innate leadership qualities. Within a short time, the GOU would play a role in the coup that would propel Perón to the post of secretary of labour, minister of war and eventually vice-president, posts from which his ability to lead would be extended far more widely. His leadership qualities were enhanced by his considerable charisma, good looks, energy and apparently permanent good humour, which made him likeable and attractive to those who listened to him. Moreover, as Sir David Kelly noted, 'he was a brilliant improviser, with a strong political sense and much personal charm', as well as an 'opportunist'.[13] Nor did he necessarily take his own publicity seriously: as another astute observer remarked, 'I think that Eva Perón came to believe firmly in the messianic quality attributed to her by the people. She was the opposite of Perón: she always believed what she said.'[14]

Following the coup, Perón and Mercante began to concentrate rapidly on the labour sector, which was of limited interest to many of their colleagues. From their position in the War Ministry (under vice-president and war minister Edelmiro Farrell), in August 1943 Perón and Mercante were called upon to deal with a meat packers' strike led by the communist José Peter, imprisoned for his involvement. Perón and Mercante managed to negotiate an end to the strike in exchange for Peter's freedom and a pay rise. With his union links, Mercante was a key asset in the process of wooing labour, initially suspicious of Perón. Via a series of careful manouevres, in October 1943 Perón convinced President Ramírez to name him as director of the obscure National Labour Department (DNT), despite some opposition from the colonel already in post – Carlos Gianni, who had already gone some way towards attempting to implement similar policies to those of Perón – as well as some sectors of the army and the newspaper *La Prensa*, who had their own candidate. Mercante accompanied him to the Department (which became a Secretariat a month later, implying a cabinet position), and was made 'interventor' of the two government-intervened railway unions, La Fraternidad and the Unión Ferroviaria. After strong tensions with the original military interventor, relations eased substantially due to Mercante's good links to the unions and his strong negotiating skills. This also helped to bring union leaders round to Perón: railway union leader Luis Monzalvo was one of the first converts, thanks to Mercante.[15]

In addition to his negotiating skills and credibility with the unions, Mercante also brought with him to the Secretariat his young mistress, Isabel Ernst, who would be installed as secretary to his cousin, Hugo Mercante, also on the staff. Isabel, the daughter of German immigrants who began work as a teacher, would remain with Mercante until his death and the two would have a son, although legally he remained married to his wife Elena Caporale. An attractive young blonde who favoured tailored suits for work, Isabel would seem to have eventually become something of a model for Eva when she later assumed responsibility for union relations, and her work at the Secretariat was similar to Eva's later role, receiving union delegations and preparing reports on their demands before they were interviewed by Perón. With Mercante and Isabel as 'gatekeepers' and

Mercante negotiating contract demands, Perón performed the high-profile function of receiving delegations and signing contracts before the cameras.[16] (Mercante's union contacts also apparently brought him into contact with the radio artists' union, including its leader Eva Duarte, which would become crucially significant before long.)

Another Perón initiative at the Secretariat was the creation, in October 1944, of a women's division designed to improve women's working conditions. It was led by the distinguished Dr Lucila Gregorio de Lavié, who backed Perón's eventual petition for a decree granting women's suffrage. The women's division in practice did relatively little, in part because the most prominent feminists of the time were upper class and opposed to the military government; Gregorio de Lavié herself was sharply criticised by her peers for accepting a post in the Secretariat and for backing the proposed 'suffrage by decree'. At the same time, despite a significant presence of women in the workforce, and a clear disparity between men's and women's wages, women were less of a presence in unionised sectors in particular, and thus less readily mobilised via government measures. Unlike the United States and Britain, for example, where World War II had seen the mass incorporation of women into the workforce to replace the men fighting the war, Argentina was neutral during the war and no such displacement occurred, leaving women as a relatively less important component of the labour force for some years to come.

Despite initial doubts on the part of unionists, Perón himself was not long in winning them over, above and beyond Mercante's efforts. Cipriano Reyes, the meatpackers' leader who would later become a staunch enemy of both Perón and Mercante, would later note that

> at first, Perón didn't appear to be an authentic revolutionary, but his intelligent sensitivity stood out […] He knew how to get close to the people, talk to the people and think like the people. Why? Because he had the innate qualities of a leader (*caudillo*) and something impossible to hide: the vital charisma to stand out among his peers.[17]

By the end of 1943, Perón was the most famous and most attractive face of the government, and its keenest advocate of social welfare policies that had been long disregarded. The January 1944 San Juan earthquake would provide yet another stage from which to confirm his leadership.

 CHAPTER 6

Political Earthquake

A T 8.48 PM on Saturday 15 January 1944, an earthquake estimated at some 7.4 on the Richter scale and lasting for 40 seconds hit the city of San Juan, 875 kilometres to the west of Buenos Aires in the Cuyo winery area of the country. The town, which had already been partially destroyed by an earthquake in 1894, still had a number of old adobe structures as well as newer buildings from around the turn of the century; an estimated 90 per cent of its buildings collapsed on 15 January, as well as all telephone, telegraph and road services. The earthquake was Argentina's worst ever natural disaster, leaving around 10,000 dead, 1,000 orphans and one-third of the province's population homeless. It was felt as far away as Buenos Aires, where it caused light fixtures to sway and buildings to shake; shortly thereafter radios interrupted their broadcasts to report the tragedy.

President Ramírez put the Secretariat of Labour and Welfare in charge of co-ordinating relief operations, and Perón, via radio, called a meeting for Monday 17 January of representatives of various sectors, including banking, industry, commerce, sports and the arts, in order to organise fund raising activities. One of those who attended, as part of a delegation of actors, was the radio actress Eva Duarte, who appears to have crossed paths with Perón for the first time on that occasion. According to Perón's various and often unreliable memoirs years later, 'I remember she was not sitting in the front row, and she wore a very simple tailored suit.' She said 'no festivals; we'll go out to ask for money directly, without offering anything [...] We'll say to people: our brothers are in need, let's help them! We have to get money from those who have it.'[1] She was 'a young woman who looked fragile, but with resolution in her voice [...] her eyes bright as if with fever [...] I felt that her words conquered me; I was almost subjugated by the warmth of her voice and her look.'[2] 'I liked this woman's way of thinking and acting. She was practical and had new ideas.'[3] Taken with her determination and insistence, Perón supposedly encouraged her to organise the fund-raising, and she took at least partial responsibility for co-ordinating offers of assistance, for example from a group of Red Cross nurses.

Some details are clearly inaccurate – Perón in various interviews describes Eva's 'long blonde hair', when in fact she remained a brunette at this date – whether wilfully so or because Perón shared with most other people the tendency to lose track of precise events years in the past and his memories were edited by time. However, while the exact circumstances under which she made such an impression are blurred, Perón would later insist that 'from the first I realised that I was faced with an extraordinary person [...] I was not attracted by the beautiful woman, but the good woman. Of course, she incorporated the two extremes: beauty and goodness.'[4] What is clear is that, whatever the precise circumstances of their first meeting, Perón fell in love. The terms in which he spoke of her bear no relation to his tepid recollections of his first wife or his apparent indifference to other passing relationships like that with María Cecilia Yurbel. Not the most spontaneous or passionate of men, Perón was smitten.

A week after the earthquake, on 22 January, actors and actresses, including Eva, walked the streets of Buenos Aires with collection plates asking for donations. They were joined by members of the army and, on Saturday afternoon, by Perón himself in his white summer uniform, who walked along the exclusive Florida shopping street chatting with passers-by and collecting donations. The fund-raising events of the 22nd ended with a marathon benefit concert at Luna Park stadium (first and foremost a boxing arena) at which most of the best known artists of the day performed, including the tango singers Libertad Lamarque and Hugo del Carril. By most accounts, after an initial contact at the Secretariat in the context of a crowded meeting, this was the event that cemented the inseparable relationship between Perón and Eva, although this is the only point on which all those accounts agree.

Despite Eva's supposed lack of enthusiasm for holding a benefit concert, she and her friend Rita Molina attended Luna Park; some reports say that Eva performed with her radio company, although in comparison with many of the stars who performed she was relatively little known (particularly for a well-heeled and well-paying audience – Eva's *radioteatros* were generally considered to be fare for the domestic servants). Depending on the version, Eva may or may not have accompanied Colonel Imbert, who was seated with Perón. According to the more anti-Peronist version, Eva saw her chance to slip into one of the VIP seats next to Perón (either occupying a seat vacated by President Ramírez or his wife, or one that had initially been intended for Libertad Lamarque, depending on the source) and seized the opportunity to attach herself to him. Other versions suggest that the young master of ceremonies, Roberto Galán, who was reluctant to accede to Eva's request to allow her to recite poetry, presented Eva and her friends to Perón as 'part of the welcoming committee' and pushed them towards the empty seats next to Perón and the other colonels.[5]

By contrast, Mercante's son insisted repeatedly that his father was responsible for the seating arrangements that brought the two together. According to this version, Mercante had met Eva in her role as representative of the radio actors' union and was impressed with her, sending her and her delegation through to meet Perón in his role as 'gatekeeper'. At Luna Park that night, anxious to keep Perón away from the designs of another actress, Mercante saw Eva in the crowd and dragged her over to sit in the empty seat next to that reserved for Perón. 'Tito' Mercante would later claim that he had often heard Eva reminisce over Mercante's role in introducing her to her husband, a favour which lay behind her strong affection for the man she would call 'the heart of Perón'. 'Mercante, do you remember at Luna Park when you led me by the hand to sit me down next to Perón? I was so scared! But, you were inspired, no?!'[6]

Typically, Perón himself had a slightly different memory of events, telling Enrique Pavón Pereira years later that

> Evita managed to get a sympathetic master of ceremonies [presumably Galán] [...] to put her in one of the exclusive seats. [The tango composer and conductor] Homero Manzi hastened to introduce us when I had already identified the intrepid personality of my lovely neighbour.[7]

This may or may not be the case, or Perón may have remembered the details somewhat hazily – or he may have had his reasons for wishing to cut Mercante out of the 'official version', given the eventual falling-out that would later see Mercante virtually erased from Peronist history. Radical intellectual Arturo Jauretche's version would tend to bear out the involvement of Homero Manzi: Jauretche claimed that Eva and her friend had been outside waiting to get in, and that Manzi let them through and gave them access to the VIP seats, with Perón and Imbert subsequently inviting the two to dinner.[8] In general, all of these versions reject the supposition that Eva arrived as Imbert's mistress and dumped him for Perón; they all coincide either in claiming that Eva's friend was Imbert's mistress, or that Imbert had nothing to do with it at all. However the approach took place, most versions coincide in reporting her first words to him, surely enough to attract the attention of almost anyone: 'Thank you for existing.'

For her part, Eva referred to the events only as 'her marvellous day', although she later told Vera Pichel that 'I saw the empty seat and ran to it, without thinking whether it was correct or not I sat down [...] When the show ended, Perón invited me to get something to eat. I accepted and we went.' According to Eva, Perón laughed at her approach: 'he very gallantly said that he liked decisive women'.[9] Whatever the truth of the details, Perón and Eva sat together at Luna Park that night. Whether she in fact said 'thank you for existing', or 'I am nothing', as some say, or made a lengthier speech in which she swore never to leave his side 'if, as you say, the cause of the people is your own cause', the fact is that the two left Luna Park together. After dining together, probably with Imbert and Rita Molina, they were 'a couple'.

Apart from the many political and personal interests involved, it is hardly surprising that time may have elided some of the facts surrounding the first meeting. Probably all the versions have some element of truth and some invention. As already noted, Perón was not notably addicted to the literal truth ('the only truth is reality' was one of his famous aphorisms) and may well have deemed it desirable to edit history. Moreover, Mercante's son Tito, in later life, tended to exert himself to place his father in the central role in all things Peronist – not unfairly, given Perón's later tendency to excise Mercante's crucial role from the official history. Thus, his assertion that Mercante played the key role in bringing the two together cannot automatically be accepted in its entirety, although the Peronist deputy Rodolfo Decker would also claim that Mercante had noted Perón's interest in Eva and had engineered the meeting.[10] Roberto Galán himself would become something of a long-term Peronist hanger-on, including during Perón's long exile, and his version is not automatically credible either.

Doubtless the truth contains elements of various stories. Most likely Eva came to the Secretariat in her role as representative of the radio actors and Mercante, in his role as gatekeeper, ushered them in to see Perón, on whom the first contact made an impression even if he did not charge Eva with 'organising everything'. Although it seems highly unlikely that she played a key role in organising the Luna Park benefit, given the involvement of a number of bigger stars, probably Eva was close at hand and may have asked Galán to let her perform in order to gain some career mileage. Someone (Mercante?) pushed her towards the VIP seats, while someone else who was nearby when Perón arrived to take his seat (Manzi? Galán?) made the introduction for their first one-to-one conversation. Regardless, a brief first acquaintance in the context of a generalised meeting gave way to an opportunity for closer acquaintance. Although most likely neither went to Luna Park in the expectation of such an important meeting, the relationship would not be broken until Eva's death in 1952 – if then.

Despite Perón's usual cautious nature, the irregular relationship became official almost immediately. A few days after the Luna Park benefit, Perón and Mercante, in uniform, visited Eva at Radio Belgrano and a photo of the three appeared in *Radiolandia*. (However, a solo visit by Perón to the station a month later was not considered appropriate for public consumption: Perón reportedly became angry when a photographer shot him and Eva together at the studio, without Mercante as cover, and the photographer was later obliged to hand over his roll of film.) In more concrete terms, Eva appears to have lost little time in removing 'Piraña' from the scene. According to María Cecilia's sister Laura, she had returned to Mendoza following the earthquake, and on arriving back in Buenos Aires had found Eva installed in her place in the flat in Arenales Street. 'She was terrible', according to Laura,[11] and never again let Piraña or any other member of the family have any further contact with Perón, who, according to some versions, came home one afternoon to find María Cecilia gone and Eva in situ. Eva herself recalled that

> when I moved in I found a surprise. A 20-something girl was there. Perón had brought her from I don't know where, and the absolute rogue introduced her as his daughter [...] He didn't have time and didn't remember to say goodbye.[12]

Indeed, 'since he liked decisive women – I hadn't forgotten that – I packed her things in a suitcase and sent her back to her province without any further formalities'.[13] María Cecilia had no choice but to return to Mendoza, where she eventually married, and died in 1989. Shortly thereafter, Eva found Perón a flat adjoining hers in Posadas Street, in the exclusive Recoleta district of Buenos Aires, and he rapidly moved in. Thereafter they used one for meetings and the other as their residence, a thinly veiled cohabitation that in 1940s Buenos Aires was unthinkable, in particular for a high-profile army officer and an actress of dubious reputation. He would also sneak her into his military quarters hidden in the boot of his car, to the great amusement of both.

While the anti-Peronist 'black myth' would later pillory Eva for her actions, the reality is that she saw her chance and she took it. After a long period of struggle, poverty, job insecurity and tenuous relationships, she would not let such a 'good catch' slip away and she acted decisively (apparently encouraged by Perón's supposed attraction to 'decisive women'). In her own later remarks to friends, Eva noted that, by the time the Luna Park evening ended, the two were already talking as though they had known each other for years, and she was entirely smitten with the colonel. Indeed, the relationship could be said to fit within the pattern of her earlier romances. From an early age she was drawn, not surprisingly, to older, influential men – such as José Franco and Emilio Kartulowicz – and, as in the case of Kartulowicz (like Perón, a tall, handsome and athletic man in his forties), she became possessive if not obsessive. Fortunately for her, Perón took the relationship more seriously than 'old Kartulo', who had found Eva too 'clingy' to allow him to get on with other romances easily.

In many respects their personalities dovetailed in both the personal and political spheres: Perón was more calculating and more cautious, while Eva was more impetuous, often temperamental and passionate. This contrast in personalities would lead to anti-Peronist jibes that Perón was a weak and effeminate coward and his wife the 'dominant male', but in fact, although even Perón could not always control Eva's temper (assuming that in fact he wanted to), the balance of impulsiveness and calculation was often effective. Perón's natural tendency to avoid commitment, and occasional impulse to withdraw from confrontation altogether, was in fact admirably balanced by two of his most intimate collaborators: the impassioned Eva and the cool-headed, determined Mercante. On the other hand, what they had in common was an often difficult and solitary youth (dominated by strong-willed mothers and absent fathers) that had taught them both to be self-sufficient and somewhat suspicious of others, although Perón was the more reserved and Eva, one of five siblings, the more spontaneous. According to the Jesuit Hernán Benítez,

> I always had the impression that their love must have had a central point: the encounter of two people profoundly wounded in their sex. Joined together by sad, puritan childhoods, rural with no bucolic charm [...] I think love had surprised both of them: Perón because he thought it was a subject already passed and forgotten, and Eva because she had never known it until then.[14]

Eva was still an insecure young woman, well aware that she was still never far away from losing her job, her income or her man. She was also well aware that Perón was undoubtedly seen by many as one of Argentina's most eligible men – a handsome widower and army officer, a power within the government and, already, a potential presidential candidate – and could have had his choice of many other women, most of them more suitable choices for a man in his position. She was jealous, with reason, and could not tolerate competition of any sort – hence the rapid dispatch of Piraña back to Mendoza and the blocking of all contacts with her family. She was also demonstrably jealous of Aurelia and her ten-year marriage with Perón, who doubtless remembered her with affection, and of his continuing relationship with her family. (According to some versions, Aurelia, on her deathbed, had made Perón promise to marry her sister María,[15] and there are claims that he did indeed propose to her unsuccessfully before meeting Eva. Moreover, his former sister-in-law would become a colleague at the Secretariat of Labour and Welfare.) Another potential 'competitor' close to home was Perón's cousin Mercedes Perón ('Mecha'), with whom he had a close relationship and to whom he may also have proposed unsuccessfully at one stage. A fellow officer purportedly sought to enlist Mecha's help to dissuade Perón from persisting with the relationship with Eva; according to this version, Mecha met Eva at a tearoom in Buenos Aires and subsequently informed the officer that she could not imagine 'anyone with greater merit to marry the colonel'.[16]

Then there was also Blanca Luz Brum. Blanca Luz, an Uruguayan communist, poet and political activist with a turbulent love life, had worked with radical groups in Chile, Peru, Mexico and Nicaragua before coming to Argentina in 1943, where she began working in the propaganda department of Perón's new Secretariat of Labour and Welfare. During this early period, before Perón became president, she continued to be an important political collaborator who was greatly respected within the Secretariat and among the trade unions, even as Eva continued to work as a radio and film actress with only minimal protagonism in the political and union spheres where she would later become paramount. However, while Blanca Luz was an important influence and (like, to a degree, yet another blonde, Isabel Ernst) played a role that would later fall to Eva, it is unlikely that she represented a competitor to Eva on the romantic side. Certainly she fell far outside the pattern of women that Perón could later claim to have 'formed' politically; indeed, at this stage of their respective careers, she had far more political experience than he, and was probably far more a valued colleague than a potential marriage partner.

On moving in with Perón, Eva's political education began. Whether or not she had had some political initiation with Damián Gómez, the anarquist in Junín, or with the socialist Agustín Magaldi, Eva had not hitherto exhibited any significant interest in politics – despite Marcos Zucker's surprise at her involvement with 'military and political personalities' and Loris Zanatta's frequent references to her 'dense networks of contacts'.[17] (Even more implausible are claims to the effect that she had acted as a Nazi spy, thanks to her good contacts with the military government; in practice it would appear that a young radio actress not known for her discretion would have been a questionable conduit for delicate relations between Nazi Germany and a neutral country.)

Despite his later claims that he immediately recognised her as an 'extraordinary person', it is not at all clear that Perón's initial intention was to prepare Eva for a political role, although he would later claim that her 'solid' early education and the 'artistic formation that greatly developed her sensitivity'[18] made her well suited to the role. She had 'sufficient intellectual level to "understand" and also adequate evolution to "proceed"'.[19] Until that time, as Perón would later note, 'the woman was quiet at home, without intervening at all in public affairs, whether for lack of political rights, lack of imagination or just to avoid suffering our inveterate *"machismo"*'.[20] However, while he would later claim credit for having 'invented' her, and does indeed merit credit for having been creative enough to see the potential of women in public affairs, it seems more likely that at this stage she was a sounding board for his ideas rather than a political partner in embryo. However, for a young woman who had so often not been taken seriously, or been used as a one-night stand, and whose intelligence was unformed but often recognised, even this was a different kind of relationship, a different kind of respect, from what she was used to, and one to which she responded. And while Perón may again have edited his memories in order to cast himself in the best possible light, there is no question that he was ahead of his time in thinking creatively about a political role for a woman (and for women more generally, even if their most important role in the main was to vote for Perón).

Eva's political education was also furthered by her unexpected presence at the political meetings held at the Posadas flat. Although she initially limited her participation to serving coffee and then sitting quietly at the back, even this was startling and disconcerting to the all-male attendees, most of whom were army officers, lawyers and career politicians of far higher intellectual standing than she, even leaving aside the question of gender equality. According to Arturo Jauretche, a leading member of the young Radical faction FORJA who joined the Peronist government, 'I wasn't a friend of Eva's [...] she regarded me with respect but she didn't like me. Poor thing, she distrusted intellectuals. It's understandable. They've wanted to paint Eva as a little whore, but it wasn't like that.'[21]

The mores of the time were far stricter, and respectable men (especially high-ranking members of the government) did not live openly with mistresses, whether they were married or not. Moreover, even respectable married women (especially army wives) did not intrude on their husbands' political meetings and would have withdrawn quietly after leaving the coffee on the table. To make matters worse, Eva was an illegitimate child, poorly educated and badly spoken, and an actress of somewhat ill repute – one they probably assumed was sleeping with Perón to further her career – and the fact that Perón allowed her such leeway and was apparently under her influence was shocking and worrying. (Perón's frequently quoted witticism, 'What do they want me to do? Go out with an actor?', doubtless did nothing either to amuse or reassure them.) One of the officers in question would later refer to her as 'one of those annoying girls who go around all the time pestering everybody to give them a small part.'[22]

Perón's apparent enjoyment of flouting convention, and the risks it implied for the government's reputation, only made matters worse, as did Eva's rising confidence, which soon led her not only to attend meetings, but to express her views vociferously. Nor was disapproval limited to the officer corps, and by extension their wives (who doubtless exercised some influence in more subtle and traditional ways). Trade union leaders already uncertain of whether to throw in their lot with Perón also expressed considerable discomfort, and apparently asked Isabel Ernst to speak to Eva about the damage the situation was doing to Perón's reputation – an overture that was predictably not well-received by Eva.[23] As the relationship progressed, Eva's tendency to keep family contacts around her would also worsen the situation, with brother Juancito drawn into Perón's inner circle; the promotion of Oscar Nicolini, presumably at her initiative, would provoke a crisis that nearly ended Perón's nascent career, as will be discussed below. However, one assumption can clearly be made from all this: Perón was in love with Eva, otherwise such an ambitious man would scarcely have maintained (and publicly) a relationship that seemingly could only damage his political aspirations.

In addition to the beginning of her political education, this time also represented virtually the only period in which Perón and Eva enjoyed a considerable degree of domesticity. Perón had known a stable domestic environment only during his first marriage, while Eva could be said not to have known one at all, at least in the most conventional sense, despite Doña Juana's impressive efforts to bring up her family as a single mother. Eva presumably had had little experience at cooking during her years in rooming houses, but both tended to prefer simple meals and during these months they were able to enjoy steak, salad and red wine at home. Thereafter, once Perón had won the presidency and Eva had begun her own singular career, their time for domestic tranquillity largely vanished. But for the early months of their relationship they were able to enjoy some quiet times together, Eva often dressed in Perón's pyjamas and with her hair loose or in two plaits when they were at home alone. Juancito also became, at least from time to time, part of this family existence, doubtless moved both by his 'duties' as big brother and his desire to take advantage of new and potentially valuable connections. (There is an amusing scene in Paula de Luque's 2011 film *Juan y Eva*, where Juancito, at the dinner table, attempts to strong-arm Perón into a commitment to his sister, and Perón tells him calmly but in no uncertain terms that he does not respond to pressure, particularly from a boy 20 years his junior. Although the film is a fictionalised account, the scene rings true: Perón did not react well to pressure and might indeed opt for the opposite course of action to that being sought, as Eva and Mercante were both well aware.)

However, apart from the enjoyment of this new and exciting romance, domestic bliss and the stirring of some new political convictions, Eva did not disregard her career. The month after the Luna Park meeting, she began a new segment of her series of famous women in history, playing Queen Elizabeth I and, a month later, Sarah Bernhardt. Perón's visit to Radio Belgrano shortly after their meeting alerted the station's owner, Jaime Yankelevich, to the fact that Eva was now the protégée of the government's strongman, and in April it was announced that her salary would rise to the record level of 35,000 pesos (a whopping 8,750 dollars at the then exchange rate) per month. The situation could easily have gone the other way: on 26 January 1944, the same day that Perón and Mercante visited Eva at the station, Argentina finally broke relations with Germany and Japan, and the ensuing political crisis threatened to bring down the government. However, the primary victim of the fallout was President Ramírez, who was replaced by his vice-president, Edelmiro Farrell, on 24 February. As a result, Perón replaced Farrell as war minister and, eventually, in July, as vice-president. Meanwhile, he also maintained his post as secretary of labour, giving him significant control over the two main pillars of political power – the armed forces and, increasingly, the trade unions. In April, Eva was named president of the new Argentine Radio Union, which was officially recognised by the Secretariat of Labour and Welfare a month later.

With Perón consolidated in power, at least for the present, Yankelevich doubtless felt that currying good relations with Eva could only be beneficial, even if no direct pressure was brought to bear to increase her salary so spectacularly. Even if Yankelevich was shrewd rather than browbeaten, and even though it was by no means her principal motive for attaching herself to Perón, it is clear that Eva did not hesitate to use the relationship to further her career when possible. Argentina's poor relationship with the United States had for some time represented a complication for the Argentine film industry: celluloid was imported from the United States, and wartime shortages resulted in sales of raw film being rationed. Allied countries such as Mexico, which had followed the US line on the Axis, received far more than Argentina, and the Mexican film industry surged ahead as a result. In 1943 and 1944 Mexico received more than three times as much celluloid from the United States as Argentina, and the number of Argentine films continued to decline as a result.[24] But thanks to her government contacts Eva could now obtain celluloid, which made her a more attractive commodity for any film director. In early 1944, it was announced that she would appear in the film *La cabalgata del circo* (Circus Cavalcade) with the stars Libertad Lamarque and Hugo del Carril. Although she still appeared in a secondary role, it was by far her largest film role to date, for which she was paid 30,000 pesos, and it was directed by the distinguished director Mario Soffici, responsible for films such as the 1939 classic *Prisioneros de la tierra* (Prisoners of the Earth), the story of the suffering of the exploited rural poor in the northern Misiones province, still regarded as one of the best films ever produced in Argentina.

The resulting film, *La cabalgata*, has no similar claims to artistic merit, and serves to confirm that Eva was not an impressive actress, although she has some moments that are relatively spontaneous and fresh (and neither Lamarque nor Del Carril deserve any acting laurels either). However, Soffici would stress that she was respectful and diligent and followed direction with discipline. The film was arguably more important for two events that occurred off the screen. One is that Eva for the first time dyed her hair blonde. From then on the hairdresser Julio Alcaraz, who worked for Estudios San Miguel where the film was shot, would continue to colour and style her hair until her death, long after he had left the studio and set up his own salon. As Eva's political star rose, Alcaraz would come to the presidential residence every morning to style her hair before opening his business. ('I was the only person to accompany Eva throughout her career: I styled her when she was an actress, I accompanied her in all her official trips and, finally, I did her hair on her dead body.'[25]) Like Perón, Alcaraz would also later claim to have 'invented' Eva, teaching her style as well as creating her iconic hairstyles. Father Hernán Benítez would also make some similar claims with respect to her social work. According to the many would-be Pygmalions surrounding her, poor Eva sometimes appears to be nothing more than their own creation. Her new blonde hair suited Eva in a way that her natural dark colour had not; it highlighted her light skin and beauty and represented a dramatic change, from a pretty but unremarkable young woman to the woman who would soon become an icon and whose blonde hair became a trademark.

The other event involved her co-star, Libertad Lamarque, with whom tensions reportedly rose rapidly and sharply. Some rumours insisted that Lamarque had had her eyes on Perón at Luna Park and resented Eva for getting to him ahead of her (although in practice, as Marisa Navarro notes, Lamarque was no sympathiser, as the daughter of anarchists, and was always opposed to the military government and Peronist policy-making[26]). Others note that Lamarque had long since made a name for herself as a diva and that she was ill-disposed to accept the attention paid to her young colleague, while Lamarque herself claimed that relations were difficult because Eva herself played the diva, failing to show up for work on time and keeping colleagues waiting (despite Soffici's remarks about her professionalism). Never diplomatic, Eva herself doubtless did not help matters by talking often and loudly about her relationship with Perón, for the benefit of anyone who would listen. Whatever the reason, the two actresses came to words if not blows. Thereafter, when Perón became president, Lamarque claimed that she was unable to get work in Argentina, although she was offered lucrative contracts elsewhere and spent most of the rest of her career in Mexico. Claims of outright persecution appear somewhat unfounded; Lamarque continued to visit Argentina throughout the Perón era without difficulty, although she never returned to live there, and died in Mexico in 2000 after a lengthy concert, film and television career.

By contrast, Eva and Perón would form a long friendship with Hugo del Carril, a leading tango singer who would become a committed Peronist, especially well-known for his recording of the Peronist March ('Los muchachos peronistas'), then as now the party's theme song. Del Carril's version remains by far the most famous and most often used, and has often tended to overshadow his long and successful recording career as a tango singer and as an actor (including a 1939 film, *La vida de Carlos Gardel*, in which he somewhat implausibly played the title role). Originally a radio entertainer, the likeable Del Carril made over 50 films and also became a noted director, whose best film was probably the 1952 release *Las aguas bajan turbias*, known in English as *Rivers of Blood* and addressing highly Peronist issues such as worker exploitation, employer greed and trade unionisation. Unlike Lamarque, Del Carril would suffer from his support for Perón and identification with the party: after Perón's overthrow in 1955, he would find himself largely blacklisted for some years (and forced briefly into exile in Mexico), although he continued to work as an actor, director and singer until the mid-1970s; he died in 1989. Del Carril may inadvertently have also planted an early seed of an idea for what would later be the Eva Perón Foundation; according to his later testimony, during the filming of *La cabalgata* he had told Eva of the letters he received from fans asking for help, to which she urged him to continue fulfilling those requests where he could.[27]

In addition to filming and her continuing series of famous women, Eva would also participate in a number of other radio series during 1944, including a crime series and various romantic stories. However, her most important new radio role was in a programme called *Hacia un futuro mejor* (Towards a Better Future), propaganda in favour of the 4 June 1943 'Revolution' and the policies of the government – or, more accurately, of Perón himself. *Hacia un futuro mejor*, which premiered on 17 June 1944 and continued every night for over a year, was written by Francisco Muñoz Azpiri, the librettist for Eva's famous women series and, since the previous week, director of propaganda in the under-secretariat of information of the presidency. Eva's role was that of 'the woman', a working class wife/mother/sister who called on Argentines to support the 'revolution'. Punctuated with military music, the programme would begin with an announcer who would proclaim 'An Argentine woman is in the city street, watching the march of time […] There are people in that street. And in that woman there is hope […] HERE are that woman and that street!'[28] Thereafter Eva would speak, with her own speech marked by sound effects and music and interspersed with excerpts from Perón's own speeches:

> I am a woman like you, mothers, wives, girlfriends or sisters […] I see the people moving […] under the leadership of the new and vigorous leaders of the Revolution […][29] The Revolution came for a reason, for something anguished and hard that germinated within […] The redeeming Revolution came for many other reasons, hunger […] the soul […] the motherland, forgotten and thirsty […] and the injustice and exploitation of the workers.[30]

This programme, which furthered Eva's own political education, would represent her first steps into the role that she would later undertake as first lady, that of propagandist and teacher of Peronist 'doctrine'. The audience for *Hacia un futuro mejor* was largely the same part of the population that would form the Peronist base: working-class and poor sectors that did not tend to read newspapers (which in general were directed at an entirely different audience of the well-off and aspiring middle classes). Even before she began her unprecedented political activity as a 'bridge' between Perón and 'the people', Eva had already gone some way to being identified as 'the woman of the people', and her message to her listeners would not greatly change over the rest of her life. As noted earlier, there is no question that she believed in the message she was delivering (probably far more than did Perón himself) and in the role she was filling. The programme also gave her the first opportunity to contribute to Perón's political plan – something that, given her limited education and hitherto scant interest in politics, she had been ill-prepared to do when she met and fell in love with Perón. Combined with her 'famous women', Eva was arguably learning about what her role could be and how she could make her own mark on politics and 'her' people. (Despite his claims to have 'invented' her, and his much greater experience, Perón himself was also still learning about politics and forming his own political persona in this period, and the two were learning in parallel at least as much as Eva was a disciple of the colonel. This in itself allowed for the development of a partnership that would have been unthinkable in any previous presidential 'couple'.)

The programme was also a precursor of Perón's talent for and use of media propaganda, then still in its infancy. Much of the Peronist propaganda machine would be under the charge of under-secretary of information and press Raúl Apold, a former theatrical agent and journalist (and possibly one of Eva's network of contacts). Apold would become a largely invisible power behind the throne ('Perón's Goebbels'), and a dangerous enemy able to destroy perceived rivals to either himself or Perón efficiently and quietly.

Perhaps unsurprisingly, in September Eva was forced to take several weeks off work on medical advice, following a period of fevered activity that included three radio programmes at any given time, as well as the filming of *La cabalgata* and accompanying Perón in his personal and political life. By October, however, she was back at work on a new novela, *En el valle hay una sombra* (There is a Shadow in the Valley), in addition to *Hacia un futuro mejor* and further famous women, and also announced a new contract to make three films for Estudios San Miguel the following year at 50,000 pesos per film. Initially it was announced that she would make a film about the San Juan earthquake, *Amanece sobre las ruinas* (Dawn over the Ruins). However, in February 1945 it was announced that she would instead take the title role in *La pródiga* (The Generous Woman), to be directed by Mario Soffici. *La pródiga*, completed in September 1945, had originally been announced as a vehicle for Mecha Ortiz, an older and far more talented actress more suited to the role of an 'older' woman who, after having led a 'sinful' and materialistic life, redeems herself through her unbridled generosity in protecting and nurturing the poor villagers surrounding her estate. However, Eva's access to celluloid may well have been a deciding factor, as well as her determination to make her starring debut in this film.

In a June 1944 interview with *Antena*, Eva had been quoted as saying 'someday I'm sure I will get the role in the cinema that I would want. In fact, I think it will be Soffici that will give me my great opportunity.'[31] Clearly she saw *La pródiga* as that role. The parallels between that role and her later incarnation as Evita are striking, suggesting that she was already beginning to perceive herself in a similar real-life role: the woman, a kind, sensitive and generous person with an obscure past, adored by her humble neighbours, is referred to as 'the mother of the poor' or simply 'la Señora'. In the film, she falls in love with an engineer and, upon eventually finding that he no longer loves her and that her money is gone, commits suicide. The film is soggy melodrama at best, full of lurid and often incomprehensible dialogue, and does Eva no favours as a showcase for her talent: she is miscast and wooden in the role, pretty but largely inexpressive and surrounded by a cast who fare little better, although, fittingly for a radio actress, she has an attractive (if somewhat monotonous) speaking voice and her diction has clearly improved somewhat from her earlier days. In the end, it would be her last film, and would not be shown in public until 1984, many years after her death: Soffici made her a gift of the final cut when it became clear that Perón would become president and Eva became his wife. However, the fact that she had made it at all generated animosity among others in the film industry, who felt that she had manipulated her connections to gain a role she did not merit, to say nothing of the officers and their wives who felt that her position as a publicly recognised paramour was unacceptable. Indeed, Perón by and large treated her in public in the same way that a legitimate wife would be treated: with evident affection and respect, and as a visible and recognised life partner. On 9 July 1945 (Independence Day) she accompanied Perón to a gala at the Teatro Colón, where dignitaries and their wives had little option but to put up with the 'affront' and accept her presence.

The fact that Eva was highly visible rankled, and the fact that her career (whether or not due to her relationship with Perón) was reaching new heights also contributed to her visibility. Eva herself did everything possible to promote this (as most actors could reasonably be expected to do), appearing on several magazine covers in 1944 and 1945 and giving a number of interviews. While many of these stories are again the sort of falsified boilerplate that could be printed about any up-and-coming starlet, some of them are more substantive. Most are geared to generating an image of her as a home-loving, quiet and cultured young woman, an avid reader and not given to nightlife (perhaps an effort to appear a more 'respectable' companion for the vice-president, although Perón and politics in general are never mentioned in these interviews and appear to be non-existent for the young radio star). Several speak of continuing to work in films or radio for only a few more years, before leaving show business either to undertake 'adventures' – including a post-war world trip or, more absurdly, a round-the-world yachting expedition – and of the fact that she is using her substantial salary to build a house in which to settle thereafter. (They would live in the two-story '*petit hotel*', in the Colegiales neighbourhood of Buenos Aires, only briefly in 1946 before moving into the presidential residence, and it would be demolished following the coup against Perón in 1955.)

Perhaps the most revealing interview was published in *Antena* in July 1944, in which she expresses her gratitude to her public and also to Radical soap, which 'gave me one of the first opportunities of my life, when nobody believed in me and I was almost unknown'. When the interviewer notes that this acknowledgement appears to suggest that she is only being fair, rather than grateful, she replies 'yes, and there is a way to be always fair [...] not to forget, and I am one of those who never forgets'.[32] Time and again, this statement would be borne out, with respect to both those to whom she felt indebted and those she felt had abused her. Another somewhat confessional statement is to be found in an odd 'open letter' published in 1944, in which she reassures her fans of her 'loyalty' to them and says that her greatest satisfaction 'would be to extend my hand to all who carry the flame of faith in something or someone and in those who encourage hope'.[33]

By the time *La pródiga* was filmed, Eva had lived through an astonishing two years or so, during which she had found the personal and professional fulfilment she had never had before. Not only had she found her soulmate, and one who had taken the trouble (and the risk) to raise her profile and to treat her as a valuable companion and support, but she had seen her career rise at a frenetic pace. Since early 1944 she had made two films and worked most of the time on three daily radio programmes, as well as finding time to attend to the home, participate in political meetings and cultivate a more elegant and imposing image. During this period she had begun to have some of her wardrobe made by the rising young designer Paco Jamandreu, who designed her clothes for some of the early functions she attended with Perón. (Jamandreu, a highly visible and frequently cross-dressed homosexual at a time when this was even more shocking and unthinkable than the idea of the vice-president cohabiting with an actress of doubtful origins, would remain a friend of Eva's long after she began buying couture dresses from Christian Dior.) On more than one occasion she would get him released from jail in the middle of the night and, years later, on finding him standing next to his broken-down car on a Buenos Aires street as she returned from the Foundation in the early hours, she would send him a new Packard convertible the next day. However, within a short time she would not only turn her back on the artistic career she had worked so hard to build, but she would take steps to bury it. At the same time, as she and Perón both became more famous, they were coming increasingly close to a dangerous showdown that threatened to finish them both.

CHAPTER 7

Los Muchachos Peronistas

Los muchachos peronistas,
todos unidos triunfaremos,
Y como siempre daremos
un grito de corazón:
Viva Perón! Viva Perón!
Por ese gran argentino que
se supo conquistar
A la gran masa del pueblo,
combatiendo el capital.
Perón, Perón! Qué
grande sos! Mi general,
cuánto vales!
Perón, Perón! Gran
conductor!
Sos el primer trabajador!

[The Peronist Boys, united
we'll win,
And as always we'll give a
cry from the heart:
Viva Perón! Viva Perón!
For that great Argentine
who won over
The great mass of the
people, combating capital.
Perón, Perón, how great
you are! My general,
how much you are worth!
Perón, Perón, great leader!
You're the first worker!]

(The Peronist march 'Los muchachos peronistas', anonymous;
widely attributed to Dr Oscar Ivanissevich)

OVER THE COURSE of 1945 both Perón and Eva had seen their professional stars and their fame rise exponentially, along with the depth of antagonism towards them. Eva, in particular, had been gaining in confidence both personally and professionally, and her sometimes tempestuous and impatient behaviour demonstrated this. According to some reports, frustrated with Perón's slowness to formalise their relationship, she exploded at a public function at the home of the Machinandiarena family, owners of Estudios San Miguel, threatening to 'tell everything' publicly if he refused to marry her. While it is unclear what she proposed to tell, if this is true it suggests that she was unaware that nothing she could have said would have done his political career more damage than marrying her. For his part, it is likely that Perón was aware of this; the fact that, while slow to reach the altar, he did not break off the relationship for the good of his career indicates the extent of his emotional commitment. A British Embassy report to the Foreign Office two years later referred to the early assumption that the marriage was 'forced' on Perón, but went on to say that

> later evidence suggests that Perón is really fond of her and no doubt realised that marriage was essential if she was to appear in public [...] People who are in a position to know, agree that the President has an unusually deep and genuine attachment for her.[1]

Perón himself by 1945 had amassed a level of personal power that was not seen entirely favourably by many of his brothers in arms, despite the fact that he still commanded substantial sympathy and support within the army. In particular, in his role as secretary of labour he had developed the start of a personal power base through meeting union demands and cultivating leaders likely to be loyal to his cause. This was facilitated by Decree Law 23.852, which restricted official recognition to only one trade union in any field that would be able, for example, to participate in collective bargaining. This allowed Perón to recognise those unions whose leaders were sympathetic or pliable (and to promote rival leaders where they existed), and their members in turn would receive substantial benefits in terms of pay rises. Perón focused his efforts in particular on sectors where unionisation was thus far limited, or where he had a ready 'in', such as the railway unions with which Mercante had close ties (and which worked in a sector dominated by foreign, i.e. British, interests). Moreover, he implemented long-dormant socialist-sponsored labour legislation to improve working conditions and limit Saturday work. The benefits brought by Perón's tenure were especially obvious in sectors involving the greatest mechanisation and concentration of labour, notably the import-substitution industries that sprang up during the 1930s and tough, 'dirty' work such as slaughterhouses and shipyards.

Among the reforms brought in by Perón (working in tandem with Mercante) were the 1944 Estatuto del peón (the rural workers' statute), which gave rural workers unheard-of rights such as minimum wages, sick pay, Sundays off and minimum food and housing conditions, as well as a new system of labour courts introduced in November 1944. These measures were seen by many as unacceptable intervention in employers' rights, in particular in the case of rural workers, many of whom lived in virtually feudal conditions, practically enslaved by employers whose company stores kept them indebted. So although Perón's labour measures focused to a considerable degree on the urban working class, they also held key importance for workers in the interior provinces – allowing, for example, for the establishment of the first sugar workers' union in Tucumán province – and also for the landed elite that, like Robustiano Patrón Costas, had been the virtual lords of their domain for decades.

Perón's insistence that these reforms were necessary to avoid revolution fell largely on deaf ears among the business community, which never accepted his contention that concessions were required to maintain social peace, or his claims that the risk of communist ascendancy and revolutionary general strikes might have spilled over into violence. Nor were they convinced by his observation, in a speech before the stock exchange in August 1944, that

> for workers to be more efficient, they must be managed with the heart [...] [I]t is only necessary that the men with workers under their orders reach them by that path, to dominate them, to make them true collaborators and co-operators.[2]

In June, over 300 firms under the auspices of the Rural Society and the Argentine Industrial Union issued a communiqué condemning the social and labour policies espoused by the government at Perón's initiative. However, the clear opposition to Perón by business leaders only served to convince the workers that Perón was their only guarantee in the face of their employers' implacable desire to return to the *status quo ante*.

For her part, Eva's self-confidence had been increasing along with her political education and 35,000-peso salary at Radio Belgrano, something that did nothing to endear her to Perón's political and military colleagues. Her increasing outspokenness on political issues, even in the confines of the Posadas Street apartment, caused incredulity and ire, while her famously salty vocabulary and lack of protocol were becoming virtually a question of state for some members of the military government. In one incident, for example, she attended a swearing-in ceremony at Government House (the Casa Rosada), in which she leaned on the president's chair, draping her arm over the seat back. According to one officer present, in an interview in 1966, 'the army, and I don't know if this is understandable now, was not accustomed to such things.'[3] In fairness, above and beyond the degree of sexism and social snobbery in this attitude, it must be recognised that Eva was not easy for the armed forces to swallow. She was hardly self-effacing, she was often abrasive and she could treat Perón's colleagues with great informality, but also exceed the boundary of informality and fall into arrogance and disrespect. This was probably as deliberate as it was a question of ignorance; certainly in the near future she would demonstrate as first lady that she had the capability to learn to manage protocol perfectly when she deemed it necessary. She was ill-qualified to intervene in politics to the extent that she did, and the fact that she enjoyed calling attention to herself would grate on their nerves, as even Perón's own tendency to call attention to himself to the detriment of military *esprit de corps* was beginning to do.

At the same time, accusations that Eva's family were becoming too influential were already beginning to spread, with Juancito now incorporated into Perón's circle of collaborators and widely suspected of using his contacts for black marketeering purposes. In fact, with the exception of a visit to her sister Erminda in Junín in 1936 and a visit to Buenos Aires by Doña Juana a few years later, Eva had had little face-to-face contact with her mother since she left Junín in 1935, and it is thus difficult to say how truthful this claim was at the time. (According to other testimonies, Eva had little time for her family, except Juancito, and kept her mother in particular on a tight lead. 'Eva kept the Duarte family hopping. She never loved them and tried to be with them as little as possible. Doña Juana, the mother, was addicted to gambling.'[4]) However, there was a perception in the army that Perón – and by extension the government – was being prejudiced by the

interference, first in his life and then in the affairs of state that he managed, of the Duarte family, that family of obscure origins [...] [W]e could not allow government resolutions to be influenced by a family like the Duartes. We were convinced that it was our duty to stop the nation falling, above all, into the hands of that woman, as it did.[5]

It was this perception that prompted the crisis of October 1945.

Although the military was still largely divided over Perón, much of the middle and upper class and the landed aristocracy were by this time whole-heartedly opposed to the government in general and to Perón in particular, as its most visible and activist element, boasting the posts of vice-president, war minister and secretary of labour. President Farrell himself was seen by and large as a mere figurehead. By the latter half of 1945, pressure was growing for a return to elected government, with demands for the govern-ment to be turned over to the Supreme Court until elections could be held, and calls for a radical shift in social policy. These demands came to a head on 19 September, with the massive March for the Constitution and Liberty, with estimates of the numbers involved ranging from 65,000 to 500,000 marchers, which brought together anti-Peronists from across the spec-trum (although the overwhelming impression gleaned from photos of the event was of the well-heeled nature of the participants). The purpose of the march was ostensibly to demand civilian government, though 'such hostile cries as were uttered, were all directed against the person of [...] Colonel Juan Domingo Perón'.[6] Clashes between the police and university students (anti-Peronists) also rose alarmingly in the latter part of September and early October, and on 26 September Farrell imposed a state of siege, which did not prevent a massive occupation of the universities that led to some 1,600 arrests.

The military government was not the only target of the students' con-tempt: the opposition's disdain and dislike were increasingly focusing on the working classes, which had become more visible and confident and whose demands for political representation were becoming more stri-dent. The student slogan '*Alpargatas* no, books yes' was clearly classist and helped to convince those workers who were still vacillating that their interests were ineluctably linked to those of Perón. (*Alpargatas* are canvas, rope-soled shoes used by the poor; while the message may have been intended somewhat differently, it was denigrating and offensive in the extreme.)

Rising tensions were also stirred by two other political events. One involved a 'spontaneous' demonstration outside Perón's flat in July, call-ing for him to run for president. Despite Perón's denials, both civilian and military opponents were alarmed by the turn of events and senior military figures promptly demanded that anyone planning to run for office resign any public function immediately – a warning shot that Perón blithely disregarded. The other was the appointment, between April and September 1945, of Spruille Braden as US ambassador. 'Mister Braden', 'who was not a career diplomatist […] came to Buenos Aires with the fixed idea that he had been elected by Providence to overthrow the Farrell-Perón regime'.[7] Inappropriately for his supposed diplomatic mission, Braden quickly became identified as the virtual leader of the Argentine opposition to Perón, which emboldened the opposition but 'eventually defeat[ed] its own object by rallying the forces of nationalism and anti-American feeling round Colonel Perón'.[8] (Braden himself, who left Argentina in September to take up the post of under-secretary of South American relations, would maintain the anti-Perón campaign from Washington. In his later memoirs he would note that he never met Eva, but would refer to her only in the terms of the oligarchic opposition, quoting a well-known lewd joke about her and describing her as a member of the 'world's oldest profession' and as a 'demagogue'.[9])

With pressure rising among at least some sectors of civil society (those with the greatest economic influence) and much of the military leaning in favour of an orderly retreat to barracks, it was announced on 5 October that Eva's friend Oscar Nicolini would be named as director general of post and telecommunications. The appointment was signed not by Perón, but by interior minister Hortensio Quijano, one of a group of civilian politicians from the Radical Party who had thrown their support behind Perón and taken up posts in government. However, it was widely supposed to have been the work of Eva – despite the fact that, as Marysa Navarro points out, Nicolini was a 30-year veteran of the department and was working as director general of radio broadcasting, making him a reasonable nominee for the post.[10] Nevertheless, this apparent evidence of Eva's influence, and the fact that an officer at the key Campo de Mayo barracks, Lieutenant Colonel Francisco Rocco, also wanted the post and was passed over, was the detonator for the crisis that followed.

The next day, Perón received a visit at the Posadas Street flat from the head of Campo de Mayo, General Eduardo Avalos, a member of the GOU and hitherto at least partially a Perón ally. However, Perón refused to bow to pressure from Avalos to withdraw Nicolini's appointment (claiming, implausibly, that the decision had been Quijano's), and Eva, present for at least part of the discussion, did nothing to alleviate tensions. On the contrary, she apparently pushed Perón to stand his ground, even urging him to retire from the army and government and leave his comrades in arms to sort out their own problems. Her intervention, and Avalos's later reports of her comportment, only served to inflame military hostility towards Eva and, increasingly, towards her lover. Perón and Avalos agreed to meet at the War Ministry on 8 October – Perón's 'official' 50th birthday – at which time Avalos would be accompanied by his colleagues from Campo de Mayo. However, they were surprised to find themselves heavily outnumbered by other officers called in by Perón and Mercante, and Avalos was astonished when a vote of confidence was proposed and he himself lost. This only served to increase the wrath of Campo de Mayo, which demanded Perón's immediate removal and prepared to back up the demand with tanks.

Thereafter events moved with remarkable speed. Under increasing pressure from the army, on 9 October Farrell asked for Perón's resignation from his three government posts. Perón added his own request to retire from the army, and it was announced that his resignation from government would be followed on 12 October by a decree calling elections for April 1946. Most other ministers also withdrew from the cabinet in the following few days. These moves led to increasing confidence on the part of the opposition, and rising demands that the government pass to the Supreme Court, while on the part of trade unions concerns increased at a similar rate. The latter concerns were fanned, quite deliberately, when on 10 October Perón was given permission to give a farewell speech to the staff at the Secretariat. Forewarned by Mercante, union leaders mobilised some 15,000 workers who congregated in front of the Secretariat (Eva among them); the speech was also broadcast by radio.

Despite his apparent total defeat, Perón scarcely sounded like a man withdrawing to private life. In a carefully calibrated speech, he reminded the workers of the numerous social and economic benefits they had enjoyed since he had become labour secretary, and noted that in his last act as secretary he had signed a decree increasing salaries. Hinting in a not overly subtle fashion that workers' gains might be threatened by his departure, Perón called for the workers across the country to remain calm, but added 'I ask for order so we can go forward in our triumphant march; but if it is necessary, some day I will ask for war'.[11] Press comment notwithstanding (that the address would be Perón's swan song 'at least as far as can be foreseen'[12]), for any astute observer the speech pointed to a tactical retreat rather than an admission of defeat. His enemies at Campo de Mayo certainly came to this conclusion and were incandescent with rage with

Farrell for having permitted Perón this defiance. Calls for his arrest rose, and with them concerns over a possible assassination attempt.

In addition to the severe tensions of the preceding days surrounding Perón's future and personal security, Eva would rapidly discover the fragility of her own position. Following Perón's ouster she was dismissed from Radio Belgrano and all her programmes taken off the air. (Whether this was because Jaime Yankelevich had been biding his time to get rid of her, or whether he felt it prudent to do so in order to maintain good relations with the now Perón-less authorities, is an open question.) After years of struggle and a relatively brief period of security, she was again 'out' and facing the prospect of being blacklisted for an indefinite period, as well as the fear that Perón (and possibly she herself) could be in mortal danger. Her understandable reaction in the face of all this was to pressure Perón to go into exile in Uruguay, abandoning his nascent political career and his campaign for workers' rights – an outcome that he himself had threatened on more than one occasion and that Mercante feared, even as he also feared the possibility of a violent end.

In fear of an attack, following Perón's speech they spent the night at her sister Elisa's flat, before leaving the following morning for the island of Tres Bocas in the Tigre delta, north of Buenos Aires, accompanied by Juancito and Rodolfo Freude, the son of the Nazi agent Ludwig Freude who owned the residence in Tres Bocas. Their respite in Tigre would prove brief: on 12 October, the new police chief, Aristóbulo Mittelbach, arrived with Mercante and orders to arrest Perón and return him to Buenos Aires. Mercante himself had opted to tell Mittelbach of their whereabouts, believing that Perón would be safer in his custody than in the hands of others. On their arrival they found Perón and Eva arm in arm near the water; the return to Buenos Aires was punctuated by Eva's ever-increasing weeping.

On arrival at the Posadas flat, Perón shaved and accepted his arrest, although objecting to the order that he should be held by the navy, far more hostile to him than the army. As he left the flat under arrest, in the early hours of 13 October, Eva suffered a new attack of hysteria and, according to some versions, attacked the officers who escorted Perón and had to be forcibly detached from him after a last long embrace. Mercante accompanied Perón to the gunboat *Independencia*, where Perón asked him to look after Eva before being taken on board and transported to Martín García, the island where Yrigoyen had been held following his overthrow in 1930. Mercante himself, while concerned for Eva, would have little opportunity to look after her, finding himself detained on 13 October and largely out of action for the next few days. However, his earlier efforts with the trade unions, while Perón and Eva were in Tres Bocas, would bear fruit even as he was left *hors de combat*.

With few resources left and facing the real prospect of losing the love of her life, Eva did what little she could in the midst of her personal crisis. As she would later note in her ghosted autobiography, 'I went out into the street looking for friends that could still do something for him', and 'I never felt […] so small, so insignificant as in those eight days'.[13] She sought out the lawyer Juan Atilio Bramuglia, an adviser at the Secretariat of Labour, lawyer for the railway union Unión Ferroviaria and later Perón's foreign minister, in the hope of presenting a writ of habeas corpus. She never forgave Bramuglia for refusing, on the grounds that Perón at liberty might be in more danger than in custody and that, moreover, he would not take the risk that Eva might put her own interests above those of the country and seek to take Perón off to a safe exile. On one of her forays into the street, as she rode in a taxi she was recognised by a group of students who dragged her out and beat her, a 'baptism of pain that purified me of all doubt and all cowardice'[14] (if indeed she could ever have been accused of cowardice, which was never obvious among her many evident defects). At risk of worse attacks, she began sleeping at the home of her friend Pierina Dealessi, arriving late when Pierina returned from the theatre and then disappearing during the day. According to Pierina later, 'she didn't know if they had killed him or if he was a prisoner. She told me that they had threatened her too.'[15]

Perhaps emboldened by the turn of events of recent days, the opposition proved to be more effective in recruiting support for Perón than even Mercante and union leaders like Cipriano Reyes, Luis Gay and Luis Monzalvo. Following the 12 October holiday, employers deducted the day from workers' wages, telling them 'to go and ask Perón for it'. On 12 October itself, a large group of well-heeled ladies and gentlemen congregated in front of the Círculo Militar, the elegant officers' club on the Plaza San Martín, reiterating the demand that the government be handed over to the Supreme Court and shouting down officers who attempted to explain the government's planned post-Perón course. A group of elegant but over-excited women even attacked an officer entering the building and left him badly battered and bleeding. By evening the police (most of whom were Perón supporters) had intervened, and a subsequent shoot-out left

numerous wounded and one dead. The events clearly illustrated that revenge would be taken on Perón's supporters, and that in effect they had no
guarantees unless and until he returned to power. Moreover, on 13 October,
Perón's replacement as labour secretary, Juan Fentanes, suggested that labour policies would be reviewed and would seek greater 'equity' between
labour and capital, hardly a reassuring sign.

Despite his parlous situation, Perón still enjoyed the support of some
in influential positions, including Eduardo Colom, who ran the tabloid
newspaper *La Epoca*. On 14 October *La Epoca* published an open letter
from Perón to Avalos demanding to know the reasons for his arrest and
calling for his immediate release. This generated enough popular disquiet
to unnerve the government, not all of whose members were altogether
anti-Perón, and produced denials that he was in fact under arrest. However,
this claim was not believed – in particular after Mercante himself was also
detained – and worker protests began to mount.

Meanwhile, a prolifically epistolary Perón, still in Martín García, wrote
letters to Farrell, asking him to expedite his retirement from the army, and
to both Mercante and Eva. All these letters indicated that his inclination at
this time was to withdraw from politics, retire from the army, marry Eva
and live quietly far away from it all. The letter to Eva, in particular (a copy
of which was given by Mercante to the historian Felix Luna many years
later), has been widely reprinted and appears to have been the sincerest of
the many writings left by Perón, as well as remarkably emotional for a man
characterised throughout his life by his emotional distance.

> Today I know how much I love you and that I can't live without
> you […] Today I've written to Farrell asking him to expedite my
> retirement. When it comes through we'll get married and go away
> somewhere to live quietly […] If it doesn't come through I'll arrange
> things some other way but we'll end this unprotected state you are
> in now.[16]

After fulminating against the disloyalty of his comrades in arms, he pro-
poses to return with Eva to the Chubut of his childhood – not, it would
seem, the intention of a man contemplating his political resuscitation – and
urges her to look after herself: 'Nothing must happen to you because then
my life would be over […] [D]on't worry about me; but love me a lot because now I need it more than ever.'

The letters were carried by Perón's physician, the army doctor Captain Miguel Angel Mazza, who examined him on 14 October and reported that the prisoner's health was in danger owing to the climate on Martín García – a manoeuvre which resulted in his transfer to the military hospital in Buenos Aires on the 16th. The letters themselves were intercepted, which has led to speculation as to whether they were written with the intention of throwing the opposition off the scent, given the likelihood that they would fall into other hands. However, Perón at that moment was not expecting a rapid political comeback and, as his actions made clear following his release, his intention to marry Eva was sincere (and the retreat to Chubut would probably have been implemented as well, if the events of 17 October had not intervened). Had this not been the case, he could easily have jettisoned her on his return to power, accepting that she was a political liability at this stage and that his personal ambitions might have seemed better served by this course. Equally, Eva had already seen the perils involved in her relationship with Perón, losing her employment and any protection during his temporary eclipse. A woman with long experience of surviving, she too could have ended the association at this time and sought alternatives that would have given her at least a modicum of security. Neither did so – and indeed, the rancour that was targeted towards them both if anything united them more closely than before.

Perón arrived at the military hospital in the Palermo neighbourhood of Buenos Aires early on the morning of the 17th, and was installed in the quarters of the disgruntled hospital chaplain, where he changed into pyjamas and awaited events. Although Eva was not permitted to see him, she spoke to him by phone from downstairs and, reassured of his safety, also returned home to await events. At this point, neither Perón nor Eva played an active role in the remarkable events that were developing.

Although the CGT leadership had shown some reluctance to cast its lot too definitively with Perón, at the grassroots level union members were taking matters into their own hands. Already on the 15th, the Tucumán sugar workers' union FOTIA had declared a strike, and on the 16th the CGT central committee met to consider a similar measure. A group of CGT representatives met with Avalos, warning him of the increasing ferment, only to be assured again that Perón was not under arrest, but simply in custody for his own protection, and that the benefits obtained by the workers under his tenure would be respected. A meeting with Farrell elicited a similar response, although this did not alleviate union concerns that the government might be turned over to the Supreme Court, as the opposition was demanding, and thence to a new oligarchic government. Nevertheless, the CGT hierarchy continued to hesitate, concerned about the effects of calling a general strike exclusively for the purpose of gaining Perón's freedom. In the end, the committee voted to call a 24-hour general strike for 18 October without mentioning Perón, but rather in defence of the gains made by labour since 1943.

At this point, however, the CGT's central committee had little more control over the situation than the increasingly unsettled military government. The demonstrations that broke out on 16 October took on a new momentum on the 17th. On that day, thousands of workers from the factories in the industrial belt around Buenos Aires, and from as far away as La Plata, marched on the capital to demand Perón's return – an unprecedented event that, despite the organisational efforts of Mercante, meatpackers' leader Cipriano Reyes, telephone union leader Luis Gay and railway leader Luis Manzalvo, was largely spontaneous and astonishingly peaceful. As they approached the capital, their numbers increased as workers from each factory downed tools and joined them. As they approached the Riachuelo, the odiferous and toxic river that separates the capital from the province, and that receives the effluents from industries and slums alike, there were efforts to raise or close bridges in order to stop them, but they swarmed across nonetheless, some commandeering boats and, supposedly, some hardy souls throwing themselves into the nauseous water to wade across. Some others commandeered buses and trolleys to take them to the centre. Perhaps most strikingly for many of the participants, the police who lined the route did not try to stop them; many even shouted 'Viva Perón!' This added to the emotion of the event: it was the first time that most of those workers had felt the police were on their side. It was also the first time that significant numbers of women participated in a political act, marching with their men and children towards the Plaza de Mayo.

Most of those who marched had never before seen the centre of Buenos Aires and the stately Plaza de Mayo, where they congregated. However, while the 'zoological deluge', as the Radical legislator Ernesto Sammartino would later call it, came as a shock to the middle-class *porteños* (many of whom saw the event as the long-dreaded nightmare come to pass), the crowds were not hostile or aggressive but rather joyful. British Ambassador David Kelly would later recall that, as he approached the Casa Rosada in his official car, 'the crowd made way readily on seeing the flag, contenting themselves with shouting through the window in a friendly fashion: "Long live Perón and down with Braden"'.[17] The impeccably oligarchic Delfina Bunge de Gálvez also noted that 'it was the feared mob [...] [But] they looked good-natured and calm. There were no hostile faces or raised fists.'[18] Moreover, despite the scorn with which the marchers were viewed by much of the press and well-heeled public – in particular, the fact that some weary walkers took off their shoes and soaked their feet in the fountains in the Plaza de Mayo – one of the more striking things about photos of the participants is how many were wearing suits and ties, in keeping with the solemnity of the occasion. However, the fact that many did not have jackets (unthinkable in formal Buenos Aires) led their detractors to refer to them as '*descamisados*', shirtless ones – the term that for Perón and Eva would thereafter become a political identification and a virtue rather than a defect. They came in their thousands 'to recover their leader at the cost of whatever sacrifice'.[19]

The crowds continued to grow in the Plaza de Mayo throughout the afternoon and into the evening, insisting that they would stay there until Perón appeared. Perón, for his part, was apparently as surprised as anyone by the events, repeatedly asking visitors to the military hospital if it was true that there were really many people in the plaza. However, he was not so surprised as to play his hand carelessly, and waited for some hours, disdaining pleas from Farrell and other members of the government to speak to the workers until the crowd had likely reached a peak. Avalos himself, presumably through gritted teeth, was forced to appear on the balcony of the Casa Rosada to assure the crowds that Perón had been released. Finally, at 10.30 pm, Perón and Farrell appeared on the balcony together and embraced before a euphoric crowd generally estimated at some 300,000.

In order to gather his thoughts to improvise a speech, Perón asked the crowd to sing the national anthem. The speech he finally gave was emotive and effective in the extreme, announcing that he would leave the army:

in order to put on civilian clothes and mix with that suffering, sweating mass which with its labour makes the greatness of the country [...] I want now, as a simple citizen, mixing with this sweating mass, to press everyone against my heart as I could with my mother.[20]

Faced with questions from the crowd as to where he had been and what had happened, Perón found the opportunity to be magnanimous, saying that he had already forgotten it. Asking the crowds to remain for a few minutes longer so that he could remember the scene, Perón sent his greetings to workers in the provinces and asked the demonstrators to disperse peacefully and take a holiday on the 18th, when the general strike was already planned – generating the well-known rhyme *'mañana es San Perón, que trabaje el patrón'* ('tomorrow is St Perón's day, let the boss work'). The crowds began to thin, and Perón went home to the Posadas Street flat where Eva was waiting.

As the author Félix Luna would observe years later,

> I think I would give ten years of the life of Félix Luna in exchange for one day, one single day of Juan Perón. In exchange, for example, for that day in October, when he appeared in the Plaza de Mayo and received, in an unforgettable roar, the purest and most beautiful thing that a man with political vocation can aspire to: the love of his people.[21]

Thereafter, 17 October would be known as 'Loyalty Day' in the Peronist calendar, although the annual commemorations would become increasingly structured and ritualistic, unlike the spontaneous nature of the first incarnation – one of the last truly spontaneous events associated with a Peronism that in government would lose its creative and improvisational side to become increasingly rigid. However, the mythic event of 1945 remained highly emotive for all those involved, whether as participants or observers, for decades thereafter, a unique case in which the working classes came – peacefully – to the defence of their leader and did so successfully in the face of opposition from the military and the oligarchy. With 17 October, the possibility that Perón might have retired with Eva to Patagonia or to exile in Uruguay was gone forever, and Argentine history changed.

Despite efforts by both Peronist and anti-Peronist mythmakers in later years to attribute a major role to Eva in organising the events and mobilising the workers – either to demonstrate her loyalty to her man and 'her' workers, or to show that she had dragged the weak and dependent Perón back to power in order to extract her revenge – there is no real evidence to support this. (Cipriano Reyes directly denied it, although his later break with Perón and Eva and his tendency to omit other union leaders from the history of 17 October may well have coloured his version.) Some trade unionists claimed that Eva met with union leaders in the run-up to the 17th, and even that she was driving around on the 17th exhorting the workers to strike. Textile worker Mariano Tedesco would later say that 'she saw everyone and shouted at them "we have to convince the boys that we have to rescue the colonel"', while her friend Vera Pichel would claim that she was the 'promoter of the march', going to the unions and demanding concrete action.[22]

In Eva's obituary on 27 July 1952, the newspaper *La Nación* similarly failed to find out exactly what role she had played in 17 October, saying vaguely that she had 'moved actively in the shadows' and that 'what she did in the course of that decisive week as the one who stimulated the partisans will undoubtedly be recognised later by detailed chronicles.'[23] Eva herself claimed no such credit, saying that 'the people came out on their own. It was not Perón's wife.'[24] In practice, as many historians have noted, Eva was a radio actress who as yet did not have the relations with union leaders that she would later develop; indeed, many of those leaders shared with the army a degree of distrust and disapproval with respect to Perón's mistress, as Isabel Ernst's intervention at the request of unionists would indicate. (Indeed, according to her own later version, Isabel Ernst herself played some role in events, helping to rally support while Perón and Mercante were both detained, contacting trade unionists to pass the 'message' that they should go onto the streets and that the police would not intervene as they were in this instance on the workers' side.[25]) As Pierina Dealessi also noted, Eva was largely without support or allies at the time, without even a job, and at risk of violence. Though certainly she attempted to help Perón through seeking a habeas corpus petition via Bramuglia, and doubtless approached others she hoped could help, at this stage she was simply not Evita the political leader who could have mobilised workers and their leaders alike. If anything, her very helplessness in the face of Perón's arrest appears to have been one of her greatest frustrations. According to Rodolfo Decker, 'she accompanied the process spiritually'.[26]

With 17 October, however, their brief downfall was reversed; Perón announced his presidential candidacy for the elections called for 24 February 1946, while he was also reinstated into the army and promoted to the rank of general. Before launching his campaign, however, Perón and Eva had a few days' rest and, on 22 October, he made good on his promise to marry her at a civil ceremony at their Posadas Street flat, with Juancito and Mercante as witnesses. However, the marriage itself raised difficulties, given the need to produce a birth certificate: this would demonstrate that Eva was illegitimate and her name was Ibarguren. In the days before the civil ceremony, Eva's sister Elisa apparently arrived at the registry office in Los Toldos and told the official there that it would be worth his while to produce a fraudulent birth certificate for the woman who would almost assuredly be first lady. Following his refusal, some nights later lights were seen in the registry office, and it was later discovered that her birth certificate had been torn out of the record book. Thereafter, a new birth certificate appeared, indicating that she was born María Eva Duarte to married parents in Junín on 7 May 1922. The marriage certificate also contained other inaccuracies, describing Perón as 'single' rather than 'widowed' and claiming that the ceremony took place at Doña Juana's house in Junín, which it also gave as Eva's domicile.

The subsequent religious ceremony in La Plata similarly proved complicated. (Under Argentine law, all marriages must be performed by the registry office to be legally valid, with any religious ceremony permitted only after the civil service.) On 29 November, Perón failed to reach the altar of San Ponciano church after hearing of a possible attack on his life. The ceremony subsequently took place on 10 December, although the bride and groom were forced to sneak in through a side door to avoid the crowds. The wedding was conducted by Father Hernán Benítez, the Jesuit who had given last rites to Perón's first wife Aurelia and who would become Eva's confessor and adviser, and, curiously, took place at 20.25 – the hour at which Eva would later famously 'enter immortality' on 26 July 1952. This was followed by a short and informal honeymoon in San Nicolás at the property of a friend, Román Subiza, before the couple returned to live briefly at the house Eva had purchased in Teodoro Garcia, in the Colegiales neighbourhood of Buenos Aires. Eva would later remember the honeymoon as a time of being alone together, walking in the country, talking, drinking *mate*, listening to music and going to bed early. She wore no make-up and wore trousers and one of Perón's shirts; it would be one of the last times they could enjoy such a quiet time together.

*****

Although Eva's own role in 17 October was limited by her circumstances, the events forever marked her identification with the *descamisados* and the lifelong 'debt' she owed them. 'For nearly eight days they had Perón in their hands […] From the time Perón went until the people recovered him for themselves – and for me! – my days were days of pain and fever.'[27] Claiming that during his imprisonment Perón had virtually commended his *descamisados* to her care and that they in turn had rescued him both for themselves and for her, Eva goes further, saying that she can find no greater way of expressing her love than by 'offering a bit of my life, burning it for love of his *"descamisados"*. This is my duty of gratitude to him and to all of them and I fulfil it joyfully, happy, as all duties imposed by love are fulfilled.'[28] Even at the *Cabildo Abierto* in August 1951, she referred in her speech to the fact that 'I have in my heart a debt of gratitude with the *descamisados* who on 17 October 1945 gave me back light, life, my soul and my heart when they gave me back the general.'[29] It could be argued that the crowds that turned out did so for themselves and for Perón, rather than for Eva, but from this time she would increasingly see herself – and come to be seen – as virtually synonymous with the *descamisados* whose place in Peronist mythology had now usurped that of the armed forces. From this moment on, nothing was too great a challenge to repay that debt.

Many have doubted whether Eva seriously viewed this new role as anything other than a new acting part, though the fact that she never attained such depths of feeling or sincerity in her career as an actress must surely suggest otherwise. Others have questioned the shift away from a largely frivolous career that had absorbed her ambitions until that time, to something far more serious and all-consuming. In itself, this is not so surprising. Eva left home with the obsession of becoming an actress at the age of 15, an age when many people who later assume considerable responsibilities are still largely frivolous. Indeed, as a provincial teenager with a passionate desire to succeed, to 'be somebody', the examples around her were limited. Feminists like Cecilia Grierson and Alicia Moreau de Justo came from cosmopolitan and educated backgrounds. Without in any way diminishing their remarkable achievements, having brothers and friends who went to university and made careers might have prompted a feeling of 'why not me?', even if most of those potential role models were male.

In Eva's case, even the young men around her in Junín were limited in their opportunities (Juancito's career as a travelling salesman could hardly have inspired dreams of glory), and the young women even more so. The one obvious example of women triumphing over poverty and adversity, and becoming famous, was the film star, brought to Junín courtesy of fan magazines and matinees at the cinema. This, then, was the model she adopted. Whatever her interests at 15, politics was not a serious career option for the youth of Junín of either gender. (Even assuming the relationship with the anarchist Damián Gómez was real, as noted earlier the anarchist view of women's role at the time was one of nurturing and feeding the male activist often on the run, hardly a career inspiration for an ambitious girl.) What Perón taught her, and what 17 October conveyed to her, was a different and far more important career option, far more rewarding, but one in which the burdens imposed by the roles of political leader and virtual saviour were also far heavier.

This increasing self-image as a representative of the people virtually chosen to 'save' them single-handed had a substantial element of narcissism, one that may be found to a greater or lesser extent in many activists whose combination of altruism and egoism permits them to achieve things few people would even attempt. That narcissism, passion and drive would provoke both good and bad, and would leave few people indifferent.

CHAPTER 8

First Lady

THE IMPENDING PRESIDENTIAL elections announced for 24 February 1946 brought a rapid end to Perón and Eva's honeymoon and their incipient domesticity. Given the unusually high-profile role that Eva was to play in the campaign (and thereafter), they also required rapid changes in other spheres: Eva's past as an actress of dubious repute was rapidly swept under the carpet and erased from official history. As noted earlier, her final film *La pródiga* was not screened until 1984 and director Mario Soffici handed over the print of the film as a 'wedding gift'. Jaime Yankelevich, the owner of Radio Belgrano, was asked to annul her contract, and he also made her a gift of all the publicity photos of her held by the radio. (Destruction of her past, and the photographic evidence of it, occurred both when she came to power and after the military overthrew Perón in 1955, accounting for the fact that photographs of one of the most famous and most photographed women of her time are comparatively scant; official photographers who managed to hide some of their negatives from the 'Liberating Revolution' would eventually become a key source of images.)

Just as she had erased Los Toldos from her history, describing herself as born in Junín, Eva would continue to make it clear that she wished to bury the 'artistic' career that had previously been her obsession; former colleagues and others who reminded her of those days or referred to her previous incarnation were rapidly frozen out.[1] This careful removal of human details from her life would carry on, on the part of both admirers and detractors, to such a degree that the image left to history has become somewhat inhuman. The 'antis' give her no credit for any human sentiment and paint her only as a vengeful and malevolent harpy, base and virtually subhuman, while the 'Evitistas' have tended to present an ever more ethereal figure emanating love and sacrifice, and seemingly without defects, failings or bodily functions.

Doubtless a part of this effort reflected Eva's desire to be a suitable wife for her presidential candidate husband, not least given that she seems to have already had it in mind to take an unusually active role in politics. On 14 December Perón was declared the presidential candidate for the recently formed Partido Laborista, while the allied Junta Renovadora faction of the Radical Party proposed the dignified elder statesman Hortensio Quijano as his running mate. This move effectively eliminated the faithful Domingo Mercante, who had doubtless expected the vice-presidential nod, from the ticket, but was deemed by Perón to be necessary to guarantee the Junta Renovadora's support. Quijano was finally formally nominated to second Perón on 15 January 1946.

Perón and Eva passed their first Christmas as newlyweds already in political mode, as on 26 December he left on a campaign tour on a special train, 'El Descamisado', which visited Rosario, Córdoba, La Rioja and Catamarca in rapid succession. On 28 December, Eva herself embarked from Retiro station to join her husband in Santiago del Estero, becoming the first candidate's wife to participate thus in a campaign. (A photo of Eva leaving from Retiro, published in the newspaper *La Epoca*, became the first public acknowledgement of their marriage.) They spent a sweltering New Year's Eve in Santiago del Estero before arriving in Santa Fe on New Year's Day and then again in Rosario. By some accounts, Eva's main intention in travelling to Santiago was to intervene in the choice of the Laborista candidate for governor of Buenos Aires province, against the unions' choice of Juan Atilio Bramuglia, the lawyer who had refused her request to present a petition of habeas corpus when Perón was held in Martín García. Although Eva has been reported as having intervened in the selection of other candidates in favour of Radicals, in this case her support went to Mercante; she had formed a good relationship with him, as noted above, and an even better opinion of his loyalty to Perón. This behaviour, unusual in the extreme, already began to be a source of irritation for other forces in the Laborista Party, notably meatpackers' leader Cipriano Reyes. However, despite Perón's initial refusal to interfere with the party's choice of candidate, Mercante eventually became the candidate for governor.

Further lengthy rail tours of the interior provinces followed, with Perón and Eva visiting San Juan, Mendoza, San Luis and Córdoba provinces in

January before returning again through Santa Fe. Eva reportedly declined to show herself in Junín, the first stop en route to San Juan, but otherwise campaigned enthusiastically, waving from the window and clasping outstretched hands even when Perón retired to his berth. However, while she received flowers at stops and smiled tirelessly, she made no speeches, although she reacted angrily and even violently when members of their security attempted to keep the crowds back too roughly. Perón, for his part, made speeches attempting to adopt a less radical tone than in the past, in a bid to broaden his support base and to acknowledge the backing of more centrist groups like the Junta Renovadora. His discourse, while justifying reforms in favour of the working classes, promised to be favourable to capitalism as well, while also stressing his democratic convictions and the Catholic inspiration of his doctrine. The latter was doubtless influenced by various priests who surrounded Perón, but primarily by the Jesuit Hernán Benítez, who would later take much credit for Perón's focus on the Papal encyclicals in his labour policy. According to Benítez later, 'from '43 we were united by the same social passion. The suffering of the poor hurt us both equally, in our souls.'[2] (Benítez, in later life, was given to perhaps exaggerating his influence over Perón, who throughout his life was prone to cut and paste bits of different ideologies that came to hand and appeared useful, but his role in emphasising the 'profoundly Christian' nature of Peronism was undoubtedly significant.)

On 27 January the couple survived a scare when a railway worker was able to remove an explosive device that had been left on the track. Similar attacks affected the so-called 'Tren de la Libertad', the train that carried the opposition candidates José Tamborini and Enrique Mosca on their own campaign trail. Tamborini and Mosca had been chosen by the so-called Unión Democrática, an unwieldy alliance of parties including the conservative groups, Radicals, Communists, Socialists and others whose only point in common was their antipathy towards Perón. Indeed, their alliance with the conservative oligarchy against Perón, the putative representative of working-class interests, would do long-term damage to the Socialist and Communist parties in Argentina, for decades seen as having betrayed their supposed natural constituency.

The slogan of the Unión Democrática, 'for democracy, against Nazism', was fairly uncontroversial in its sentiments, but the tacit equation of Perón with Nazism, while readily accepted by many sectors, was anathema to most of his supporters, many of whom could have been charged with being ingenuous but not with being Nazi sympathisers, and further polarised the campaign. Moreover, the Unión Democrática received the enthusiastic but ill-advised support of the former US ambassador, Spruille Braden, now back in Washington. On 12 February the State Department published the so-called *Blue Book* (officially titled *Consultation Among the American Republics with Respect to the Argentine Situation*), which allegedly documented links between Perón and some of his colleagues with members of the Third Reich. An inflammatory document that played well with the opposition, the *Blue Book* was also an obvious interference in domestic politics, coming less than two weeks before the presidential elections, and gave Perón a highly effective campaign slogan – Braden or Perón – as well as the excuse to launch a response, the *Blue and White Book* (*Libro azul y blanco*), denouncing imperialist intervention.

At the same time, Perón could arguably be said to have received support from a higher power: in November 1945, the Catholic Church issued a pastoral letter ordering the faithful not to vote for any candidate in favour of divorce, secular education or separation of Church and State. Although this was a standard instruction before all Argentine elections, the Unión Democrática subsequently came out in favour of all of these steps (it must be remembered that the Radical Party had long been considered anti-clerical by the Catholic hierarchy). The military government's early efforts to adopt measures favourable to the Church, such as religious education and the cleaning up of radio dialogue and tango lyrics, together with Perón's own frequent references to the Church's social doctrine, would stand him in good stead, although in practice the electoral numbers would appear to have been on his side in any case.

After being a decorative but silent presence during the campaign trips, Eva would make her debut political speech on 8 February, at a meeting of Perón's women supporters (who did not have the vote) in Luna Park, the site of her meeting with Perón only two years earlier. The women gathered there had expected Perón, who was ill, and his wife was poorly received: despite the efforts of some of the organisers, Eva was shouted down repeatedly and those present did not hear her speech, written by her former scriptwriter Muñoz Aspiri, as they continued to shout her husband's name. (On leaving Luna Park many continued to cause a disturbance and were dispersed by the police with tear gas.) However, the text of the speech, which is reproduced in various sources, gives early indications that Eva's role would be different to that of any of her predecessors: 'I, as a woman of the people, which I can never forget, will fight at the Colonel's side.'[3] Moreover, although she obviously had much to learn as a political speaker and the occasion can scarcely be counted a success, it is striking to note how rapidly thereafter she would become a highly accomplished and effective speaker, arguably outstripping even her husband. The unpleasant experience did not stop her leaving for Rosario with her husband the following day for a campaign trip, in which the return journey was disrupted by an attempt to derail their train. Nor did it stop her from rapidly becoming

> the motor and the executor of Perón's projects, the best student, the best disciple [...] She was born to be a leader, she was *Evita Capitana*. Marvellous. The things she said came from her soul, a girl who didn't go to secondary school [...] *Evita Capitana* because she led, she carried, she was the motor of the National *Justicialista* Movement.[4]

Perhaps to the surprise of the Unión Democrática, the 24 February elections, widely touted as the cleanest in Argentine history, did not crown a President Tamborini. With over 2.7 million votes cast, Perón received nearly 1.48 million, although the official count was slow and the final official result was only announced on 8 April, during which time Tamborini claimed to be the 'certain' winner. (Also during this interval, Eva's old friend Anita Jordán, with whom she had shared boarding house rooms, dressing rooms and clothes, died of cancer on 20 March, arguably marking a symbolic end to her earlier life and a shift to a different type of companion.) Due to the system of the electoral college, which under the constitution gave greater relative weight to smaller provinces, the margin was even greater, with Perón winning 309 electors and Tamborini only 72. Moreover, Peronist candidates won the majority of governorships, with the exception of the provinces of Córdoba, Corrientes, San Juan and San Luis (the latter three provinces all governed by personalist leaderships of long standing, despite Perón's high-profile role in sending aid to San Juan after the earthquake only two years previously). In Congress, the Peronists gained 109 seats in the Lower House, to 49 for the opposition (44 of them Radicals), and 28 of 30 Senate seats.

After the election results became known, Eva made her first official radio speech as the wife of the president-elect, in which she effectively set out her stall in terms of women's (and her own) role in politics and promised to fight for women's suffrage:

> The wife of the President of the Republic, who speaks to you, is no more than another Argentine, *Compañera Evita*, who is fighting for the demand of millions of women unjustly subordinated in [...] the desire to elect, the desire to watch over, from the sacred space of the home, the marvellous march of their own country [...] It is necessary to establish equal rights, as women already sought and almost spontaneously gained equal responsibilities [...] To serve the *descamisados*, the weak, the forgotten, is to serve [...] those whose homes knew want, impotence and bitterness [...] [W]omen must vote [...] The vote for women will be the weapon that will make our homes the supreme and inviolable surety of public conduct.[5]

Also from this time, Eva began the first steps in what would later be her prodigious social programme, visiting factories in the company of Mercante's secretary Isabel Ernst, and also with Lillian Lagomarsino de Guardo. Lillian, the daughter of a wealthy family that owned the first company to manufacture men's hats in Argentina, was married to Dr Ricardo Guardo, a dentist who was an early convert to Peronism and was elected to the Lower House in February 1946, becoming the president of the chamber. The Guardos were unusual among their social class for their early Peronist sympathies and often found themselves ostracised by their acquaintances, but for a period became close to the president-elect and his wife. Lillian would later recall her first encounter with Eva, in the autumn of 1946, when Perón invited the couple to their weekend home in San Vicente. Eva 'was wearing two braids and a pyjama belonging to Perón [...] She looked like a child, with no makeup and much more refined, despite her outfit, than many people said.' However, Lillian also rapidly became aware that Eva was already heavily involved in politics. 'I was impressed by her, by her beauty and her manner. In effect, she talked all day about politics, about this person and that one, about this post and that one. She was on top of everything.'[6] This tendency to meddle in politics and to express opinions about appointments did not go unnoticed by others either, and would rapidly generate resistance even within many Peronist circles. Lillian also noted early on that Eva was fascinated with '"complications and intrigues" and was extremely distrustful' but that:

in her life, before everything else, were the most needy, the most humble. She was extremely intuitive, she immediately understood people's suffering and their needs [...] She had a special charisma with the masses, and her message always reached them, because it was clear, but *fundamentally because it was sincere.*[7]

That sincerity is difficult to doubt, despite the fact that the anti-Peronist camp invariably accused Eva of being only a self-serving and vindictive woman who used her role to enrich herself and increase her own power. However, that sincerity, both in her gratitude to Perón and in her reaction to suffering, does not imply that she did not in some way create and play a role; she herself (or her ghostwriters) admitted in *La razón de mi vida* that the role of First Lady María Eva Duarte de Perón was merely formal and thus simpler than her role as Evita: 'Eva Perón, the wife of the president, whose work is simple and agreeable [...] receive honours, gala functions [...] Evita, wife of the leader of a people that has deposited all of its faith in him, all its hope and all its love.'[8]

It is perhaps inevitable that this was so. Ambitious to take a more active part than the decorative and only occasionally seen first lady to which Argentina was accustomed, she had no real previous role model (limited in her knowledge of international affairs, and largely 'anti-Yankee' by predisposition, she would scarcely have thought of Eleanor Roosevelt) and had no option but to create that role for herself. The heroic role she created was deeply felt and carried through to the end, but someone who came to be referred to as the 'Lady of Hope' or the 'Spiritual Leader of the Nation' is not simply behaving as a 'real person'. Although her detractors would later claim that she was simply acting a public role, this by no means explains her absolute dedication and fervour. As noted by the anti-Peronist sociologist David Viñas, 'she had a vital experience analogous to that of the *"cabecita negra"*. She also arrived from the interior looking for work, with a past full of necessities behind her. For that reason she profoundly understood the later process.'[9] Indeed, she shared the experience of the many poor people uprooted and adrift in the big city seeking relief from poverty. At the same time, however, there is no doubt that the experience of being an actress, even a bad one, stood her in good stead in a public role for which most potential first ladies would not have been prepared. She knew how to speak in front of an audience, how to hold a stage, and she knew about image. While this professional use of image was decried by her enemies, this is now something deeply embedded in politics which surprises no one; politicians in the West spend large amounts on image consultants in order to appear at their best in the mass media that were only just becoming a major political factor in Perón and Eva's time.

Moreover, Eva's preoccupation with image must also be understood in context. The largely Catholic and *machista* culture of Argentina at the time, especially among the less sophisticated classes, was premised to a significant degree on roles rather than individuals. Women, even in their own thinking, were frequently placed in the role of self-abnegating wife or mother (the latter in particular largely interchangeable with saint in the popular imagination), the devoted woman supporting her husband as comrade and helpmeet, or alternatively as sinner or slut. This can be taken further – for example, with no modern experience of warfare, the Argentine military was made up of men playing the role of officers, rather than actually working as professional soldiers. While this type of creation arguably had less resonance for some sectors, such as hard-working immigrants seeking to progress or more cultured elites (for many of whom Eva was simply a negative personage, a whore to their more elevated roles), it was a reality of a sort to which many others, and Eva herself, responded. As Libertad Dimitrópulos notes, she broke the existing mould of women as either poor or great ladies, and created the political woman.[10]

One of the few roles usually assigned to the first lady was to act as chair of the Sociedad de Beneficencia, the aristocratic charity established in 1823 that still oversaw, inadequately, much of the country's educational, health and charitable infrastructure. To those august ladies the thought of Eva as their chair was anathema, and it has been widely claimed that they refused to countenance the idea. Purportedly they offered the excuse that she was too young, prompting her to suggest that they invite Doña Juana to take up the post. Be that as it may, Eva never acted as president of the Sociedad and would soon become the head and heart of a far greater undertaking while the Sociedad was to be wound up.

In point of fact, moves had been made in this direction as early as 1943, not due to the wrath of Eva but because the Sociedad, a voluntary body made up of wealthy ladies with no particular professional experience in social work, and which in fact received much of its funding from the state, had become completely inadequate to the task of managing a rapidly expanding social infrastructure network. In late 1946 it was disbanded and its functions were absorbed by the Health Ministry and others. The government intervention in the Sociedad was decreed on 6 September 1946 and Armando Méndez San Martín, a widely questioned Peronist operator who would later play a key role in the Eva Perón Foundation, was appointed to liquidate it. However, it must be said that, while the Eva Perón Foundation made every effort to operate in a way completely different to the 'humiliating' behaviour of the Sociedad, it was equally inappropriate for this quasi-private social justice organisation to have oversight of such a broad range of schools, hospitals, orphanages and other facilities, even though many of these were eventually turned over to the government on their completion. In fact, the two organisations had some very similar shortcomings and crossed accusations between Eva and the ladies of the Sociedad, relating to unsupervised government largesse, lack of oversight and questionable spending decisions, have more than an element of pots calling kettles black.

In the weeks before Perón's inauguration, Eva, together with Isabel and Lillian, visited several factories, as well as attending meetings in her husband's former 'empire' in the Secretariat of Labour. As noted earlier, Isabel Ernst, an attractive blonde given to tailored suits and the business-like hairstyle later adopted by Eva, had already gained considerable experience in dealing with trade union delegations, holding initial meetings and preparing reports for Perón and accompanying union representatives to meetings with the then vice-president. Eva as yet lacked this experience, and apparently a degree of tact in dealing with delegations, but as ever she was quick to learn. Lillian's somewhat reluctant presence at these events was less readily explicable, given that she had no experience of such activities and would have preferred to be at home with her children. Nevertheless, Eva frequently called her and asked her to accompany her to the Secretariat, saying that she felt much more 'tranquil' with Lillian there. Insecure, Eva was embarking on a high-profile and ill-defined role and doubtless felt in need of guidance from these women – her other role models were all men – both in terms of union politics and, in Lillian's case, in terms of etiquette and proper comportment. Whatever her often arrogant and rude behaviour, Eva was extremely conscious of wanting to be a credit to her husband and, increasingly, to her people, and wanted to be sure of how to behave correctly in situations for which her early education and prior experience had given her no preparation, and on which her family and earlier friends could give her no guidance. Over time, however, Isabel and Lillian would both become distanced from her inner circle. In the particular case of Lillian, who would accompany her to Europe in 1947 as her constant companion, Eva may have felt that she knew too much of the fears that Eva sought to conceal – perhaps mistakenly believing that courage required having no fears at all, as opposed to facing them.

Another manifestation of Eva's insecurity over protocol in this period was the fact that she asked Ricardo Guardo for recommendations as to a suitable designer to make her clothes for the inauguration and related formal events, and even asked him to accompany her to visit Bernarda, a distinguished dressmaker whose elite and largely anti-Peronist clientele would not approve of her agreeing to dress the new first lady. Guardo, apparently in no small discomfort, accompanied Eva and vetted her wardrobe choices, rejecting an evening dress proposed for a gala at the Teatro Colón on the grounds that its somewhat military-appearing adornments would look inappropriate at an event full of officers in dress uniform.

On 4 June, Perón was finally sworn in as president, three years after the 'Revolution of 4 June' that had indirectly brought him to power. Wearing a black, fur-trimmed suit and a tense expression, Eva was flanked by Lillian and by Quijano's wife María Teresa, whose arm she clutched fiercely. However, at the official banquet celebrating the inauguration, Eva's off-the-shoulder dress (whether or not it represented a small lapse in judgement by Guardo) caused some scandal, owing to the fact that Cardinal Santiago Copello was seated next to her bare shoulder; the cabaret artist Sofía Bazán would rapidly satirise the incident by appearing on stage in a similar dress with a cardinal bird perched on her shoulder. Famously, following the inauguration Perón and Eva invited the Guardos to see the presidential residence, the 283-room Unzué Palace, where Perón challenged Guardo to a race to see who could slide fastest down the imposing banister rails of the central staircase. Later Eva took down her hair and braided it and sat on the bed in Perón's pyjamas while the four talked about the inauguration. For the months immediately following this time, the Guardos would be virtually constant companions, invited to lunch or dinner on an almost daily basis, while Lillian accompanied Eva and her husband pressed Perón's agenda in the Lower House.

Arguably the off-the-shoulder dress made little difference to the way in which Eva was viewed by 'polite society', which doubtless saw the dress as but one more sign of her vulgarity. Indeed, during this period, she had yet to find her style for this new role, and her tastes were somewhat more suitable for a *radionovela* actress than for a first lady or for a serious working woman. For the only time in her life, she had put on weight and in some photos looks decidedly plump – one could argue that this reflected the fact that the early months of her marriage were the happiest and most secure she had known – and the penchant for exaggerated, flowery dresses with large accessories and elaborate hats was not especially becoming.

Although the shift to blonde hair was flattering, the exaggeratedly complicated pompadour style of the 1940s starlet was not. Eva was a small, fine-boned woman who, only a short time later, seemed effortlessly elegant, whether in haute couture ball gowns for formal occasions or in her iconic tailored suits. But at only 27, and with only a background as a provincial teenager and a moderate career as a radio actress behind her, it is hardly surprising that she may have floundered somewhat before finding the classic style that remains identified with her – although even this did nothing to stop the malicious innuendoes and social stigma she faced. If anything, Eva and her style may have been more distressing to sectors of the middle classes (notably upwardly mobile immigrants) than to the aristocrats who ran no risk of being associated in any way with her or her image, or with her poor provincial followers – they did not suffer from the 'humiliating fear of being confused' with them in the way that the middle classes did.[11]

On taking office, Perón himself faced a favourable panorama, with strong voter support, a substantial congressional majority and a country that came out of World War II as a creditor in an unusually solid economic position. However, his power was never nearly as great as often supposed by either his supporters or his detractors, primarily because his supporters did not on the whole include Argentina's major economic interests, who retained a substantial share of economic power and at least some degree of political leverage (notably in the international arena). Moreover, his party was a recent creation, lacking a large body of experienced figures, and included a number of different groupings whose interests did not necessarily coincide. This may have contributed to a large degree to his determination to quash potential sources of opposition as rapidly as possible. On 23 May 1946, even before his inauguration, the parties that had supported him, including the newly created Partido Laborista, were unceremoniously dissolved and a single official party – briefly the Sole Party of the Revolution and subsequently the Peronist Party – was created. As a result, meatpackers' leader Cipriano Reyes, who resisted the move, would become the only Laborista representative in Congress; the party disappeared after his two-year term ended in 1948. (Reyes would become a victim of one of the more nefarious moves of the first Peronist government, once he had passed to the strident opposition after 1946. In 1947 he was the target of a machine gun attack, and in September 1948, after leaving Congress, he was detained on trumped-up charges of masterminding a plan to assassinate the first couple, severely tortured and imprisoned until Perón's overthrow in 1955.)

Similarly, the CGT came under rising constraints, as the 1945 law of professional associations allowed the government to withdraw legal recognition from any union considered troublesome. Nevertheless, the trade unions would remain Perón's key support base, and his government never tired of pointing out the difference between the repression of the past and the close relations between labour and government that had replaced it. On 1 May Perón, Eva and Mercante led the annual May Day parade, together with workers' delegations.

Speaking to a group of university supporters (never his most enthusiastic support base) in 1947, Perón himself reportedly recognised that 'my government is full of robbers, grafters and persons incapable of directing the progress of the nation […] [T]he party must be reorganised with trained, honest men who put patriotism above everything else.'[12] However, the lack of an established party and his own propensity to eliminate potential competitors did limit the number of competent and honest candidates to participate in his government – and limited the longevity of even those few, as Domingo Mercante and Ricardo Guardo would discover. Perón's first cabinet included some highly competent figures, including Foreign Minister Juan Atilio Bramuglia (Eva's nemesis) and the former head of the DNT, José Figuerola, who became Perón's secretary of technical affairs. Unfortunately, the far less competent and arguably less honest included Miguel Miranda, a successful industrialist who became economy minister (and possibly the commerce minister, Lillian Guardo's brother Rolando Lagomarsino). Not long after taking office, on 21 October 1946 the government announced its Five-Year Plan, focused on increasing national investment and production and also on significantly increasing the state's role in the economy. Despite being criticised as corporatist, the early part of the Perón government saw some considerable achievements, such as an average rise in real wages of around a third in the first three years of government, as well as a similar increase in GDP.

However, the unions that had supported Perón were, perhaps unrealistically, disgruntled to find that on becoming president Perón no longer had time to attend to worker delegations at the Secretariat as he had done before. Into this gap stepped Eva, who moved into an office in the Central Post Office (the area of influence of her friend Oscar Nicolini) and launched the María Eva Duarte de Perón Social Aid Campaign. Soon she became involved in labour negotiations, receiving delegations and overseeing the signing of labour contracts. Shortly after Perón's inauguration, she began visiting factories and union offices, often accompanied by Isabel Ernst, as well as visiting the poor and distributing clothes and toys; she also accompanied Perón to every public engagement, activities that came as a surprise to those accustomed to the traditional invisible Argentine first lady. Her role rapidly became visible enough that it was noted in international media such as *Newsweek*, while for his part the Radical legislator Ernesto Sanmartino (who had described the crowds of 17 October as a 'zoological deluge') presented a draft bill on 22 July stipulating that 'wives of public functionaries [...] cannot enjoy any of the honours or prerogatives enjoyed by their husbands, nor represent them at public events'.[13] Needless to say, the bill did not pass. However, the furious activity may already have begun to take its toll; in August she was forced by illness to miss an event in her honour at which the Association of Hospital and Private Sanatorium Personnel named her Argentina's First Samaritan – the first of a lengthy list of such titles to be bestowed on her during her brief but meteoric career.

On 23 September, she moved from the Post Office to Perón's old office at the Secretariat of Labour, where her public role began to take off in earnest (and which she would forever refer to as the 'Secretariat', despite its having gained ministerial status). According to Vera Pichel, the queues of people waiting to see her had overwhelmed the Post Office and made normal activities impossible. When she broached the subject with Perón over dinner one evening, he told her to move to his former office, where she would have more room – and where she would inherit the symbolic significance of his work on earlier labour reforms. She said to Pichel:

> you realise that that office is historic? I'm crazy with happiness that he's given it to me. I'm going to work so that my *descamisados* feel that they have me at all hours ready to help them with whatever they need. You see how serious I am? It's the new office that's changed me.[14]

Once there, she began arriving at the office early in the morning – greeting her staff with a rapid 'hello boys' – to receive delegations and individual requests, often for jobs that she would meet by charging ministers with finding public sector posts for those supplicants. She maintained a list of potential vacancies, as well as a supply of banknotes to give to those who reached her office, in order to alleviate immediate needs or ensure that they could travel home. This style of work would become more professionalised but would not change in essence until years later when her illness made it impossible for her to continue.

This first year of Perón's term also marked the first anniversary of 17 October, and Eva's first major role in the events commemorating it. The festivities began with a parade of bus drivers, who drove their buses and honked their horns around the Casa Rosada for several hours. The main event, in the Plaza de Mayo at 9.00 pm, involved speeches by both Perón and Eva from the balcony, although these were delayed by a 15-minute ovation from the gathered crowd, who chanted 'neither Nazis nor fascists, Peronists!' A week before the 17th, Eva also made a speech in which she returned to a theme that would be resolved the following year: 'I speak to all the women of my country who work and struggle hard for their home [...] For all of them, the right to vote is essential.'[15]

Eva ended 1946, her first year as wife and first lady, with another debut, a solo visit to Tucumán that marked the first of a constant series of tours throughout the interior of the country (as Buenos Aires tends to refer to the rest of Argentina's provinces). She made the trip with Isabel Ernst and a delegation that included the trade unionist Mariano Tedesco, of the textile workers' union, and travelled throughout the province. Tedesco would later recall his fear on making his first flight; Eva, seeing him, said 'look, Marianito, I'm flying for the second time and I'm just as scared as you are'.[16] On her arrival she and her companions were kept waiting inside their aircraft for some time owing to the huge crush of people who had come to see her; some were killed, crushed against the railings set up around the provincial government house to keep the public back. Eva and the rest of her delegation only learned of the tragedy later, when Perón, worried about her reaction, sent a telegram; thereafter,

> Eva found out about everything and was determined to go to the morgue to see the victims. When she got there she fainted, but recovered rapidly and, stubborn and obstinate, went to see the dead one by one. That night she didn't eat.[17]

Although by the end of 1946 Eva was not yet the figure she would become, and the Peronist government was not yet the overarching machine that it would become, the year was an apprenticeship for both. Her break with the type of genteel activities that had characterised past first ladies was in process and was perhaps inevitable, given that Perón's election itself represented a break (or at least a partial one) with past presidencies and a demand for change – change that encompassed social justice rather than charity, as Perón and Eva would themselves have described it. With Perón described as 'the first worker', and dedicating more of his time to relations with trade unionists than cattle barons and industrial potentates, Eva could scarcely have dedicated her time to 'bridge-canastas' to raise money for the Sociedad de Beneficencia, even had she wanted to. Although Perón's power was substantially less great than sometimes imagined – economic power remained largely in the hands of anti-Peronism – he came to government with substantial public backing, a congressional majority, a favourable economic situation and relatively little political baggage in terms of party or alliances, and with the expectation that the 'New Argentina' would be led by new leaders. The lack of baggage, and the degree of improvisation that still characterised the Peronist government, gave Eva space to occupy a new and expanding role.

While in some aspects it may now look far less innovative than it appeared at the time, the Peronist government was arguably Argentina's first modern administration (despite justifiable criticisms that it was populist and authoritarian and played on sometimes primitive social and nationalist prejudices), and a modern first lady was not out of keeping with the 'winds of change' approach it assumed. Moreover, its overbearing approach to media propaganda might be understandable given the fact that traditional print media were stridently opposed to the government. However, whereas Perón was sometimes seen as 'heretical' in his approach (the word is Daniel James's[18]), he kept his heresy within reasonably acceptable bounds. Eva, for her part, was the far more heretical (and Manichean) of the two, both in her very existence and in her discourse. That 'heresy' would become more marked from 1947, as she grew into her new role and expanded it, taking over from Perón the personal contact with labour and support for increasingly radical demands that he, as president, could no longer undertake, and gradually surpassing him in the role. However, it would also help to cement the hostility to Peronism of many powerful social sectors, reducing the president's margin for conciliation and focusing that hostility on Eva.

CHAPTER 9

Europe

O N 6 JANUARY 1947, Eva participated for the first time in handing out
toys for Epiphany, something that would later become a nationwide
and iconic operation for the Peronist government, with millions of
fruit cakes and bottles of cider, adorned with photos of the presidential couple, distributed to homes throughout Argentina for Christmas. Although
her activities remained relatively small-scale at this stage, she was already
attracting considerable attention, not all of it favourable – not least from
the armed forces. A British Embassy report as early as 10 February 1947
noted that she 'has every sign of being a woman of considerable intelligence and ambition as well as beauty'.[1]

The 'secret account' referred to in Chapter 4 and produced by the
Embassy a few weeks later, on 7 March, cites claims that Eva was already
seen as linked with 'the most corrupt elements' of the government and that
her three brothers-in-law had received plum posts – not to mention her
brother Juancito, the president's secretary. Blanca's husband, the lawyer
Justo Alvarez Rodríguez, would become a member of the Supreme Court
(and Blanca herself inspector of secondary schools), while Elisa's husband
Major Alfredo Arrieta became a senator and Erminda's husband Orlando
Bertolini became director of customs. (Doña Juana herself had apparently
discovered a passion for gambling and maintained a reserved place in the
casino in Mar del Plata – normally the preserve of the 'oligarchy' – as well
as a government employee charged with keeping her supplied with chips.)
The report noted that Eva's 'sudden elevation to the position of president's
wife has gone to her head', and that she had gone so far as to register
'El Peronista' as a trademark in her name for a wide range of products,

doubtless a potentially lucrative move. Somewhat paradoxically, the writer expresses 'doubt whether her influence is very great in questions of out-standing political importance but, short of this, it is certainly considerable'. Nevertheless, he suggests that she was already campaigning for women's enfranchisement – indeed, she returned to this topic on 27 January in a speech promising that the law was close to adoption – and that she could potentially be a candidate for Senate in future.

Moreover, the report notes that her office in the Secretariat of Labour (re-ferred to as the 'benevolent section') was already distributing some 500,000 pesos per month (then around 122,000 dollars) – a modest amount in com-parison with the later spending of the Eva Perón Foundation, but still suffi-cient to extend her political influence to a considerable degree. Possibly due to her continuing insecurity, or to the fact that her position had 'gone to her head' (or because women in positions of authority were viewed with suspi-cion at best), the report notes that she was generally regarded by colleagues as '*antipática*' (unpleasant), unlike Perón, 'who is liked by all around him'.[2] Nevertheless, allegations of unpleasantness and corruption notwithstanding, there is no doubting that she was already sincerely dedicated to her 'benevo-lent' works. Alicia Dujovne Ortiz refers to an early visit to one of the worst *villas miserias*, in the Villa Soldati district of Buenos Aires, where she was so appalled by conditions that she returned three days later and remained there until the entire slum had been burned to the ground, rehoming the residents in new flats.[3] There they became part of the urban legend fuelled by anti-Peronist gossip, claiming that the slum dwellers moved to new homes ripped up the parquet flooring to use for barbecues. However, Eva was always adamant that the poor must be taught to aspire to and to value better things, even if that meant replacing the parquet until they learned to do so.

For the writer at the British Embassy, those 'most unscrupulous and corrupt' elements of the government included Rolando Lagomarsino, Lillian's brother and commerce minister, with whom Eva was 'seen at her worst', while 'both she, her family and her clique are believed to accept "graft" in reasonably large amounts'. This is seen as one of the key reasons for military hostility to the Duarte family, although in practice this may have been due more to the military perception that Perón was increas-ingly distancing himself from his allies in the armed forces in favour of his wife's family and broader circle of influences.[4] In either case, the British Embassy remarked to the Foreign Office that 'unless a curb is placed on her activities they may someday contribute to her husband's downfall'.[5]

This military concern reportedly led to espionage aimed at ascertaining Eva's involvement in corrupt dealings – notably fraudulent transactions in the nationalised telephone company, attributed to board members named by Miguel Miranda, Perón's 'super-minister' and an Eva ally. As head of the Central Bank, Miranda had loaned Eva the money to acquire the small newspaper *Democracia*, which would become her own mouthpiece and the first specifically Peronist newspaper. Concerns also potentially surrounded the Argentine Trade Promotion Institute (IAPI), created in 1946 to centralise trade and foreign exchange transactions, notably through compulsory purchase by the state (at below international market prices) of export crops, which were then sold abroad by the state. Both Eva and Lagomarsino, as well as Miranda, were suspected of involvement in fraudulent activities by a body that unquestionably lent itself to such things. (Lagomarsino was, like Miranda, one of the few industrialists who supported the government and were seen as knowledgeable in economic management. There has been no suggestion that either his sister, who had no involvement either in the family firm or in politics, or her husband Ricardo Guardo, were guilty of corrupt activities.)

According to the Embassy, the view was 'that the army and police chiefs do not wish to remove Perón, but to control him by changing his ministers and eliminating his wife from politics. The threat of publicity might be sufficient to achieve this purpose.' However, 'unless the military can discover sufficiently damning evidence against Perón's wife with which to blackmail him, it is difficult to see how they can bend him to their will'.[6] Whether or not the allegations had substance, or were above all a ploy to curb elements around Perón that did not respond to military interests, these machinations make clear to some degree the climate of intrigue in which the government operated, with espionage, blackmail and power plays emanating from the armed forces, economic elites and other sources, as well as from the so-called 'Duarte group'. Without justifying the increasingly authoritarian tone that would be adopted by the government, it is perhaps understandable that Perón felt the need to centralise his own control.

The desire to remove Eva from the scene temporarily, in a bid to reduce military tensions and scrutiny of her activities, is one of the motives sometimes cited for her trip to Europe in mid-1947. Perón himself received the invitation early in the year, from Spanish dictator General Francisco Franco, but determined that his own participation in an official visit to Falangist Spain was diplomatically inconvenient at a time when he was seeking to carve out a position of non-aligned power in the post-war period. (Although Perón would eventually spend 12 years of his exile as a reluctant and unwelcome guest in Franco's Spain, the two men reportedly met only once and there was no love lost between them; Perón had seen the results of the Spanish Civil War at first hand and was critical of the Franco government's social attitudes.) Notably, foreign minister Juan Atilio Bramuglia, of socialist origin, appears to have pointed out the inconveniences that could arise from a state visit at a time when the Franco regime was largely shunned and under sanctions in the post-war period. However, according to most sources, the president suggested that his wife might travel instead in representation of the government. Hernán Benítez claimed to have made the suggestion, to which Franco – keen to attract Argentine aid, primarily in the form of food, to his hungry country – agreed enthusiastically, promising to receive her personally with the honours due a head of state. At the beginning of February, the Argentine press reported that the first lady might visit Spain; in March the visit was officially confirmed and by May it was announced that she would depart for Madrid on 6 June.

As usual, there are many versions of the real reasons surrounding Eva's European trip, another of which is Perón's desire to distract her from a personal tragedy that was weighing on her in 1947 (although Lillian Lagomarsino de Guardo would deny this categorically, saying that she was happy and enthusiastic when they departed for Spain[7]). Again, there is speculation that she had lost a pregnancy, that she had found she could not have a baby, that some past experience in a similar vein had returned to the fore. In practice, the motives may have been less dramatic than either a miscarriage or a corruption scandal – the occasion may simply have presented itself, and been seized upon as an opportunity to show Peronist diplomacy and the opulence of its situation on a world stage. Indeed, already in October 1946 the Perón government had committed to substantial shipments of wheat to Spain in both 1947 and 1948, and the opportunity to show Argentina as both benefactor and possible leader of Hispanic nations at a time of Spanish weakness was not to be passed up. However, with an eye to avoiding giving the impression of an exclusively Argentine–Spanish tie (or axis, as it would be ominously described), Eva's planned trip was broadened, with official invitations from Italy, Portugal and France. Although these invitations fell well short of the head of state honours accorded by Spain, and she visited as the wife of the president rather than an official guest of those governments, they gave the trip greater prestige. The possibility that Great Britain might be added to the list was also mooted as a prestigious option, and in June the Foreign Office indicated that she was expected to visit in an unofficial capacity, although in the event that visit would not take place.

Much of the organisation was left to Father Benítez, who travelled to Madrid in April and then to Rome, where he met with Vatican secretary of state Cardinal Montini (later Pope Paul VI) and arranged for Eva to have an audience with Pope Pius XII. Benítez himself attributed much of the motivation for the trip to the 'need, on the part of the Argentine government, to strengthen its diplomatic relations with the Vatican', in particular because the Argentine hierarchy, traditionally tied to the 'oligarchy', was not entirely supportive of the Peronist administration. This at least was indeed the case: although much of the Catholic hierarchy had welcomed the initiatives of the military government that took power in 1943, and elements of the hierarchy and the Catholic right more generally had hoped that Perón might prove to be an Argentine Franco who would turn Argentina back to a traditionally clericalist posture, it was clear by this time that this was not the case. Moreover, suspicions were already rising over Perón's tendency to adopt a religious element in his social doctrine, which hinted that the government was seeking to occupy moral ground normally conceded to the Church, and over his attempts to co-opt Catholic and Christian tenets as inherently Peronist. In any case, given that active Catholics in Argentina tended to belong to classes that were not supporters of the government, on the whole, there was relatively little common ground between much of the institutional Church and the government. In addition, of course, the first lady's dubious origins did little to improve the relationship. Although culturally a Catholic and eventually a 'tertiary sister' of the Franciscan order, Eva was fond of noting that she did not waste time sitting in pews instead of acting, and that she was not a '*chupacirios*' – literally a 'candle-licker'.

However, this was not the only significance of a Vatican visit. Under the Lateran Treaty, an official invitation from the Vatican would automatically imply an official invitation from Italy – which, in turn, would facilitate an invitation from France. As early as February, Benítez travelled first to Spain, and then to Rome, to organise the trip. His own activities and public statements would bring him into conflict both with Franco (whose government he defined as a 'pro-oligarchy dictatorship, with military backing', as opposed to Perón's 'pro-poor dictatorship, with the backing of the workers') and with the Jesuit authorities in Argentina, who warned him that parents were threatening to remove their children from Jesuit schools owing to his high-profile relationship with the government. In Rome, the head of the Jesuit order forbade him from appearing in public with Eva and from writing her speeches. Nevertheless, according to Benítez, in April he had an hour-long audience with Pope Pius XII, who was extravagant 'in expressions of gratitude towards our president and praised him without reservation' (although he demanded to know whether Perón and Eva had married in church before consenting to the audience).[8] Benítez himself would later be ordered by his Jesuit superior to remain in Spain after Eva's trip ended and would finally leave the order as a result of his relationship with the Perón government.

A still uncertain Eva evidently decided early on that she would not undertake such a daunting task as the 'Rainbow Tour' (in which she proposed to represent a rainbow rather than axis between Argentina and Spain) without assistance, and in late March she approached Lillian Lagomarsino de Guardo to accompany her. According to Lillian much later, Eva told her only that they would go to Spain for two weeks (informing her only later, already in Spain, that the trip would be extended by some two months). Even this briefer itinerary was not welcome for the mother of four, and she attempted to persuade Eva to leave her out of the committee. Nevertheless, Eva began to press Guardo to make Lillian change her mind, and eventually Perón himself was obliged to intervene, telling Lillian that Eva would not go without her. Bowing to the pressure, aware both of Eva's own enthusiasm and of the importance of the trip, Lillian agreed to put her family on hold again.[9]

Although the thought of Eva as Argentina's representative in Europe, in whatever capacity, was anathema to the upper classes, for her humbler followers the trip was important. When it became known that she would go, a group of poor women turned up at the offices of *Democracia*, asking that Eva be given their message that she should wear her hair in a chignon, the style that suited her best, when she went to Europe. It is not clear whether she received this message, but it is certain that she travelled with the same conviction as that held by the delegation of women, that she was representing them in Europe and that, as the representative of Perón and the *descamisados*, it was imperative to carry the trip off successfully. (Eva would use her over-elaborate pompadour hairstyle for much of the 'Rainbow tour', only in the latter part of the trip beginning to appear with a sleeker hairstyle. Lillian Lagomarsino would later claim to have encouraged

Eva's hairdresser Julio Alcaraz to adopt a more elegant style that suited her better, although Hernán Benítez would also be credited with influencing her more austere style. In practice, Dior's 'New Look' had anything but connotations of austerity in Europe – the metres of fabric used in his long, wide skirts represented the fact that the austerity of the World War II period was over. However, the more classic Dior look Eva would adopt on her return from Europe, both more elegant and more businesslike, would be the image of her remembered by history, saving her from appearing as dated as a Hollywood starlet from the 1940s.) In a reception the day before her departure, she made her representational intentions clear, saying 'I go representing the working people, my beloved *descamisados*. On going, I leave them my heart.'[10] By contrast, the Conference of Socialist Women issued a resolution stating that they did not consider themselves represented by Eva, at home or abroad.

On 6 June Eva boarded a Spanish DC-4 at the airport in Morón, together with a substantial delegation including Lillian, Eva's speechwriter Francisco Muñoz Aspiri, her hairdresser Julio Alcaraz, a doctor, her maids and a rowdier element formed of her brother Juancito and Alberto Dodero. Dodero, a shipping millionaire who had benefited substantially from the government's policies and was a close friend of the presidential couple, would reportedly finance most of the trip. On setting off, Eva severely lectured the delegation on the importance of maintaining the dignity required of representatives of the Argentine state and people, warning that anyone who failed to do so would be sent back. According to Lillian, Eva retained her suspicious nature and was dubious about the loyalty of many, even asking Lillian to hand over the cash she carried with her for the duration of the voyage, although she denies having seen Eva write a letter during the course of the long flight.

Nevertheless, most other sources claim that she set about writing a long letter to her husband, whom she was leaving for the first time, and in which she expressed her adoration ('idolatry') for him and her fears that she might suffer some accident. She urged him to look after her mother, Isabel Ernst and Domingo Mercante, because 'he adores you'. She continued:

> I struggled a lot in my life with the ambition to be someone. I suffered a lot, but then you came and you made me so happy that it seemed like a dream, and since I had nothing else to offer you but my heart and soul, I gave them to you completely.

She also warned him about the activities of Rudi Freude, the son of Ludwig Freude and suspected of Nazi links, claiming that he had sent someone to Junín to look into her background.

> I swear it's an infamy (my past belongs to me, but at the hour of my death you should know it's all lies) [...] I left Junín when I was only 13. How low to think something so vile of a girl! It's totally false.[11]

Like the letter Perón wrote to Eva from Martín García, the content of the text raises many questions but leaves little doubt of the profound love expressed there. What it is that Rudi Freude supposedly tried to find out about her in Junín is unclear. The statement that she left at 13 is inaccurate, but would suggest that he was digging for information on the rumours describing her mother as the madam of a brothel, and possibly on her purported relationship with the anarchist Damián Gómez. Clearly her fears and insecurities were still very much with her, despite her rise to power and the firm backing of her husband. This was a difficult way to begin what was already a difficult assignment for a small-town girl with little education or sophistication: representing her country (and her husband) before heads of state, with the eyes of the world's media on her.

However, the inherent difficulties were not readily apparent to observers. On arriving in Madrid on 8 June, where she was awaited by a multitude of 300,000, including Franco and his aristocratic wife Carmen Polo, Eva greeted her hosts before kissing the stewardesses on the cheek in thanks for their service, then greeted the remaining delegation of dignitaries and reviewed the troops 'as if she had done nothing else all her life'.[12] Riding in an open car with Franco, Eva's triumphal entrance into Madrid took four hours, as thousands of people thronged the decorated streets, threw flowers and shouted 'Viva Spain! Viva Argentina!' According to Lillian, Franco himself would later say that he was 'more impressed by her aplomb and personal control than by the reception', even though 'we've never seen anything like it here before'.[13]

Despite her extraordinary poise in public, in private Eva's feelings were another matter. After retiring to her palatial guest suite, she phoned Lillian and asked her to come to her room to talk and to write in their diaries together. Although Lillian tried several times to leave, even when she thought Eva was finally asleep, Eva called her back repeatedly on one pretext or another before finally admitting 'Lillian, I'm afraid'. Lillian would sleep in a chair in her room for three nights before asking Carmen Polo to arrange another bed for her in the same room, after which two imposing four-poster beds were accommodated and both women were able to get some sleep to recover from the demanding schedule of the visit.[14] These sleeping arrangements would be maintained throughout the Rainbow Tour.

The visit to Spain, a personal triumph, must also have been both exhausting and exhilarating – and doubtless cemented Eva's conviction that there was nowhere like Perón's Argentina. Argentina in 1947 had emerged post-war as a wealthy country that was rapidly modernising, while Europe (notably Spain) was anything but. Notably also, Franco's Spain made little effort at the Peronist concept of 'social justice', not least given that, for Franco, the poor and left-leaning were the defeated foe in the Civil War and still the enemy. Despite being an official visitor, Eva lost no opportunity to lecture Franco and his wife on the importance of social justice, a discourse that must have wearied the Caudillo rapidly – just as Carmen Polo rapidly tired of Eva's demands to visit poor neighbourhoods to talk to the Spanish *descamisados*. Her first public speech on the need for social justice came on Monday 9 June, the day after her arrival, when she addressed the crowds after being decorated by Franco with the Great Cross of Isabella the Catholic, Spain's highest honour. Speaking on the balcony of the royal palace, she made what was doubtless an odious comparison, albeit indirectly, noting that 'Argentina is marching forward because it is just with itself, and because in its battle for bread and wages, it knew how to chose between the false deceptive democracy and the real distributive democracy'.[15] The popular enthusiasm she generated, among crowds who had heard little of social justice from the *franquista* regime, was genuine and powerful. It must also have been a thorn in the side of her host – to whom she remarked at one stage that 'if you ever need to attract crowds, just call me'. Her habit of arriving late at events planned in her honour can also only have been a source of irritation to her hosts, and probably reflected both her insecurity (arriving late was a means of demonstrating her importance) and the fact that she was more interested in her improvised visits to factories and slum dwellings than in the gala events Franco had planned for her.

However, while the Peronist government would doubtless have fulfilled its promises to provide grain and meat to Franco's Spain even without Eva's visit, the need for those foodstuffs, at a time when Spain was left out of the Marshall Plan and hunger was a serious issue, put Franco in the unusual and uncomfortable position of having to tolerate some impertinence from his illustrious visitor. Nevertheless, Carmen Polo was somewhat more intolerant of the situation and tried to elude outings with Eva as much as possible, in particular where these involved working-class neighbourhoods whose inhabitants she referred to as 'reds'. Eva herself

> responded that [Doña Carmen's] husband did not govern due to the votes of the people, but through imposition of a [military] victory [...] I told her how Perón won the elections and how he governed, because the majority of the people had decided it.[16]

Thereafter, Eva lost no opportunity to comment at every palace she visited that it should be turned into a hospital. On being informed by her military escort that she would surely weep with emotion on seeing El Escorial, Eva said nothing, but following the visit she would tell him 'I didn't weep at all. On the contrary, I thought what a wonderful home for orphans El Escorial would make, what a vacation colony!'[17] (Her failure to weep also won her a wager with Franco, as a result of which he presented her with a priceless tapestry from the Prado.) She was also unable to avoid commenting on her revulsion at a bullfight held in her honour, remarking on the unfairness of the fact that the bull was always killed regardless of whether it 'won' or 'lost' and describing the tradition as 'barbaric'.

Despite such complications, the visit to Spain represented a constant series of gala events which Eva in general managed with substantial aplomb. Following the awarding of the Cross of Isabella, she was feted with regional dances in the Plaza Mayor, after which she was given a traditional costume, set with jewels, from every region. She attended a gala function of Lope de Vega's masterpiece *Fuenteovejuna*, visited Toledo and Segovia and made a radio address to her *descamisados* in Argentina before beginning, on 15 June, a tour of most of the rest of Spain (this time sans the doubtless relieved Franco family). Before departing, she made a radio speech to the women of Spain, promising that the twentieth century would be remembered as the 'century of victorious feminism' (something of an odd concept in 1940s *franquista* Spain) and calling on them to work together 'to implant in the world the fundamental rights owed to human beings [...] I have not come to form an axis, but to stretch a rainbow to all peoples, as befits the spirit of a woman.'[18]

The same night, 15 June, Eva attended a moonlit dance performance at the Alhambra in Granada, also visiting the tomb of Ferdinand and Isabella and giving a speech to some 3,000 factory workers. Other members of her delegation participated in less respectable events, and trips by Dodero and Juancito to cabarets and other nocturnal pursuits produced protests from Spanish diplomacy and an explosion from Eva, who threatened to send them home. This visit was followed by travels to Seville, Vigo, Santiago de Compostela, Zaragoza (where she left her gold and diamond earrings as an offering to the Virgin) and Barcelona, the last stop on her itinerary, where she was rejoined by Franco and where she arrived several hours late for a performance of *A Midsummer Night's Dream* held in her honour. Again, Lillian attributed this to her insecurity and her need to demonstrate her own importance (something to which she also attributed Eva's enthusiasm for receiving costly gifts), as well as her belief that her other activities such as visiting slums and factories were more important than the official agenda. However, it may also have reflected exhaustion and the nerves of which there were occasional signs despite her poise. On her departure on 26 June, she broadcast a final speech on Radio Nacional, recognising that the 'homage of colossal proportions' she had received did not glorify her herself, but

> the woman of the people, until now always dominated, always excluded and always censored. You have exalted yourselves, Spanish workers [...] Poverty can never again be a barrier to anyone in achieving their aspirations and the triumph of their ideals. I leave part of my heart in Spain.[19]

Despite Eva's hyperbolic tendencies, which involved freely strewing bits of her heart around, and the obviously self-serving nature of the visit for both the Peróns and the Francos, there is no doubt that Eva carried off the visit with remarkable success, and even less than favourable sources praised her triumph. *Time* magazine noted that 'even without gold and wheat, the Argentine rainbow would have been well received in Spain' and recognised that her reception was far more genuine than the usual obligatory enthusiasm organised by the Franco government, while its competitor *World Report* compared her with Eleanor Roosevelt, breaking with the 'tradition of passivity' among Argentine women and taking a stand for feminism and women's suffrage.[20] Even the US Embassy in Spain noted that 'personally, the Señora may have had something of a triumph. It is recognized that she carried out a difficult task with poise and intelligence, and that she is a force of importance in her country.'[21] (Eva herself was self-deprecating in interviews during the tour, saying that she understood little of art or music, that her favourite pieces of music were 'the shortest' and that her favourite author was Plutarch, whom she had not read but had learned about from her husband.) From here on, however, the Rainbow Tour would generate more mixed reviews.

As Eva was not a state visitor to Italy her reception was far more modest, although the fact that on her arrival in Rome she was greeted only by the foreign minister, Count Carlo Sforza, the wife of the prime minister and the Argentine ambassadors to Rome and the Vatican must have seemed a small affair by comparison. Without an official agenda in Italy, she was received by a group of some 5,000 gathered in front of the Argentine embassy – most of them well-wishers, although with some anti-fascist voices among them. These were raised mostly by the workers' central across the road, who sang the Red Flag and shouted slogans against Perón and Mussolini. Some 27 arrests were made, and Eva would later intervene to ask for their release. Her activities were limited primarily to receptions, luncheons, visits to an orphanage and various charitable works, and a performance of *Aida*. Speaking at a reception offered by the Italian Suffrage Association, she highlighted the need for women's voting rights as a defence 'of our homes, as a supreme guarantee of good public administration'.[22] In a similar vein, speaking to the Italian National Women's Association on 28 June, she said 'I have a name that has become a battle cry throughout the world [...] I want to say that women have the same obligations as men and therefore we should also enjoy the same rights.'[23] However, while speaking in favour of women's rights, she also expressed her opposition to divorce.

However, the 'main event' of the Italian trip was Eva's audience with Pope Pius XII on 27 June. Dressed in a long black gown and veil, Eva was escorted by an august group, including three bishops and five members of the Papal nobility, to her 20-minute audience, the length of time granted to queens by Vatican protocol. In that interview she told the Pope of her work for social justice and was then given an escorted tour of the Vatican. The Pope gave her a rosary, the usual gift on such occasions, and the following day awarded Perón the Order of the Grand Cross of Pope Pius IX, 'in recognition of the help President Perón has been giving the peoples of Europe through Vatican organisations'.[24] However, she did not receive the title of papal marquise she purportedly desired, and according to some versions she agreed in advance with Dodero a system of code to inform him of the decoration she had received and the size of the donation that should accordingly be made. With only a rosary to show for the visit, the donation was minimal. According to Benítez, the reason for her limited success was the smear campaign mounted against her by members of the Argentine oligarchy (not least, through the reproduction of 'scandalous' photos and rumours dating back to her days as an actress which apparently shocked and horrified His Holiness).[25] At the same time, it must be borne in mind that Eva had at the time scarcely begun her social work and it had not yet assumed the scope or the high profile it would later achieve; that she did not receive a papal decoration for it does not automatically represent overt hostility on the part of the Vatican.

Despite this, according to Perón's later recollections, Eva would recount the visit to him saying that:

> the Pope seemed to me to be a vision […] He told me that he followed your work, that he considered you a favoured son and that your policies put in practice in a more than praiseworthy way the fundamental principles of Christianity.[26]

Moreover, 'Sra de Perón was accorded the most elaborate Vatican reception extended to a visiting dignitary since the war' and also received His Holiness's thanks 'for the aid Argentina has given the war-stricken nations of Europe, and for Argentina's collaboration in the relief work of the Pontifical Commission'.[27] However, 'the Pope, although occasionally permitting photographs of himself with distinguished visitors, did not do so on this occasion'.[28]

If Benítez and Eva were received at least cordially by the Vatican in 1947, despite the opposition of the Argentine oligarchy and members of the hierarchy, this appears to suggest that the Holy See was interested in seeking financial assistance and a potential country of exile for European refugees, rather than that it explicitly favoured the government. According to one Vatican official:

> in view of Vatican interest in Argentine assistance as a supplier of relief to Europe and a receiver of displaced persons, it is not surprising that the Vatican should have received in such good part the Argentine effort to dramatize and intensify its good relations with the Vatican.[29]

In particular, some of those 'displaced persons' reportedly included for-mer Nazis and war criminals, and there are strong allegations that at least some Argentine officials made a lucrative business of selling documents to some of them. A list of refugees accepted by Argentina following Eva's Vatican visit included the Croat Uztachi leader Ante Pavelic; others, such as Adolf Eichmann, made their way to Argentina with or without help from the Holy See or the Argentine authorities. Pope Pius XII himself has been accused of Nazi sympathies, notably in John Cromwell's 1996 book *Hitler's Pope*, although others have rejected this claim. According to Uki Goñi, Eva may also have met former SS commando Otto Skorzeny in Madrid, although this is unconfirmed.[30]

While there is no question that numerous Nazis made their way to Argentina (including before the 1943 coup) and that Perón saw many of them as a source of industrial and scientific advancement – as did the United States – it remains far from clear that this represents evidence of pro-Nazi convictions, as opposed to indifference, on the part of either Perón or Eva. Not least, it is worth noting that both Perón and Eva made numerous statements condemning anti-Semitism, and Perón made consid-erable efforts to involve the Jewish community in his movement, notably through the Argentine Israelite Organisation. As Raanan Rein notes, Perón 'was the first Argentine president to legitimate the mosaic of identities of different ethnic groups in his country. He saw no incompatibility between being a good Argentine, a good Jew and supporting Zionism or the State of Israel.'[31] In 1951 Israeli Labour Minister Golda Meir would come to Argentina to thank the Eva Perón Foundation for donations of clothes and medicine to immigrants to Israel.

According to Lillian Lagomarsino, the evident hardship faced by Italy in the post-war era made Eva determined to cut the official visit short, mind-ful of the cost, and after a brief visit to Milan to see the Argentine stand at the Industrial Exposition she returned to Rome and cancelled planned vis-its to Venice, Florence and Naples before taking a ten-day private holiday at Dodero's rented villa in Rapallo.

Independently of the Vatican diplomacy involved in the audience with the Pope, two events of significance occurred during Eva's ten-day holiday in Rapallo. On 6 July Perón formally announced his government's foreign policy, known as the 'Third Position' – the timing carefully chosen to co-incide with the Rainbow Tour. Although the Third Position had already been tacitly revealed when Perón restored diplomatic ties with the Soviet

Union on taking office, while simultaneously assuring the United States of Argentine support in any eventual conflict between the two global powers, it became the government's formal position in international affairs even as debate over ties with Franco continued. Neither specifically pro-Western nor pro-Soviet, the Third Position was 'an ideological position which is in the centre, on the right or on the left, according to specific circumstances'[32] – in other words, a typically Peronist attempt to play both sides and find a middle ground between conflicting interests. While in some respects a forerunner of the non-aligned movement, the Third Position was also another Peronist attempt to set a political course for other Latin American countries to follow (which they proved reluctant to do), as well as to maintain the option of playing the 'Yankee imperialism' card while also promoting Peronism as a bulwark against communism. In line with this desire to play a leading role in Latin America and the Hispanic and Catholic world, Eva's visits to Spain and the Vatican were a key element in this strategy, even if it ultimately proved unsuccessful.

The other event that occurred during the holiday was the final breakdown of attempts to organise an official visit to Great Britain. Although the Foreign Office reiterated that Eva was expected and that her visit would be welcome, the fact that she would not be formally received by the Royal Family (because they were on holiday for the summer, if for no other reason) and that the government had not held official visits since the war appears to have swayed her to stay away. (The fact that one of the last such official visits was organised for none other than Eleanor Roosevelt may also have influenced her, if she felt that the US first lady had received greater deference.) She may also have been concerned over her lack of language skills, which had not been an issue in Spain but which increased her insecurity. There was also unquestionably opposition from left-of-centre circles in London, although the business and finance sectors were happy to receive a representative from such a lucrative partner as Argentina. If credence is given to Benítez's own claims of influence, his anti-Anglo Saxon views, which Eva no doubt shared, may well have also played a role; he would later claim that the visit had never been considered, despite substantial evidence to the contrary.

Whatever the decisive reason, the visit was not to be. Instead, on 17 July Eva and her delegation travelled somewhat surprisingly to Lisbon, where she met unofficially with two scions of exiled royalty: former Italian King Humberto and Spanish Prince Juan de Borbón, the latter an affront to Franco. (When this was pointed out to Eva, she merely replied, 'if the fat guy doesn't like it, that's too bad'.) The unofficial visit was not well received by her former hosts in Spain and Italy, and was taken as a sign of arrogance, while Portuguese dictator Antonio Salazar was more interested in ties with the West than in 'an alliance of weak Catholic nations'.[33]

On 21 July Eva flew from Lisbon to Paris to carry on with the more significant part of the tour, where she was received at Orly by foreign minister Georges Bidault (who could not resist exclaiming over her youth and beauty) and stayed at the Ritz. The early part of her stay was marked by a lunch with President Vincent Auriol and a visit to Notre Dame, where her meeting with the Papal Nuncio, Msgr Angelo Roncalli, who would later become Pope John XXIII, became the subject of diverse and probably apocryphal versions. According to some, they had only a brief meeting at a reception which merited little comment on either side. According to Benítez, however, the future pope would tell her in his presence, 'Señora, continue in your struggle for the poor. But don't forget that that struggle, when it is undertaken seriously, ends on the Cross.'[34] Vera Pichel, for her part, cites a conversation with Eva in which Eva supposedly referred to her visit to Notre Dame and 'the words of the one who later became Pope John XXIII', despite the fact that Roncalli did not become pope until 1958, six years after Eva's death.[35]

Before leaving Paris, Eva would preside over the signing of an Argentine loan to pay for French imports of Argentine foodstuffs, the usual range of visits to hospitals, schools and social welfare institutions, and visits to Napoleon's tomb and Versailles. She would also receive the Legion of Honour, a tribute that the Parisians scathingly attributed to the need for Argentine wheat rather than any personal attributes of the recipient or her husband. However, on 23 July she fainted, and cut short other planned activities, including a visit to Louvre and a fashion show. Warned that the latter would be deemed frivolous, she nevertheless left her measurements with the house of Christian Dior and others. However, the visit was a mixed success, not only because of her evident fatigue. Uncomfortable with her lack of French, Eva was forced to depend on Lillian as interpreter, becoming exasperated when she felt that Lillian did not expound on the subjects she considered of interest. Moreover, the Argentine ambassador and his wife, as well as some members of the government and their own spouses (notably Suzanne Bidault), clearly demonstrated some contempt for the first lady and her background (and possibly jealousy over her youth and good looks). The French diplomatic corps reportedly believed that on arriving in Paris she would understand 'the international hierarchies' and the secondary place assigned to Argentina – apparently disregarding the fact that it was France that needed Argentine assistance at the time and not the opposite.[36]

Abandoning Paris, Eva and her entourage travelled to the Mediterranean for several days' holiday, interrupted by a rapid visit to Monaco (where Eva again expressed her fears to Lillian and barricaded them into their room at night). In San Remo, according to the later claims of the Greek shipping magnate Aristotle Onassis, they may have met and, according to his own version, had a brief fling that culminated in his giving a 'donation' to 'one of her favourite charities' – the obvious suggestion being that he paid her for sex. This seems more in keeping with Onassis's own arrogance, sexism and braggadocio than with any notion of reality (at least it suggests that he was consistent in his treatment of women, and his desire to acquire them as valuable possessions as a result of their fame or position). Eva may have felt herself valued through receipt of costly gifts, but at this stage in her life she was surely no longer interested in being involved in a one-night stand that could have done nothing to benefit her position and, on the contrary, could have caused her, her husband and her political cause great harm. Onassis, who had emigrated to Buenos Aires as a young man and began to make his fortune there, was an old friend of Dodero's, and a meeting in San Remo is not implausible, though given Eva's reluctance even to go to the casino on the grounds that it was frivolous and not respectable, worse behaviour scarcely seems likely – especially given the constant enforced presence of Lillian in her boudoir.

During the Monaco visit, it was announced that an official invitation to Switzerland had been received. Arriving in Geneva on 3 August, they spent five days touring the country and visiting the UN headquarters there. On one occasion, when travelling in an open car with Swiss foreign minister Max Petitpierre, Eva and her host were the target of a tomato-throwing protester. When asked later if she had been afraid, Eva responded 'when one is representing a state, one cannot be afraid' – somewhat to Lillian's bemusement.[37] The visit to Switzerland also gave rise to widespread rumours that the actual purpose was to open a Swiss bank account to hide the Peróns' ill-gotten gains – something categorically denied by Lillian Lagomarsino and that seems in any case implausible, given the last-minute nature of the trip and the fact that such a high-profile plan to open a secret Swiss bank account would surely defeat the purpose. (Another rumour surrounding the visit was that it involved negotiations to allow passage to Argentina of former Nazis then residing in neutral Switzerland – although here too its high-profile nature would seem unnecessary and counter-productive, particularly given that the first lady's presence was scarcely necessary for the negotiation of such a deal.[38])

The Swiss stop marked the end of the Rainbow Tour; from there Eva flew to Lisbon and Dakar and boarded a Dodero ship, the *Buenos Aires*, for the return journey. However, her diplomatic round was not yet finished: on arriving in Rio de Janeiro she attended the so-called Rio Conference that produced the Inter-American Mutual Assistance Treaty, and the Foreign Ministers' meeting, where she attended the speech by US secretary of state George Marshall. Her presence distracted substantially from the speaker, while she also dined with President Gaspar Dutra and was honoured by the Lower House of Congress.

This stop may also have represented the beginning of the end of her friendship with Lillian, who arrived in Rio nervous at the fact that her husband would be there as part of the Argentine delegation, and that Eva would resent the demands Guardo would make on his wife's time. This intuition appears to have been correct, and in fact Lillian would soon be spared the demands made by Eva on her time, while Guardo would soon be replaced as leader of the Lower House by Eva loyalist Héctor Cámpora. Within a few days of their return to Buenos Aires, Lillian had no further contact with Eva, although after Perón's fall in 1955 Guardo would be forced into exile for a time. Nevertheless, the Brazilian leg of the tour was apparently as successful as the European visit, and a final press conference made clear that Eva increasingly dominated the niceties of diplomacy and media work, at least when she wished to. Her responses were 'politically correct' – she said that her impression of Franco was 'the same as all the other heads of state' and that she was equally impressed by the *descamisados* of all countries. However, when one reporter asked about her artistic career she froze and replied 'after the important questions asked by your colleagues, I find yours out of place', and abruptly ended the press conference.[39] After an overnight stop in Uruguay (another round of receptions, charity visits and presidential meetings), on Saturday 22 August Eva finally arrived, weeping, in Buenos Aires where she flung herself into her husband's arms.

Alicia Dujovne Ortiz notes dismissively that Eva was bored by the wonders of Europe and the great people she met. This is in part true, but it is hardly surprising or unique to her. While Argentina's wealthy had the custom of leisurely trips through Europe to absorb culture, make purchases and show off their wealth, and many middle-class Argentines whose parents had emigrated had the dream of seeing the countries their families had left (and perhaps showing off how much they had prospered), Eva did not fit into these categories. Rather, her identification was with the Argentine poor, who had few dreams of Europe – if their ancestors had come from there, in most cases they came from desperate poverty and had no memories to recount of the glories of Europe. Many Argentines (and others) still board the plane for Europe when they feel they can afford it but without any specific interest other than being able to say that they have been there, that they have ticked important sights off a list. Like many of her compatriots, Eva was not a cosmopolitan; she was a small-town Argentine who had never been further than Montevideo. Indeed, in Eva's case, she probably had no 'sights' in mind, but the reception she received was important for her personally and for Argentina – while much of what she saw in Europe led her to feel that Argentina under Perón was superior in its pursuit of social justice, and that no effort should be spared to advance further in that area.

While her hosts may have hoped that a close encounter with the 'international hierarchies' would be a humbling experience, in practice she emerged with a greater sense of superiority than before. Eva visited much of Europe as a benefactress (a role that she enjoyed, however sincerely she played it), not as a beggar, and the poverty she saw compared unfavourably to the moment of prosperity that Argentina was then enjoying. Moreover, with the exception of the hardcore anti-Peronist sectors, many Argentines – not only her *descamisados* – were pleased by the international attention gleaned by Argentina as a result of her visit and pleasantly surprised by her aplomb in carrying it off.

At the same time, Eva's personal image, not only as an elegant and beautiful woman, but as a political leader and statesman (the term 'statesperson' seems an anachronism in this case), was cemented during and after the visit, and her prestige began to overtake that of her husband. Although she never hesitated to describe herself in public as a 'simple woman' and Perón's 'shadow', in practice she was fast becoming a confident, charismatic, iconic figure on her own terms. Lillian Lagomarsino categorically denied suggestions that Eva was intimidated during her European tour by fears that she was not politically Perón's equal,[40] but she also recognised that as the voyage progressed Eva became increasingly self-confident and autonomous, despite still seeking approval in private. Moreover, she recalled that Eva would tell her during the trip that she aspired to 'be someone in history', an ambition that was already in place but may have been cemented by her passage through Europe.[41] Lillian, of course, also noted her need for attention and approval, seen in part through her desire to receive expensive gifts that demonstrated her 'value' – an insecurity that would leave a worrying opening for corruption (not to mention annoyance for her friends).

Speaking four days after her return, Eva would say:

> I took to Europe the spiritual message of the Argentine workers who work for greatness and do not fight in fratricidal contests, but for high ideals [...] I have seen the Old World and have contemplated its desolation, the difficulties and the impoverishment that Old Europe offers.[42]

This would give new impetus to her nascent campaign for social justice. It would also, perhaps, mark the end of at least one phase of a love affair and wedded bliss. According to Hernán Benítez,

> I believe I saw them in love, sentimentally very united, until the year '48. After that, power and political passion led them down parallel but different paths [...] San Vicente was left behind [...] By '49 it was clear that their lives were parallel but different [...] What happened was that she had taken a different path. She had begun to soar on her own, which he was intelligent enough to respect.[43]

 CHAPTER 10

Enter Evita

T HE EVA WHO returned from Europe on a Saturday and saluted her followers with the promise that she would be back at work on Monday
'with more energy than ever to continue being the spiritual bridge
between the descamisados and General Perón'[1] was not the same Eva
who had left for Madrid two months earlier. A once pretty but unremarkable young girl who in her early period as Perón's partner had become a
slightly plump and overdressed young woman, the Eva who returned from
Europe was the more ethereal, iconic beauty generally remembered today.
Physically slimmer, more streamlined and more elegant, now using her
trademark tailored suits and chignon, she was also, according to Perón's
later memories, more politicised and more politically sophisticated, and
increasingly focused on a political and social mission that would dominate
the rest of her life. She was rapidly becoming Evita.

Although some have attributed this transformation to an early aware-
ness of an incipient illness that would soon curtail her life, this does not,
on the face of it, appear a likely explanation. The change, and the mission-
ary zeal it brought, may to some degree have reflected a feeling of disillu-
sion following her European tour. She would not have been alone among
Argentines in expecting that Europe would offer a more exalted or more
awe-inspiring reality, and the reality of post-war Europe must surely have
disappointed (even as the teenaged Eva's illusions about Buenos Aires had
been quickly dashed). On the one hand, this tended to confirm her belief
that Perón's Argentina was a beacon for the world (and she would later tell
Perón that Europe was old and had nothing to teach), but on the other it
was a let-down – as was, perhaps, the fact that even her remarkable reception could not hide the reality that she, Perón and Argentina were not of

transcendental importance in Europe. Indeed, as in France, it was assumed that seeing the glory of the Old World would make her understand her proper place, while the ability to supply food was vastly more significant than the supposed example set by Peronist doctrine.

Despite the apparent 'road to Damascus' effect of her European trip and her shift to a more austere wardrobe, it is worth noting that Eva did not also lose her enthusiasm for jewels – whether because this represented a vestige of coquetry and glamour that she was unwilling to suppress, because, as Lillian Guardo suggested, she felt valued as a result of being given valuable gifts, or because something inside still felt that having assets against future need was some guarantee of security. In any case, she would continue to accrue expensive and highly visible jewellery for the remainder of her career, often in the form of gifts from governments, or from individuals, politicians, businessmen or others seeking favour in the government's eyes (a strategy that speaks to her influence over decision-making, if not to the quality of that decision-making). Alberto Dodero was a frequent donor, either directly or through his wife, the former US show-girl Betty Sundmark. Betty, a sometime friend of Eva's, would later note that whenever Eva admired a piece of jewellery she was wearing, she was happy to make her a gift of it in the knowledge that her husband would re-place it with a larger one.

This somewhat mercenary fascination with jewellery would become yet another subject of malicious gossip and criticism among the anti-Peronist ranks, given the whiff of corruption, the tinge of vulgarity evident in some of her jewels and the longstanding rumours concerning what else she might have bought and sold in her days as an actress. The notion of a 'kept woman' or, worse, coaxing jewellery out of admirers in exchange for favours fitted well with the so-called 'black myth' surrounding her past that was whispered about in good society. One prominent proponent of that myth was the writer Jorge Luis Borges, who would insist until the end of his life that Doña Juana had operated a brothel in Junín and that Eva was 'a common prostitute'. Borges, a great writer who believed himself 'differ-ent', and by inference superior, to his countrymen by virtue of his English ancestry – a frequent belief among *porteños* which in fact gave him far more in common with his compatriots than he believed – was a lifelong, fierce anti-Peronist whose criticisms were sometimes well-founded and sometimes not. He hated Perón and Evita and they returned the favour; the Peronist government removed the blind writer from his post as head of the

National Library and gave him the post of poultry inspector instead. While this was a vindictive act that justified his feelings about the government's authoritarian nature, he would later do little to burnish his own democratic credentials by frequently expressing his fulsome admiration for Chilean dictator General Augusto Pinochet – 'a gentleman', in Borges's opinion.

In this period, the private Eva became increasingly subsumed into the public *compañera* Evita (or Eva Perón, as she would describe herself on formal occasions). In her earlier life, glimpses of the private individual were more frequent, from her day-to-day contacts with colleagues and friends and occasional confidences with close contacts like Lillian Guardo or Vera Pichel. Now, with her public mission increasingly absorbing all of her waking hours (including many that should by rights have been sleeping hours), it becomes more and more difficult to separate the two personae, as time for family, friends and even her husband became time she perceived as stolen from more imperative activities. Here the person – still a very young woman of only 28 – merges with the activist, the symbol and the campaigner, a figure of extraordinary energy and executive capacity, whose many errors can be at least partly attributed to her age and inexperience, and to the vertiginous activity and genuine passion that consumed the private girl whose time for chats over coffee, weekends at San Vicente and private entertainments was no more. That fanaticism and obsession (and self-obsession) with her responsibility for addressing the ills affecting millions of Argentines doubtless reflects a considerable degree of narcissism, but it is also readily traceable to Doña Juana and her sewing machine.

Even before her European experience, Evita had, as noted earlier, become extremely active in relations with the trade unions, visiting factories, receiving delegations at the 'Secretariat', as the Ministry would forever be for her, hearing petitions and accepting donations. However, the rhythm of this activity now became astonishing. For example, as counted by Marysa Navarro, in the weeks following her return Evita received 12 different delegations on 17 September, 8 on 30 September and 30 on 1 October.[2] Every morning she would receive union representatives, often until well into the afternoon, hearing demands while employees took copious notes. Her own memory was prodigious, and she remembered names, faces and personal histories in a way that greatly facilitated these talks. Her role in negotiating processes would continue to increase and her talent for the process was widely recognised: even in the early stages, when her understanding of labour issues was more limited, her personal sympathy was able to overcome elegantly the difficulties of that interview [...] At times we had to repeat the same thing several times, until suddenly she understood the whole problem and gave us a solution that we had not even remotely thought of.[3]

Later, it would also become customary for her to be present when new collective labour contracts were signed, most of which boasted improvements in working conditions, paid leave and other benefits in addition to wage increases.

Moreover, while it had already become common for unions seeking favours to make spontaneous donations in cash or in kind for her charitable work (initially known as the Doña María Eva Duarte de Perón Social Action Crusade), it thereafter became customary for unionised workers to donate collectively the first days or weeks of their wage increase in recognition of her efforts on their behalf. Speaking on 28 November 1947, she remarked that 'my assistance campaign is a foretaste of the work dreamed of and initiated by General Perón'.[4] At the same time, she received individual petitions from those seeking help – often jobs, which were usually resolved by resort to a list of vacancies in public ministries. Above and beyond these activities, her public speaking schedule was expanding, from a total of 20 speeches in the first five months of 1947, before her trip, to 78 public speeches over the course of 1948.[5]

Evita's increasingly significant links with the trade unions were originally a response to the inevitable shift in relations implied by Perón's move from the Secretariat of Labour to the presidency. Following his election Perón was obliged to some degree to be 'the president of all Argentines' and his day-to-day activities obviously extended well beyond the question of labour relations and welfare. Evita was uniquely placed to fill that vacuum, in part because she was perceived as an instrument of, rather than a competitor to, her husband, but also unquestionably because of the natural talent she displayed for the role. Perhaps more significantly, as over time her relationship to organised labour became closer than Perón's, it gave her great influence over one of the government's main pillars of support – all the more crucial because her relationship with the other main pillar, the armed forces, was turbulent at best, and her most effective means of exercising power (in addition to her husband's backing) was to maintain a hold over the CGT, the only other corporation able to counter the sway of the military. However, despite Perón's later claims that she was a 'marvellous instrument' but 'my product, I made her, I prepared her to be what she was',[6] there is no question that her own innate abilities and charisma were crucial to her ability to play that leadership role (undoubtedly, in addition to the space opened to her by her husband). Moreover, she was buttressed by the loyalists she was able to place in strategic positions, like Oscar Nicolini as minister of communications and her brother Juancito as the president's private secretary.

One of the casualties of Evita's increasing leadership role was Isabel Ernst, who had come to the Secretariat with Mercante in 1943 and had remained after he became governor of Buenos Aires, serving both as trade union secretary of the presidency (in practice, interviewing unionists and accompanying them to meetings with the president) and as Evita's private secretary. Initially Isabel served as a mentor (although she was five years younger) to an Eva eager to learn from her experience with the unions and also from her early small-scale experience with responding to petitions for assistance, which she had attempted to address on an ad hoc basis within the Secretariat. Many noted the fact that, from early on, Isabel used the type of suits and hairstyles that would later be identified with Evita, and that she was a constant presence behind Evita in her office and at visits to factories and union offices. According to one witness, 'the role she played in Eva's first contacts with workers is fundamental. Isabel […] had deep knowledge of the "language" of the workers. She spoke to them as equals […] she knew how to reach them.'[7]

However, as in the case of Lillian Guardo, it may be that once Evita felt more secure in her own handling of public situations she was no longer willing to have a mentor or potential competitor nearby; indeed, many reports speak of her rebuking Isabel sharply in the presence of others. According to some:

> initially, [Evita] was completely dependent on Isabel's superior knowledge and experience […] However, she soon came to resent the other woman's competence and her cordial relations with the union men and government officials. On several occasions, she lashed out at her assistant in public.[8]

At the same time, Evita's close relationship with Mercante's legitimate wife Elena Caporale, who as first lady of the province took an active role in her social justice programmes, may have soured relations with Isabel, Mercante's long-time mistress.

> It is probable that her relationship with Mercante [...] provoked her later relations with Eva Perón. I also think that Isabel Ernst could never have stood out while Evita was in charge of labour policy [...] Eva Perón did not accept second figures.[9]

There are mixed reports of Isabel Ernst, with some saying that 'the young and beautiful blonde secretary had become a favourite with the union men frequenting the office, who took to calling her Isabelita'.[10] However, others defined her as 'an authoritarian character, who followed Eva Perón's trajectory step by step until 1947. In all the graphic testimonies from the period, Isabel Ernst appears close to Evita, a few steps behind, wearing similar dresses and using identical hairstyles.'[11] Evita's maid Irma Cabrera would later say that 'Isabel Ernst was an apathetic and indifferent German. She did not know how to make people like her', and would attribute her departure to the comments surrounding her romance with Mercante.[12] According to another sceptic,

> it was never clear what job that woman did. She always wore a plaid skirt with a jacket. She was very masculine, she used short hair and flat shoes. Thin and military-looking. They said she was Domingo Mercante's girlfriend.[13]

Whatever the truth of the matter, there is little indication of an identifiable break in the relationship – indeed, in the famous and possibly apocryphal letter that Evita wrote to her husband en route to Madrid, she asked him to 'look after Isabelita' and to give her a cash present and a better salary in recognition of her loyalty. However, Evita's increasing independence and high-handedness probably made it clear that Isabel's career in the government was nearing an end. In 1949 she became pregnant, at Mercante's behest, and resigned from her posts, moving to a semi-rural location in the southern part of Greater Buenos Aires, where she kept chickens and cows. Isabel would remain with the married Mercante for the remainder of his life, accompanying him into exile both in 1953, after his governorship ended, and in 1955, after Perón's overthrow, when she lived in Uruguay for several years, also on a smallholding. She would later move to another rural area, in Córdoba province, where she finally married several years after Mercante's death in 1976, and where she died in 2000.

Nor was Isabel Ernst's departure the only shift to come. On the contrary, Evita's influence in government was already extending to cabinet personnel, and she was widely believed to be behind the departure of Foreign Minister Juan Atilio Bramuglia from the cabinet in early 1949. Bramuglia, a talented statesman who received international recognition for his chairing of the UN Security Council during the Berlin crisis, was unquestionably one of the few genuine stars of the cabinet. However, he had earned Evita's longstanding antipathy by refusing to present a writ of habeas corpus in favour of Perón in October 1945, and later by opposing her Rainbow Tour. In practice, Bramuglia had managed to survive Evita's ill will for some considerable time so long as Perón considered him a useful collaborator, and stories that Perón supposedly encouraged her to plot his ouster suggest that she was a useful tool rather than the driving force behind his departure. Nevertheless, the story boosted fear and loathing of Evita's power in anti-Peronist circles (and that of information and press under-secretary Raúl Apold, allegedly her co-conspirator), and her role, not long afterward, in undermining Buenos Aires governor Domingo Mercante may have been more tangible.

If Isabel Ernst's role in government was ending by 1949, Evita's was soaring. Her influence over the trade unions, a key pillar in the Peronist movement, would soon be greatly enhanced by her absolute dominance over two institutions that were her own creations and her great passions: the Peronist Women's Party and the Eva Perón Foundation.

CHAPTER 11

Las Muchachas Peronistas

Las muchachas peronistas
con Evita triunfaremos
Y con ella brindaremos
nuestra vida por Perón.
Por Perón y por Evita,
la vida queremos dar
Por Evita capitana y por
Perón general.
Eva Perón, tu corazón nos
acompaña sin cesar
Te prometemos nuestro amor
con juramento de lealtad.

[The Peronist girls will
triumph with Evita
And with her we will offer
our lives for Perón.
For Perón and for Evita,
we want to give our lives
For Evita our captain and
Perón our general.
Eva Perón, your heart
always accompanies us
We promise you our love
with an oath of loyalty.]

(*'Las muchachas peronistas', anonymous; the 'female' version of*
the Peronist march 'Los muchachos peronistas')

SHORTLY AFTER EVITA'S return from Europe, on 9 September 1947 Congress adopted Law 13.010 granting women the right to vote. As noted earlier, as early as 1946 Evita had begun speaking in favour of votes for women, albeit largely as another facet of women's role of defending the home (as well as due to women's participation in the demonstrations of 17 October). This was in marked contrast with earlier anti-feminist arguments that women's suffrage would take them away from their natural role in the home and family, although in line with Socialist Doctor Alicia Moreau de Justo's earlier contention that women were crucial to the moral

1. Eva Perón and her siblings dressed for carnival, 1921

2. Practising film star poses in Junín, aged 15

3. In the *radioteatro Los jazmines del 80*, 1939

4. In early 1946: beginning married life, still in search of an image

5. With Franco and Carmen Polo de Franco, Madrid, June 1947

6. In her office at the Foundation (undated)

7. A demonstration in favour of women's votes in 1948: 'Women can and must vote. María Eva Duarte de Perón.'

8. Crowning the Queen of Labour on her last May Day

9. Presenting a decoration to Dr Ricardo Finochietto for a 'successful operation' he did not perform, January 1952

10. The *Cabildo Abierto*, 22 August 1951

11. With Perón on the balcony of the Casa Rosada, 17 October 1951

12. Being decorated by the volunteers of the Argentine Labour Institute

13. Evita addressing delegates of the PPF, 1951

14. 17 October 1950; behind Evita, Vice-President Hortensio Quijano and Governor Domingo Mercante

15. Evita meeting the families of non-commissioned officers (undated)

16. The first couple in gala mode, Teatro Colón, 1951

17. Evita receives a delegation of maritime workers, August 1951

18. The funeral of Evita, 1952

19. Learning to read in Peronist Argentina

20. A ten-story image of Evita, Buenos Aires, 2015

21. 'Not one woman less': the image of Evita used to promote a campaign against violence against women, 2014

education of both the family and the citizen. Nevertheless, women's issues per se had not been a key focus of her attention, more concentrated on trade unions and broader issues of social need.

Nor, despite the official propaganda that presented the vote as a victory for Evita, was the question of women's suffrage a new one. The women's movement had begun in the late nineteenth century, led by remarkable women like Cecilia Grierson, Alicia Moreau de Justo and Elvira Rawson de Dellepiane, the former two among Argentina's first women doctors. All of them were from well-to-do and well-educated backgrounds, often of Anglo-Argentine origin (Moreau de Justo, the wife of Socialist Party founder Juan B. Justo, was born in France and spent much of her childhood in London). Their links with the average Argentine woman were limited – as were some of their objectives, such as being allowed to practice medicine. The Council of Women, founded in 1900 by Grierson, was divided on the issue of votes for women, but after the civil code was reformed in 1926 to give women greater rights in other spheres, women's suffrage came increasingly to the fore as an issue. However, an attempt in 1932 to pass a bill granting the vote foundered on congressional divisions and would eventually languish in a congressional drawer together with other somewhat forgotten projects. (Uniquely, San Juan province had granted votes to women in the 1920s under the *Bloquista* administrations of Federico and Aldo Cantoni.)

Indeed the feminist movement, often closely linked to the Socialist Party, would suffer similar difficulties to those of the Socialists. The Socialist Party had, over the years, presented and even managed to pass a number of labour laws in Congress, but these had not been implemented until Perón came along, revived them and made them his own. Similarly, women's suffrage, which had been a longstanding demand of the (upper-class) Argentine women's movement, only gained political traction when it was adopted by Perón and Evita, regarded by and large as the enemy by those women. Also like the Socialist Party, the women's movement signally failed to grasp why their own position had had little salience for the vast majority of the working classes and why the Peronist position did. This was recognised by the Socialist writer Ernesto Sábato after the fall of Perón, who noted that 'in the Peronist movement there were not just base passions and purely material appetites: there was a genuine spiritual fervour, a para-religious faith in a leader who talked to them as human beings and not as pariahs':[1]

There was a justified desire for justice and for recognition [...] This
is fundamentally what Perón saw and mobilised. The rest is only
detail [...] It is also what our political parties continue not to see and,
what is worse, do not want to see.[2]

By the time of the Perón government, the international atmosphere was
far more favourable to women's suffrage, which was becoming more common and had been a key theme of discussion in regional forums such as
the 1938 Conference of American States. However, the largely elitist profile
of the feminist movement in Argentina was not aligned with the government; as noted earlier, Perón's moves in favour of votes for women when
he was vice-president had been rebuffed. Most of those women had subsequently backed the Unión Democrática in the 1946 elections. Similarly, the
Peronist Law 13.010 was not well received by many of those who had long
clamoured for the vote, and that it should have been attributed virtually to
Evita's single-handed efforts must have been especially galling.

Whatever Evita's efforts in this respect (which also served to legitimate
her own political role), by 1947 both the domestic and international context
were favourable to the women's vote. Within Congress there was little opposition to the measure – a single member, the legislator Reynaldo Pastor, raised
objections to the bill on the somewhat bizarre grounds that women in rural
areas could not 'abandon their domestic duties in order to vote' and that
women would find the process of having to vote particularly onerous due to
the 'physiological' conditions that affected women and not men.[3] The brief
text, voted in Evita's presence, applied to women the same civic rights and
obligations as men (except for military service), and required the executive
to prepare a voter register of women within 18 months, as well as the issu-
ance of identity documents (*libreta cívica*) to women to allow them to vote.
Perón promulgated the law on 23 September and the document was handed
to Evita at a public ceremony where she noted that 'my hands are trembling
as they touch the laurel that proclaims victory. Here it is, my sisters, sum-
marised in a few articles a long history of struggle, stumbles and hopes.'[4]

Doubtless, for the opposition, the negative view of this event went
beyond the feeling that a long feminist struggle had been neutralised by
a latecomer who was given all the credit for an outcome in which she had
invested comparatively little. 'There were about eight draft bills for the
women's vote presented by legislators, and then one day the Peronist project entered and it was approved just like that.'[5] It was also clear from the

first moment that the incorporation of a new voter base could scarcely fail to benefit the incumbent government. According to the British Embassy,

> the passage of the Bill has been greeted as a victory for the 'Revolution' and for Señora de Perón in particular. There can be little doubt that it is the hope and, indeed, intention of the Peronista party, abetted by Señora de Perón, to make obvious use of these votes when the time comes.[6]

Moreover, rumours abounded that Evita herself might stand for the Senate as a result – or worse. 'Someone has sold Evita on the idea that now that votes have been granted to women in this country, there is no reason why she should not run for the Presidency once Perón's term is over.'[7] This can scarcely have reassured the opposition – or the armed forces.

Nor was it altogether clear that women were unanimous in their desire to vote. One Peronist legislator was reported to have claimed that 'thanks to Evita [...] the average Argentine woman had become politically-minded. From tame and colourless housewives the women of Argentina [...] were now ready to take their place in the vanguard of public life.'[8] However, others suggested that Argentine women's interests 'have on the whole lain in more personal fields than politics'.[9] Indeed, the reactions of beneficiaries were extremely mixed, as illustrated by a group of women interviewed years later by Lilia Lardone: 'I liked the women's vote, because it meant a degree of independence for women.'[10] 'In 1951 it was very impressive to vote for the first time [...] the women came to vote because of Evita, Evita sent them to vote for Perón.'[11] 'Even though I didn't like her, we have the vote because of her.'[12] 'Voting wasn't something that I was enthusiastic about [...] The vote was an achievement, maybe it didn't interest me because [...] I cared little and nothing about politics.'[13] However, it was not a mystery that Evita would seek to organise the women's vote to benefit her husband: 'Evita was very clear: "this is a vote, and think carefully about what you do with it women, you are choosing a way of life".'[14]

Nor was it universally believed that her attitude was a feminist one, at least among more politically conscious women:

> If there's one thing that can't be said of Eva Perón it's that she was a feminist, despite the women's vote. Perón was God, you had to be with Perón and she was his shadow. A feminist woman doesn't talk like that.[15]

However, 'I didn't like Perón but I did like Evita. Because she wanted to improve the situation of women, she had had a very hard and very sad life.' 'If she hadn't had cancer at 33, maybe the country would have been different.'[16] Evita's frequent references to her inferior role ('I have been nothing more than the bridge I desire to be between the workers and the General') make it difficult to reach a different conclusion.[17]

Despite Evita's public career, Perón's unusual willingness to allow his wife to play such a role and the fact that his government enfranchised women nationally for the first time, it is more than fair to say that neither Perón nor Eva had any real feminist belief as it would normally be understood, nor is it realistic to imagine that they would have in light of their culture, background and experience. (In *La razón de mi vida*, Eva – or her ghostwriter – refers to feminists as 'resentful women' and says, 'I wasn't an old spinster, or ugly enough to occupy that kind of role.'[18]) However, Evita's understanding was that women had to have better options in order to avoid being condemned to the type of life her mother had experienced.

Those options were not especially to be found in a career outside the home: both the Peróns, like other Argentine analysts before them, believed that women should be able to remain at home rather than going out to work (where, if anything, they put downward pressure on wages by receiving less pay than men, and tended to 'masculinise' themselves, according to Evita). Thus, the solution was to increase men's wages so that they would be able to provide adequately for their families without a second income. As such, relatively little emphasis was placed by Evita or the government as a whole on improving women's wages or working conditions, beyond the generalised improvements in salary, paid leave and other benefits. Indeed, in *La razón de mi vida* Evita would raise the suggestion of paying housewives a salary for the work they did at home, rather than pushing them outside their 'natural' condition of wife, mother and homemaker.

The anomaly here is obvious, and not lost on Evita herself: Evita had left home at 15 to pursue an unorthodox career alone in the city, she was childless and was anything but a stay-at-home housewife, however much she attempted to present that image. Her speeches constantly cast her own role in a 'motherly' vein:

I want to be, as I said years ago, more than the wife of the Argentine president, the *compañera* Evita, if that way I can help to calm any pain in any home in my fatherland. I want to continue being the companion of the humble and the workers, the Woman of Hope [...] if that means I can bring happiness to working households.[19]

She claimed she was:

slandered and vilified every day because she was on the side of the humble interpreting General Perón, because she works from sun to sun to bring a little happiness to humble homes and because instead of leading a comfortable life she had opted to burn her life in the office of Labour and Welfare.[20]

Nevertheless, although she believed in the value of a traditional role for women in general, she also understood clearly the need for them to have other options, albeit by preference inside the home.

This was permanently illustrated by her habit of distributing her emblematic sewing machines, initially on an ad hoc basis and later through the Eva Perón Foundation, and by offering sewing and hairdressing classes at the *unidades básicas* (literally 'basic units', party offices that would be set up across the country to offer political indoctrination, legal and other advice, secretarial training, home economics and cooking, and hair and manicure services). Evita's upbringing by Doña Juana and her eternal sewing machine had left its mark, and a significant insight: women needing extra income could earn it at home if they knew how to sew or how to cut hair, and they could save on spending by making the family's clothes and cutting their hair. If this cannot be seen by twenty-first century viewers as a feminist posture, it was nevertheless a practical and a popular one:

A dressmaker recently told my wife that she had written to 'Evita' to ask for a sewing machine and that her request had been promptly fulfilled. This dressmaker was enthusiastic, saying that the people would tear to pieces anyone who tried to do harm to General Perón or to 'Evita', who had been brought to power by the will of God.[21]

Despite this preference for a more traditional family, though, Peronism did not overlook the fact that in reality many women were part of the workforce, and indeed that many of them had participated in 17 October 1945. 'Those women are the precursors of the women's vote.' 'We didn't believe in the woman, and it was the Revolution that pulled us out of that eternal error.'[22] One of the many recognitions of that significant support base was the institution of the 'Queen of Labour', chosen on May Day every year. The May Day parade in 1946 was the first time that the nation's leaders had participated, and that the event had been seen as pro- rather than anti-government. The slogan 'yesterday and today' reminded participants that the government had not always been a friend to labour. ('In our country they no longer sing foreign anthems but rather sing our national anthem, and they do not carry foreign banners, but instead the immaculate white and blue flag.'[23])

In 1947 the newspaper *El Laborista* organised the first Queen of Labour contest, in which its readers voted for the contestants (it was specified that Eva Perón had graciously ruled herself out of contention despite the obvious landslide she would have received), although thereafter the initiative was taken up by the government and the candidates were chosen by the CGT, with the winner picked by a jury including Perón. The winner would be crowned by Perón and Evita and would ride a float at the head of the May Day parade. She was required to be a 'worker', as the title implied, and capable of embodying the virtues of beauty, moral values and industry. This was yet another advertisement of the new dignity of the working classes under Peronism: women workers could be both hard-working and beautiful, desirable, well-dressed and proud of their appearance, showing that not only the wealthy and idle classes could produce women worthy of esteem. 'Before Perón, maids never had these luxuries [...] Now at least we felt like ladies.' 'When I asked my aunt "why are you so anti-Peronist?" she replied "because my servant dresses the same as I do".' 'When Perón and Evita came, they showed people how to live and people, for instance, stopped wearing *alpargatas* and used shoes; they didn't wear a torn sweater but a good one.'[24] The prime embodiment of this woman was, of course, obvious, and photos of the time demonstrate the extent to which the contestants attempted to emulate Eva in style and dress. Despite this attempt to glorify and dignify the working woman, however, much of the propaganda surrounding women's representation in the May Day parades still revolved around traditional roles as wife and mother.[25]

At an initial stage, at least, the perceived value of women as a political force lay in their role as managers of their households and household budgets. Women's role as the defenders of their home and family was a frequently repeated theme in Evita's speeches and would also become a key plank of the government's anti-inflation campaigns. In a similar vein, advertising even in Peronist magazines such as *Argentina* continued to focus on the role of women as housewives and mothers, household managers, careful consumers and defenders of the household budget, rather than as wage-earners, although the magazine also focused on the 'dignifying' of the working classes by providing guidance on fashion and 'tasteful' consumption. (As noted by Eduardo Elena, there is something somewhat paradoxical about the fact that a government based on its connections with the working class should attempt to educate those workers in what were basically middle-class, orthodox tastes and consumer patterns.[26]) Needless to say, in terms of fashion, Eva was the example to imitate, and magazines such as *Argentina* and other more mainstream women's publications, as well as daily newspapers, saw their circulation increase when they included photos of the first lady in glamorous evening dress or elegant business attire – photos that were then cut out and displayed. According to one contemporary account of a sugar factory in Tucumán, the walls were adorned with 'pictures of General Perón's wife which cover the whole factory like a rash'.[27]

The rise in real wages since 1943 had had the desired effect of boosting consumption, capacity for which would be a central element of Peronism's promise to dignify and empower the working class and which to a degree equated being a consumer with being a citizen. It was also, significantly, a useful booster of the importance of media propaganda: by 1947 over half of all households had a radio, and monthly cinema and theatre attendance rose from 1.6 million in 1940 to 3.1 million in 1947 and nearly 5 million in 1952.[28] However, productivity did not rise as fast as wages, despite Perón's and Evita's frequent exhortations to 'produce, produce, produce', and competition between domestic consumption and export markets also put upward pressure on prices. As a result, as early as 1946 inflation was beginning to undermine the real advances in workers' purchasing power. This would become a theme to which Eva in particular would return again and again in speeches:

> I want to ask you, please, we must produce, produce a lot to collaborate with General Perón and above all to meet our obligations to the fatherland in this new year. We must produce a lot, to consolidate our conquests, the only way to cement them is to produce as much as we consume.[29]

There is a problem that has us especially worried, which relates to production [... Union leaders should not consolidate] based on an uncontrolled race to gain better salaries, but on constant dedication to their duties [...] If production levels were higher, the fall in prices would be immediate.[30]

Given the fever for enrichment we are seeing today, we have only one option to cause prices to fall: superproduction.[31]

The Peronist response to this problem, in addition to 'produce, produce, produce' and calls for workers to become more thrifty, was to attempt to shift the blame for high prices onto 'usurers' and unscrupulous merchants who overcharged. In their role as the main purchasers of family needs, women were in particular charged with active vigilance over prices. Anti-speculation drives called on women to report 'speculators', whose businesses might be fined or closed down if they were accused of over-charging. While this approach was visibly not tantamount to a government policy to reduce inflation (something that risked running counter to the policy of boosting both production and consumption), the casting of inflation and wage-price problems as yet another 'war' between the people and the greedy and unscrupulous economic powers was well within the overall Peronist strategy of identifying enemies as scapegoats. And in this case, such a campaign could be targeted on newly enfranchised women who for the first time were now a constituency ripe for political mobilisation.[32]

Even though, as noted earlier, Evita's chief focus at this time was her work with the trade unions, the role of women, whether as defenders of home and hearth or as political actors, was a recurring theme in her speeches. In 1948, she noted that women, as citizens, now had both new rights and responsibilities, but that the home was where the woman could make the greatest contribution, bringing up her children to be good Argentines in the Peronist mould: 'In the schools teachers have that mission; in the home that honour belongs to the woman.' 'Everything done and to be done for the good of the nation's total sovereignty [...] is in large part conditioned on the activity of the woman in the heart of the home.'[33] By the following year, this would take a more concrete form.

In July 1949 the Women's Peronist Party (Partido Peronista Femenino, PPF) was launched, with Evita named as its president. The initiative in fact came after earlier similar moves at the provincial level, with local party bases already founded by the wives of the governors of San Juan and Buenos Aires, although these groups were later subsumed into the national party. As might readily have been expected, given Evita's organisational capacity and need for control, the PPF was far better, and more rapidly, constituted than its masculine counterpart (which was allowed no interference in the women's party – to such a degree that the wives of Peronist activists were not given leading roles), and its nationwide growth soon gave her control over two of Peronism's main support bases, together with the CGT. Perón himself called it 'so perfect and so complete that in the Argentine political arena, in all our civic tradition, there has never been a more disciplined, virtuous, moral and patriotic force than this group'.[34] Those disciplined, virtuous, moral and patriotic women had, in Eva's view, an overriding objective:

> working women, the humble women of the fatherland know that we are living an historic hour […] and in this struggle of all we women have a role: that of fighting at the side of General Perón for the happiness of our homes.[35]
>
> I feel proud, because today the woman is standing up, before this Peronist reality that we are all living and that we want for all the Argentines of the future.[36]

One of Evita's earliest initiatives was the organisation of a 'national census of women Peronists' as a basis for the PPF, for which she designated census delegates charged with overseeing the process in all 23 provinces and terrorities. The young women chosen personally by Evita, none of whom had prior political experience, were sent away from their home districts, working tirelessly for months away from their homes and families in unfamiliar territory, designating thousands of sub-delegates. They were answerable directly and constantly to Evita and not to any member of the men's party, something that caused frictions on more than one occasion. Both they and other functionaries and candidates were carefully vetted for their 'moral qualities', mindful of the scrutiny and criticism they would face. 'They said we were whores because we did politics.'[37] The purpose of the census, and the *unidades básicas*, was, moreover, not solely to detect Peronist sympathisers and assist women in processing their voting papers (60–70 per cent of whom it was hoped would join the PPF). It was also to detect needs and difficulties at the family level that could be addressed, often through the Eva Perón Foundation. Speaking on the radio in December of that year, Eva exhorted women across the country to collaborate with the census takers attempting

> to know how many women are enrolled in the Peronist cause. The leaders will emerge from the mass. The hardest working, the most self-sacrificing and the most disciplined will be those who emerge [...] I have always thought that leaders are not made: they are born.[38]

However, there was never the slightest doubt as to who would lead the women's party.

The considerable sacrifice demanded of the delegates sent out across the country bore remarkable fruit and at remarkable speed. After the first women's *unidad básicas* were opened in Buenos Aires province in November 1949 (by Mercante's wife Elena Caporale) and in the capital in January 1950, a total of 3,600 were opened across Argentina by February 1951, and staffed daily by delegates and by specialists in other services, including lawyers, doctors, hairdressers, manicurists and teachers, to offer classes in basic education, literacy, and skills such as typing and, as noted above, sewing and hairdressing. They were equipped with the ineluctable sewing machines, as well as classrooms, first aid centres and facilities for civic instruction and the training of election officials. Much of the emphasis was on home and social work rather than politics, not least to avoid frightening off women who shared the view that politics was an inappropriate sphere for women.

Moreover, in 1951, women not only voted for the first time: the Peronist Party presented six women candidates for the Senate and 23 for the Lower House, many of them emerging from the delegates chosen by Evita and the system of *unidades básicas*, and all of them elected, together with 80 women who entered provincial legislatures. (The Socialist Party presented three female candidates, including Alicia Moreau de Justo.) One of those elected, Ana Macri, would later note that Evita 'introduced women to politics, opened the doors to a new life of hopes and realisations that elevated their role as mothers and wives to political life on a par with men'.[39] The women's party would also be crucial in Perón's landslide re-election, in which he won some 60 per cent of the vote: more than 90 per cent of registered women voters turned out, and 2.4 million of the 3.8 million women voted for Perón. However, the women legislators felt that they represented Evita more than their geographical jurisdictions or the party itself.

Despite a discourse and an evident belief that was in no way feminist, Evita did note that 'it is urgent to conciliate in the woman her need to be a wife and mother with that other need for rights that as a dignified human person she feels in the most intimate part of her heart'.[40] An element of this, and of the proposal to create greater independence for women, even if only through salaries for housewives or the use of the sewing machine, doubtless reflected her own childhood experience of the dire situation facing women either chained to a 'bad' man or with no man at all. However, even if her own concept of women's place in the home was a highly traditional one – and one which reduced the options for competition that she clearly did not accept – Evita's activism generated options not previously on most women's radar. The creation of the PPF obeyed the same basic logic as that of the men's party of which it was independent – to follow and support a charismatic leader (or, in the case of the PPF, two), but it generated a space in which women could occupy a public role not previously considered by most of them. Evita chose her delegates, and later her candidates, but they developed a political role by following her, and her mere existence represented an example of taking responsibility in the public sphere that had hitherto been lacking, or limited to a certain narrow class of well-off, well-educated women with whom most of their compatriots did not identify. Despite the conservatism of much of her thinking, Evita herself was innately subversive (or heretical), and her example as a female political figure would remain paramount long after her death. 'What we wanted was to collaborate with her, not the Peronist Party.'[41]

By this time, Evita's high public profile and very real power within both the women's party and the trade union movement made her, as is often said, the most loved and hated woman in Argentina. Indeed, for the anti-Peronists, she was far more hated than the less abrasive and more apparently affable president, who was after all performing a role not very far removed from that of other men in power. In this respect, Evita acted as a real force in government, a lightning rod, but also as a red rag to the segments of popular opinion not impressed with Peronism or with Evita's flowery language of love, hearts and praise for the General (combined with ever more fiery rhetoric regarding the 'traitors' and 'oligarchs' clearly identified as the enemy). Her portraits were in hundreds of thousands of homes, and arguably caused rage in as many others. ('Every time my mother-in-law, who was anti-Peronist, went to my house she would grab the fly spray [...] and spray it at the photo.'[42] 'I think that "anti-Evaism" was stronger than "anti-Peronism".'[43])

However, in order for the women's party to perform its function of ensuring Perón's re-election, another hurdle remained: the constitutional prohibition on immediate presidential re-election. The 1853 constitution, based to a substantial degree on its United States predecessor but presiding over a very different political context, could realistically have been said to be ripe for an update by 1949, and the overwhelming Peronist majority in Congress was eager to incorporate values such as the social role of private property, nationalisation of public utilities, the rights of workers and Evita's rights of the elderly, proclaimed in that year. However, the key target of the reform, albeit unacknowledged, was Article 77, which prohibited immediate re-election of the president. Perón himself spoke publicly and vehemently against immediate re-election on numerous occasions, leaving open the belief (at least among those who did not know how to read him) that he would step down in 1952, at which point it was widely anticipated that Buenos Aires governor Domingo Mercante would be the candidate to succeed him. Nevertheless, 'bowing to popular pressure', on 3 September 1948 Perón promulgated a bill calling a constituent assembly, with elections on 5 December. Predictably, the Peronists won a two-thirds majority.

The constituent assembly began on 11 January 1949, presided over by Mercante (the most-voted candidate), who sought to be an able and respected leader of the assembly and to ensure even-handed treatment of the opposition Radical minority (led by the young lawyer Moisés Lebensohn, a native of Junín who had been an occasional paying guest at Doña Juana's table). However, Mercante, who strongly supported Perón's social policy but had a different concept of democratic practice, chose to take Perón at his word and to reject proposals to modify Article 77 in order to allow immediate re-election (despite his evident understanding that in fact Perón had no intention of being taken at his word). Here, though, Evita would be called into play, whether on her own initiative or at Perón's instigation. She urged her old friend Mercante in no uncertain terms to 'convince' Perón that he must accept the re-election clause (despite some speculation that she and some of her own unconditional supporters, such as Lower House president Héctor Cámpora, were opposed because they wished to promote Evita's own candidacy to succeed her husband in 1952). Mercante correctly read her intervention as non-appealable, and had a new draft prepared to provide that 'the president and vice-president are elected for a term of six years and can be re-elected'. Despite being roundly denounced by the Radical minority (who then left the convention and forced the Peronists to vote the constitution in their absence), the re-election provision was included, and the new constitution approved and published on 16 March 1949.

Like Evita's ubiquitous social justice and public presence, the reformed constitution was both a blessing and a curse to Perón. Both increased the government's hold on power and popular support, but also fuelled rising opposition. On the one hand, as noted earlier, Evita was even more high-profile than the president and commanded both greater love and greater hatred. On the other, the reformed constitution removed the safeguard that had guaranteed to the anti-Peronists that, however odious the government, the president's term in office was limited to six years and he would step down in 1952. Coinciding as they did with a deterioration in the economic outlook, these factors would simultaneously appear to bolster Perón's position while in fact making it more untenable in the longer term.

The new constitution also implied the beginning of Mercante's eclipse, given both rising tensions between him and Perón and the fact that Perón no longer required a credible heir. Mercante had in particular been a protégé of Evita (possibly given his supposed role in bringing her and Perón together), who often referred to him as 'the heart of Perón' and was a tireless supporter of his work in the province. When visiting Paris in 1947, according to Lillian Lagomarsino, Evita exhorted her to expound on Mercante's stellar achievements to their doubtless unenthusiastic French interlocutors, and complained bitterly when she did not hear Lillian mention his name. In the letter she supposedly wrote to Perón on departing for Madrid, she had urged him to remain close to the loyal Mercante. Even before this, when her work with the unions was in its infancy, she would often travel to La Plata, the capital of Buenos Aires province, early in the morning to seek Mercante's advice and guidance before going to her office. Although her relationship with Isabel Ernst had chilled, she had formed a similarly close partnership with Mercante's wife, Elena Caporale, who enthusiastically copied Evita in undertaking social justice work and the organisation of Peronist women in the province.

However, the cooling of the relationship with Mercante became palpable after the constitutional reform, with a sharp reduction in participation by the president and first lady in political acts and inaugurations in the province. Relations were strained further by Mercante's refusal to remain in office for an extended period under the new constitution, which would have brought gubernatorial elections into line with presidential contests on a six-year calendar, instead calling for new elections for a two-year term when his mandate expired in 1950. Moreover, the national government's decision to arrest his Radical competitor, Ricardo Balbín, on charges of contempt (*desacato*) immediately after the gubernatorial election angered and embittered Mercante.

According to Mercante's biographer Caroline Becker, Evita was the instrument used by Perón to dethrone Mercante, goaded by his planting seeds of doubt in her mind. An anecdote Becker cites suggests that in mid-1950 Perón had managed to convince Evita that Mercante wanted to replace him as president. Relations were already souring, as Evita ceased to refer to Mercante publicly as 'the heart of Perón' and increasingly took credit, on her own behalf and Perón's, for Mercante's achievements in the province. However, after Perón purportedly 'confessed' to his wife that he was unable to sleep due to his concern that Mercante wanted to take his place as president, the official campaign against him took off.[44] As was the case with Bramuglia, thereafter Mercante disappeared from official photos and his name was no longer mentioned in the press, leading to his virtual political demise; after his term ended in 1952 he left politics. Whether this was true or not, in May 1950 a British Embassy source noted that Mercante was in the 'dog house' with Evita.[45]

Stories that Perón manipulated and used Evita for such ends abound, as do stories that she manipulated him. Given that all relationships involve some degree of manipulation on both sides, this is at least to some extent plausible. Nevertheless, Evita was no fool and had a strong will and strongly held, largely inflexible opinions. However, her obsession with loyalty to Perón may have made her somewhat more easily manipulated on such points, in particular in the case of someone like Bramuglia, whom she had always hated and whose presence in the cabinet she had barely tolerated. However, in the case of Mercante, the fact that Evita was widely known for her strong loyalty to those she herself viewed as loyal would suggest that something significant – whether Perón's 'revelatory dream', Elena Caporale's activism or some other factor – must have happened to convince her that he was no longer a friend. Or perhaps this shift was facilitated by another consideration: Mercante's putative candidacy to succeed Perón was not only a potential threat to him, but also to Evita, if she and some of her loyalists were beginning to see her as the successor in the presidency. Arguably, by this time, the only two figures capable of representing a threat to Perón were Mercante and Evita herself. While Evita, as Perón's wife, was at least in theory more controllable, Mercante was an independent operator with his own record in office and his own support base, albeit as (like Evita) something of an appendage to Perón.

Ironically, however, in some respects it was Evita who was the greater threat to Perón, given both her own charisma and ability to inspire popular devotion, and the animosity she generated through her fame and her authoritarian attitudes that pointed up some of the worst aspects of the Peronist government (even as her social passion reflected some of its best aspects). By contrast, Mercante's lower profile did not suggest a serious leadership challenge, while his efficiency and moderation in office, which engendered respect even among the opposition, could have been said to present a more positive and less threatening image of Peronism. In Evita's case, her rising public profile and burgeoning social aid campaign gave her, together with the women's party, the tools to ensure Perón's continuity in office, and perhaps her own.

 CHAPTER 12

The Foundation

THE EVA PERÓN Foundation would become the focus of the rest of Eva's life, an extraordinary institution that barely outlived its founder, but which would become her most emblematic achievement.

As noted earlier, first Isabel Ernst and later Eva had begun responding to requests for assistance, and union delegations had already begun offering donations for that work. However, although the government had made real advances in improving the working and living conditions of organised labour, as well as some increase in the construction of schools and hospitals, the poor who fell outside the net of trade union membership remained largely in the same conditions as before, and Evita was disinclined to wait until the government bureaucracy could construct institutions for the purpose of changing this. In late 1947, the María Eva Duarte de Perón Social Aid Crusade began operating formally, and reportedly was receiving some 12,000 letters a day within six months. The Crusade distributed around 5 million toys at Christmas of that year, and began the practice of constructing free housing for the poor, giving subsidies to poor old people with no pension and building shelters for working women (above all single mothers) far from their homes or forced to leave them.

On 8 July 1948, by Decree 20.564, the Crusade formally became the María Eva Duarte de Perón Social Aid Foundation, a legal entity to manage and foment the many donations received and to channel them into sustainable programmes, in principle until such time as legislation could be passed to institutionalise pension and social welfare provision. The following month, Evita proclaimed her so-called Decalogue of the Rights of Seniors, including the rights to assistance, housing, food, health and spiritual care, clothing, work, respect, entertainment and 'freedom from worry', which would be incorporated into the reformed constitution the following year. On 17 October, she inaugurated the first residence for seniors, the Hogar Coronel Perón, with accommodation for 200 people and the type of California-style architecture and level of comfort (many would say unnecessary luxury) that would characterise most of the Foundation's installations. Another 1948 mega-project was the so-called Ciudad Evita, a city of 5,000 low-cost houses for workers, with a church, schools, hospitals and other amenities, constructed in the shape of her profile.

The behemoth that would be the Eva Perón Foundation had modest beginnings, at least in its infancy. According to Perón's never very reliable memoirs,

> for the initial funds, Eva came to me. One night at the table she set out her programme. She seemed to be a calculator. Finally I agreed. I asked her, and the money? She looked at me, amused. 'Very simple', she said, 'I'll start with yours'. 'Mine?' I said, 'What money?' 'Your salary as president.'[1]

In fact, the Foundation was launched with a donation of 10,000 pesos (then some 1,650 dollars) from its founder. According to Evita herself, her attitude at the time was:

> here I am. I want to be of some use to my people [...] When I started to see that more and more letters arrived, and men and women, youths and children and the elderly began to knock on the doors of our private residence, I realised what my 'hunch' would signify.[2]

In practice, some money had been 'rolling in' from as early as 1946, when Evita began receiving petitions at the Secretariat of Labour, and an account had been opened at the Central Bank for those donations, as well as contributions from government bodies, 'to be used for the acquisition of clothing, footwear, food, pharmaceuticals'.[3] By 1948, shortly before the Foundation formally came into being, some 12,000 letters were arriving daily from people seeking assistance. Funding also grew exponentially, with the government ceding funds from the national lottery, the casino of Mar del Plata (where Doña Juana was an assiduous visitor) and the whole of the funds received in concept of tax debts – some of them astronomical. Many donations came in kind, either from unions who donated the products they manufactured, or from companies themselves. Many of the latter were later claimed to have been coerced (the most famous case was that of the makers of Mu-Mu sweets, which purportedly proposed to bill the Foundation for supplies of sweets and rapidly found itself closed down after rat hairs were found during a surprise inspection of its factory). Nevertheless, when the military government that overthrew Perón in September 1955 urged such firms to come forward there were very few complaints – either because the contributions were not coerced, or because they had been made in concept of a bribe, perhaps with a view to gaining more favourable tax treatment. The CGT also contributed substantial funds, both through donations and through payment of a percentage of any pay increase negotiated by member unions (that is, the differential between members' initial and subsequent salary passed to the coffers of the Foundation). The day's wages for 1 May and 17 October also went into the funds. By the time of the *coup d'état* in September 1955, the Foundation's assets were estimated at some 3.4 billion pesos (over 120 million dollars), with real estate worth some 1.6 billion pesos and an annual budget of around 1 billion. Finance minister Ramón Cereijo was the Foundation's administrator, and Father Hernán Benítez its spiritual adviser, with a further staff of 26 priests. The Foundation came to employ some 14,000 people, with around 6,000 working in construction.[4]

Speaking on 17 January 1949, Evita underlined that the funds of the Foundation 'are controlled by the minister of finance because I want the social aid, as something that is eminently popular, to live in a crystal box'.[5] Despite this laudable sentiment, the Foundation's funds were never managed with any great transparency and controversy would rage for decades as to whether they were managed honestly or siphoned off to Swiss bank accounts. However, while managed at Evita's discretion and with limited accounting, the Foundation appears to have spent its vast resources, if not always prudently, at least on the projects and the people for whom they were intended. Moreover, Evita was known to be watchful of the Foundation's staff, and ruthless in dealing with anyone caught stealing. (At the same time, when a judge ordered the Foundation to make an indemnity payment to one of its employees, Evita congratulated the judge and made the payment immediately.[6]) After the 1955 coup, the military government, bent on destroying the reputation of Perón and Evita and thus their residual influence, appointed an investigating commission to look into the

Foundation's finances, whose members could scarcely have been accused of being Peronists. According to Alicia Dujovne Ortiz, one of those aristocratic ladies, Adela Caprile, came to the conclusion that:

> it was a waste, craziness, but not a fraud. Eva cannot be accused of having kept one peso in her pocket. I would like to be able to say as much of all of those who collaborated with me in the dissolution of the organisation.[7]

As with most of her activities, views on Evita's social work and the operations of the Foundation were equally black and white, and both extremes had at least some substance. According to Lardone's later interviews, some felt that 'the form of aid that she did from the Eva Perón Foundation was pure clientelism'[8] and that 'the queues of people who went to ask disgusted me. The idea that people had to beg for something for it to be given to them seemed horrifying to me.'[9] On the other hand, 'the Argentine people never received so much, and much less from a woman so pretty, so loving, who was loved so much'.[10] 'Now, years later, I recognise that there was never a first lady like her. Who committed herself to others, the weakest, those who had nothing.'[11]

The practical intention of the Foundation was not to supplant the state, but rather to provide assistance and necessary infrastructure more rapidly than bureaucratic institutions could do. In this respect, its activities were remarkable, in particular taking into account that Evita herself was to all intents and purposes in sole charge. It had specific departments dedicated to works, administration, social aid and protection, education, tourism and sports, urgent assistance, consumer supplies, agrarian development, housing, and health. According to its statutes, it was to 'provide aid in cash or in kind, grant scholarships [...] construct housing to be adjudicated to indigent families, create and/or construct educational, hospital, recreational [...] establishments [...] construct benevolent establishments of whatever type', to be transferred later to the state.[12] And so it did. Its projects included the construction of five major public hospitals, including a children's hospital in Catamarca province, where medical attention was free, as well as a burns institute, boarding schools for children who were either orphans or indigent, or who lived too far from schools to attend, temporary residences for women in need (one of those institutions is now the Evita Museum in Buenos Aires), a nursing school, and the Home for

Employed Women in Avenida de Mayo, inaugurated in 1949 with luxurious accommodation (decorated with some of the gifts Evita had received in Europe) and two low-cost restaurants. These aimed at protecting women from falling into morally questionable situations and ensuring they were not abused or exploited. At the same time, the Foundation ran holiday facilities in Chapadmalal, near Mar del Plata, and Embalse in Córdoba, which together accommodated up to 35,000 workers and their families in a single season and generated resentment among the classes whose enjoyment of such places was no longer exclusive. It organised children's and young people's football championships in which some 500,000 participated, all of whom received not only sporting equipment but careful medical check-ups, any treatment required and free travel. In the city of Buenos Aires, it constructed Evita's pet project, the Children's City, a miniature city inaugurated in July 1949, which housed up to 300 children. It was followed two years later by the Students' City, which accommodated those who came to the city to study and who had no relatives there, and which aimed to form future leaders.

At a more granular level, the Foundation – specifically Evita – continued to attend to personal petitions and the mandate of seeking 'the recovery of all persons who have fallen into misfortune'.[13] The thousands of requests received every day were read, catalogued and responded to, with either the materials requested, a visit from a social worker or an appointment for an interview with Evita. The Foundation was proud to insist that it did not discriminate against non-Peronists or seek to determine political allegiance before providing aid; in practice it can probably be assumed that convinced anti-Peronists did not petition the Foundation for assistance. Attending to these personal requests and the endless queues of supplicants would become virtually the centre of the remainder of Evita's life, to the extent that she famously often returned to the presidential residence in the dawn hours – sometimes meeting Perón in the doorway as he left for the Casa Rosada. In a bid to avoid disturbing her husband with her irregular hours, Evita moved to a separate bedroom.

In fact, the need to avoid disturbing Perón's rest may have been only a pretext. Evita's health had begun to be cause for concern as early as 1947, and in 1948 she was diagnosed with anaemia and ordered to rest, an order that she ignored. By 1949, her symptoms were evident. According to Vera Pichel, around this time Evita admitted to her that she suffered from vaginal haemorrhaging, and remarked:

why do you think I sleep alone? Because I like it? Saying I don't want
to bother Juan because I come back late is the other way around.
I come back late because I can't be with him, and I can't tell him,
because that would be like confessing that I'm sick.[14]

For a woman who had some years earlier told the same friend that her husband was 'fabulous, strong and tender at the same time. Gentle and careful
[...] Everything is like a festival [...] he notices everything [...] I have a
flower on my pillow every morning',[15] this could only have represented a
sharp change in her married life.

To Vera Pichel and others, Evita insisted that she must continue working and did not have time to look after herself, apparently consumed with
fear that she would not have time to accomplish what she saw as her mission in life. Others noted bluntly that 'Eva killed herself. She always avoided
the doctors despite her blood losses, her swollen ankles and her constant
fevers. From 1950 she had intense pains. She could have been cured and
she didn't want to.'[16] (Her hairdresser, Julio Alcaraz, also confirmed that
she carried cotton wool when she made her frequent tours through the
provinces in order to deal with the haemorrhaging.) Doña Juana herself
had suffered uterine cancer and had been successfully operated on by Dr
Oscar Ivanissevich, the education minister and Evita's doctor; moreover,
the photographer Anne-Marie Heinrich once observed that when her own
mother had a hysterectomy Evita had asked her about her condition with
evident knowledge. Therefore, it must be assumed that she was not ignorant of what her own bleeding might mean. Her way of addressing it –
by ignoring it and continuing to work at a frenetic pace – could be seen
as yet another indication of the courage that she showed throughout her
life. At the same time, it could be seen as a sign that her courage failed
her in this case, and that her fear led her to reject treatment, with tragic
consequences.

Indeed, the long hours dated from the earliest days of Evita's social
aid efforts, even before the Foundation was in full swing. Initially, donations in kind were stored in the garages of the presidential residence,
and after a full day receiving trade union delegations and supplicants she
would return to the residence and prepare care packages in response to
requests. In this she was assisted by her maid Irma Cabrera and by the
steward of the residence, Atilio Renzi, a former military man in charge
of the presidential household who would become an unconditional Evita

loyalist (remarking years later that 'Argentine history, and the fortunes of the workers, would have been different if she had not been the one who died on 26 July 1952. With Eva Perón's death the flame of revolution was extinguished – I think forever.'[17]) Dubbed by Perón *La tienda de las delicias* (the store of delights), the presidential garages became a huge stock room full of foodstuffs, clothing, medicines, mattresses, sewing machines and other necessities, where, according to Renzi, Evita's efforts were somewhat marred by the fact that 'in her enthusiasm, the *Señora* spilled more [sugar] on the floor than she poured into the paper bags'.[18]

Despite the frequent and valid criticism that Evita's work at the Foundation was clientelistic, propagandist and generated dependency among those who came to petition for what she herself insisted were no more than their legitimate rights, it is evident that this was not her prevailing motive. While she herself willingly admitted that she was partisan and 'fanatically' Peronist (not something she considered a negative characteristic), she was convinced in her own mind that she was merely putting into practice the 'social justice' that Peronism preached and that even her full and remarkable energies were insufficient to that end. In her mind there was perhaps no contradiction between the belief that the recipients of that social justice were merely receiving their due, and the fact that that aid brought with it a quota of due gratitude and fealty to the government: from Evita's point of view, both she and the rest of the *descamisados* already owed Perón a debt of gratitude for his efforts to implement social justice, and therefore there was nothing dubious about that gratitude, nor was it tied purely to receipt of a mattress or a sewing machine.

Moreover, she was convinced that in dispensing that social justice, she and Perón contributed to making the recipients less dependent by making them more aspirational. 'I want them to get used to living like the rich [...] Everyone has the right to be rich in this Argentine land.'[19] Like her mother, Evita had never been one to settle for the hand that fate had dealt her, and she believed passionately that the poor should share her upwardly mobile ambitions – this despite her conviction and oft-repeated insistence that the poor were more noble and more human than the rich. As such, when handing over the keys of new homes to her *descamisados*, she exhorted them to look after and cherish the housing that the government and their compatriots had sacrificed so much to give them – both in recognition of that sacrifice and to give the lie to the malicious anti-Peronist gossip. Unarguably, the reality often differed from her perception, as dependence on political patronage became a substitute for personal ambition and effort in many cases. Similarly, the luxurious transit homes aimed to teach the beneficiaries how they could live properly, although their inability to do so thereafter was sometimes felt as a personal failure.[20] Nevertheless, the Peronist government's record (via both the Foundation and state institutions) on public health and education, affordable housing and (non-party political) access to housing credit through the National Mortgage Bank was a strong one, as the number of modern public hospitals and the creation of the National Technological University, a polytechnic providing tertiary education for the children of working-class families, would attest.

In any case, as 1949 wore on, the spectre of Perón's unlimited re-election and the potential of the Foundation as an unparalleled political patronage machine combined to disquiet and alarm the opposition, casting suspicion on the Foundation's activities and prompting accusations, loathing and contempt. Yet while the activities of the Foundation and Evita's own role are open to legitimate criticism, this dismissive 'anti' picture disregards their genuine and remarkable achievements. According to Evita herself, it was created 'to fill gaps in the national organisation […] there are always some to fill and to do that it is necessary to be ready to carry out rapid, direct and effective action'.[21] With that intention, the Foundation built some 1,000 schools across Argentina, later handed over to the state, as well as 18 boarding schools attended by 3,000 poor children.

Her travels across the country, both on proselytising tours and to open Foundation facilities, doubtless opened her eyes to even greater poverty than she had been aware of. As noted earlier, her own origins were poor but not destitute, squalid or malnourished – thanks to Doña Juana's efforts, she and her siblings had regular meals, lived in a clean space and went to school in clean smocks washed and ironed twice a week. Colleagues recalled that the sight of indigent and hungry children in northern Argentina drove Evita to tears, fury and even greater efforts to address the problem virtually single-handed. Although she was sometimes known as 'the woman without tears' for her stoic attitude in the face of personal or social calamities (unlike Perón, who was more sentimental, at least superficially), some injustices wrung them out of her. At the same time, the conviction she inherited from Doña Juana, that it was natural to aspire to better things, was not, whatever she believed, always shared by those whose lives she wanted to improve, although this did not stop her from continuing a virtually solo campaign to instil that desire for progress.

The Amanda Allen Children's City (named for one of the Foundation's nurses, badly injured in a plane crash on returning from an aid mission to Ecuador, and inaugurated in 1949) catered to around 300 poor children, providing a miniature city with parks and plazas (many with names like 'workers' rights' and 'rights of the elderly'), dining areas and cheerfully decorated dormitories. This centrepiece of the Foundation's work – which became an obligatory stop for any illustrious visitor to Buenos Aires, often accompanied by Evita herself – was the focus of objections that went to the heart of criticisms of the Peronist government overall ('it irritated me that they built things so that children saw pretty things, instead of changing the lives of those children'[22]), but was beloved of Evita herself and was perhaps a blueprint of what she felt educational institutions for poor children should be. (Evita's Children's City differed from the so-called 'Children's Republic' constructed by Mercante's government near La Plata, which is still open to visitors today. Not a residential home for children, the Children's Republic was a more fanciful and fairy tale-like construction designed to teach children about the functioning of public institutions.)

A more substantial contribution than the Children's City was the Foundation's work in public health, constructing five polyclinics in the greater Buenos Aires area, as well as in Catamarca, Corrientes, Entre Ríos, Jujuy, Mendoza, Rosario, Salta and Santiago del Estero; it created 15,000 new hospital beds in 1952 alone. It also equipped a 'health train' which spent four months in 1951 crossing the country and providing free health services to remote communities, and constructed children's hospitals in Jujuy and greater Buenos Aires; the ultramodern Children's Hospital in Buenos Aires, which was under construction, was abandoned following the 1955 *coup d'état* (the part-finished building would become a huge slum until it was demolished in the 1990s). Moreover, the nursing schools formerly run by the defunct Sociedad de Beneficencia were combined in 1948 as the María Eva Duarte de Perón Nursing School, run by Evita's friend and close collaborator Teresa Adelina Fiora and incorporated into the Foundation two years later. (After a falling-out, Fiora would later be replaced by Evita's nurse María Eugenia Alvarez.)

By the time of the 1955 coup the nursing school had trained over 850 nurses who worked in the Foundation's medical services, although the increase in Argentina's nursing corps, from 8,000 in 1946 to 18,000 in 1953, was far less than the government's target of 46,000. The Foundation's aid services were not limited to Argentina; it sent material and medical assistance abroad, including to Ecuador, Finland and the United States (rather as Venezuelan President Hugo Chávez would later offer subsidised fuel to poor people in the United States and aid following Hurricane Katrina in 2005). Evita herself was named 'citizen of America' by the Ecuadorian government in recognition of the aid sent following an earthquake there in September 1949. According to one of Evita's nurses, 'she made me comprehend that we must be at the service of others and we should never put our head on the pillow without asking ourselves what we had done that day for our fellows'.[23]

The Foundation also excelled at constructing low-cost housing for working-class families, including 25,000 homes in the new Presidente Perón and Ciudad Evita neighbourhoods of Buenos Aires. Most of these homes tended to be in the 'California mission' style – white chalet bungalows with tiled roofs, which could be constructed fairly rapidly in line with Evita's urgent drive not to waste time. It also would eventually maintain four homes for the elderly, including facilities for work, recreation, socialising and health care. The residents of those workers' neighbourhoods, and others, could also make use of the grocery stores maintained by the Foundation, offering goods at subsidised prices as part of the government's drive to fight rapidly rising inflation. (A number of trade unions also operated their own similar *proveedurías* for their members.) The Foundation would eventually have 181 such retail outlets, most of them in Buenos Aires; although their prime focus was on providing consumer staples at reasonable prices (and with the names of the president and his wife visible all around), they also began to provide some luxury goods for their working-class customers, part of the government's – and Evita's – drive to accustom them to a 'dignified standard of living'. As the Peronist slogan invented by Raúl Apold ran, 'Perón fulfils, Evita dignifies' (*Perón cumple, Evita dignifica*).

Another stellar project, the General San Martín Working Women's Home in Avenida de Mayo (which runs between the Congress building and the Casa Rosada), was, like the Children's City, one of Evita's particular passions – doubtless, as many have noted, because it provided the sort of safe and comfortable accommodation she would have desperately yearned for during her difficult early years in Buenos Aires. With space for 500 residents, it also became a sort of refuge for Evita in the early 1950s and she often ate in one of its two restaurants late at night after she had finished a long day at the Secretariat. (The building that was to be constructed as the Foundation's permanent home was not completed until after her death, and is now the Engineering Faculty of the University of Buenos Aires.) There she was often accompanied by friends and colleagues, as well as residents and a group of young writers and poets who for a time formed the Eva Perón *peña* (literally, a folk club), where they composed poems and other works in her honour.

The group reportedly started informally when Evita invited José Castiñeira de Dios, a rising young poet who had been named under-secretary of culture, to come along to the Foundation on the grounds that it would do him good, joking that he was 'a bit oligarch'. While there, he attempted to stop a young woman with a syphilitic sore on her mouth from kissing Evita, which earned him a sharp reprimand. So impressed was he at Evita's willingness to receive the woman's kiss that he was inspired to write a poem to her called *Alabanza* (Praise), which she invited him to come along and read at one of her dinners at the Working Women's home. The *peña*, which met perhaps a dozen times, included later famous writers such as Fermín Chávez and Castiñeira de Dios, although Evita was also often accompanied by trade unionists, whom she arguably felt greater affinity with than the 'intellectuals', of whom she always harboured some distrust. Chávez would later recall:

> the Eva Perón I knew was happy, spontaneous, without artifice, what impressed was her vitality, her nervous walk, her extraordinary memory [...] At the meals more than once we saw her quick natural intelligence and the common sense with which she could overwhelm us.[24]

Here, and perhaps only here, she would relax, laughing, joking and gossiping as well as discussing politics and social welfare – perhaps reverting to an earlier part of her life when responsibility for the welfare of an entire nation did not rest on her shoulders, and offering a glimpse of a relaxed young woman rather than the tense, and intense, figure constantly in the public eye.

During long and exhausting afternoons, Evita would receive petitioners in her office, usually resolving their requests expeditiously. However, arriving as far as her imposing desk was a complex process. Of the many thousands of letters received by the Foundation every day, all were catalogued and some responses dispatched. Social workers would often be sent to determine the needs of the supplicants, and appointments would be given for them to be received by Evita at the Secretariat. Even with an appointment, however, the wait could last for hours (or more), given frequent interruptions as she met visiting delegations or fulfilled other duties as First Lady. However, once she received the petitioner, her attention to them and their needs was total. Arguably this was not the most efficient means of dealing with problems that could have been addressed by teams of employees and home visits, and would provide ammunition to those who accused her of crude clientelism. However, while this level of personalism may legitimately be criticised, it should be borne in mind that Evita was herself convinced of the need for a personal touch, to demonstrate to the poor that an individual, the First Lady, cared about them, and not simply a faceless government department.

Evita's days at the Foundation began early (although she often began receiving delegations at the presidential residence, even before starting her day's work there). After a cursory breakfast she would take her place behind her desk at the Foundation and, apparently oblivious to the noise and smells inevitably associated with a crush of people and their small children (something which many of her illustrious visitors found less tolerable), she would receive, listen, take notes, give instructions to secretaries or make phone calls to ministries, and problems would be addressed – whether a request for a job, a mattress, false teeth, a home, a bicycle or the ineluctable sewing machine.

As Castiñeira de Dios noted, she was also apparently impervious to the health risks or disagreeable quality attached to being embraced by supplicants often suffering from communicable diseases. Her maid, Irma Cabrera, also recalled:

> one day, when she was kissing a woman with sores, I brought her some alcohol so she could disinfect herself with some cotton. She wanted to kill me! It was the only time she got angry with me. She threw the bottle against the wall.[25]

On another occasion, when a woman with symptoms of leprosy gave her a kiss, the diplomat in charge of ceremony for the presidency took out his handkerchief to wipe her cheek, only to be attacked by a furious Evita who said 'don't touch me, you son of a bitch. On top of everything else you want to humiliate this poor woman?'[26]

The personal problems resolved by Evita in her office were manifold and sometimes bizarre – including, on one occasion, phoning a minister in the middle of the night to demand that he obtain a horse and milk cart for an immigrant milkman whose own had been stolen. Nor did Evita forget the more immediate problems faced by her visitors. She always asked whether they had a means of getting home, and usually supplied some cash to ensure that they did. On some occasions, she ordered her chauffeur to take them home in her own car, which sometimes meant that her car had not yet returned from a distant destination when she left the office after midnight and that she had to take a taxi. If her supply of banknotes ran out, she would turn to the ministers, secretaries and illustrious visitors in her office and ask for the contents of their wallets. (Nor was she fooled when some of her targets, knowing of this risk, hid their bankroll in a back pocket – more than once she told a hapless visitor that she wanted the thick wallet in his trouser pocket and not the meagre one he had pulled from his jacket.) These days of endless scrimmage in her office usually ended well after midnight, when she would return to the residence – often after a dinner with her friends at her haven in the Working Womens' Home – just as her husband was leaving to start his own day.

At least in the early days of the Foundation, Evita would often leave at midday and collect Perón from the Casa Rosada in order to have lunch at the residence together. However, as the pace of her activity gathered speed, those lunches became a thing of the past, and she would nibble on a sandwich and a glass of juice at her desk. The weekends at San Vicente were also largely suspended; on the rare occasions when they went, Evita would fret over her enforced inactivity and chafe at Perón's ban on the use of the telephone, often hiding herself away to make phone calls and give instructions. This was a far cry from the early days of their relationship, when they would relax, prepare steak and salad and sometimes share meals and conversations with friends like the Guardos, the Mercantes or Father Benítez. Occasionally she would make a point of taking time out of her schedule to watch a film with Perón at the residence, but even this appeared to Evita to be wasting valuable time that was needed for greater things. She was frequently heard to lament that 'I'm only sorry that the day only has 24 hours and despite my intense activity I can't be everywhere',[27] although in practice her attempt to do so was remarkable.

The state of the private relationship between Perón and Evita at this stage can only be conjectured, but while it was still apparently characterised by mutual respect and affection, it was scarcely intimate in any sense of the word. Perón would later recall that, when he pointed out to her that she was his wife and must take care of herself, she replied that her work and her care of the *descamisados* was her way of feeling, and demonstrating, that she was his wife. Regardless of this, Perón would sometimes remark, both at the time and later, that he felt he had lost his wife. A disciplined man of regular habits, Perón himself was known for his energy and for working longer hours than his predecessors in the presidency, arriving at his desk at the Casa Rosada at 7.00 every morning. However, his energies paled in comparison with Evita's driven pace, and his early-to-bed, early-to-rise habits had little in common with her hectic and unpredictable schedule, in which she tried to encompass every possible duty, whether ceremonial or private, travelling through the provinces, opening schools, hospitals and trade union facilities, giving speeches and attending conferences.

Arguably one of the few times when the presidential couple still spent time together was at state functions and galas, when Evita took on the role of 'Eva Perón'. There, she herself put aside her classic, sober working wardrobe and became glamour personified in Dior ballgowns (something that she herself admitted that she loved, one of the few frivolities she still permitted herself). Film star beautiful and elegant, she was a radiant presence at formal events, with an elegance that the society matrons who despised her could not match. Photos of these events were guaranteed to boost sales of magazines and newspapers (especially her own *Democracia*) that printed them. Perón in his dress uniform and Evita in her Dior gown made a striking couple, more elegant in appearance than much royalty and a presidential image that their supporters could be proud of. Dior himself supposedly once remarked that the only queen he had dressed was Eva Perón.

While Evita clearly enjoyed her gala wardrobe and jewels, she was less enamoured of many of the gala events she was forced to attend, given her impatience with anything that took her away from her work and her lack of interest in classical music. When asked in an interview during her 'Rainbow Tour' what her favourite musical pieces were, she had replied 'the shortest', while her erstwhile designer Paco Jamandreu would recall seeing her dressed for a gala at the Teatro Colón and eating a plate of fried eggs, saying that she could not face the opera on an empty stomach. Nevertheless, despite the number of photos still extant of Evita in gala dress, these occasions were relatively infrequent compared to her political and social action work; many photos have survived given the number of copies always sold of publications including those photos, but in fact the first couple's formal appearances were comparatively few, with both preferring other aspects of their role and neither much given to protocol and high society for their own sake.

Her long hours at the Foundation and formal appearances as first lady did not cause Evita to neglect her public speaking and trade union commitments. Volume II of her complete speeches quotes five public speeches (largely to trade unions) in January 1949 and seven in May (including the Labour Day festivities and speeches in Rosario, Santiago del Estero and Chaco, and not including related activities such as the Queen of Labour contest). In July there were five such speeches, and seven more in November, in addition to other scattered interventions and, of course, her speech on 17 October. The speeches are largely similar in the themes they touch on, including the need to increase production even at the cost of sacrifice due to moral obligations to the workers and General Perón (and, not least, to ward off the latent threat still posed by communists and capitalists). They note that, despite being a 'simple woman', she has chosen to work long hours for the benefit of Perón's people, and reiterate that

> I have only been the bridge I want to be between the workers and the General […] For that reason I want you to continue to see Evita as your *compañera* at all times, but especially in bad times. I want to be, as I said years ago, *compañera* Evita before being the wife of the president, if thus I can help to calm any pain in any home in my country.[28]
>
> I want to continue to be the *compañera* of the humble and the workers, the Lady of Hope, as the humble of my country have affectionately called me, if I can thus bring happiness to workers' homes.[29]
>
> Remember that *compañera* Evita has three ideals for which she is willing to die: the fatherland, Perón and the *descamisados*.[30]

These speeches are repetitive (as are the speaker's cadences), reminding listeners of her own devotion and Perón's constant concern for the workers, a litany that drove home the central themes of Peronism, and Evita's central role in it, to their supporters. While to other ears the discourse may sound melodramatic or patronising – or even reminiscent of Lina Lamont, the dim-witted silent film star in *Singing in the Rain* who tells her fans that 'if we bring a little joy into your humdrum lives, it makes us feel our that hard work ain't been in vain for nothing' – it must be borne in mind that the perception of its intended audience was quite different. British Ambassador John Balfour noted somewhat caustically, but not inaccurately, that:

> the vaudeville technique of the Señora – herself the embodiment of Latin American adolescence – exercises a strong emotional appeal on those numerous sections of her compatriots whom she has, as it were, promoted from the pit to seats of unaccustomed privilege in the stalls.[31]

For the believers, it represented a reassurance that the government had a face, and one that cared, for the first time, while even the repetitive quality was reassuring in the way of a frequently told story. Moreover, although melodramatic, the narrative was truthful – Evita's endless hours at the Foundation, her constant presence and her obsessive concern with her *descamisados* bore it out.

In August 1949 her interventions included opening and closing remarks at the Inter-American Commission of Women, which met in Buenos Aires. In her opening speech, Evita focused her message on peace:

> international peace will be possible only when internal peace in all nations of the world has been achieved and consolidated [...] Internal and international peace, peace through social justice, the brotherhood of nations and the happiness of its peoples are the fundamental principles that His Excellency President General Juan D. Perón applies in this region of the world that Providence baptised as the Argentine Republic.[32]

She called on delegates 'to work to achieve internal peace through annulling capitalist and totalitarian extremisms, whether of the right or left' and 'to work to achieve international peace on the basis of leaving aside antagonistic ideologies'.[33]

In her closing remarks the following day, Evita referred to 'the effort of will of all women to find solutions that lead to concrete and tangible advances in women's civil, political, economic and social rights',[34] although her more feminist statements were somewhat diluted by the usual constant references to Perón as the maximum leader of the cause. While her discourse had a predictable note of partisan propaganda, her call for political and social action and education designed to 'elevate social culture, dignify labour and humanise capital and, especially replace systems of struggle with one of collaboration' gained support among many delegates. The head of the Commission, the Mexican Amalia Castillo Lebón, would later note that:

> Sra María Eva Duarte de Perón definitively won me over to her cause, because charity when it reaches the level of integral human assistance [...] is something superior that we women feel, because we are women and no one can deny us the privilege of having our heart in the right place, always.[35]

Perhaps most forward-looking was her comment that the Peronist aim was 'for others to join the [...] Third World struggle, which must include, fundamentally, the active and lucid participation of the woman.[36]

Within an astonishingly short period of some 18 months from its formal beginning, the Foundation had become a force to be reckoned with by the end of 1949, in terms of both propaganda and its very real contribution to social welfare in the form of health care and education. It also contributed to expand other programmes already launched under the first Perón government, including the construction of vacation colonies for children and for working-class families who now enjoyed the right to paid holidays. Moreover, its founder had become a central figure, both for the Foundation and for the government, whose presence was indispensable for a range of public activities and often risked eclipsing that of her husband. This period, just before the post-war boom and Evita's own health began to weaken, was the apogee of the Peronist administration and the key to its political and emotional legacy.

However, as noted earlier, Evita's high profile and inescapable presence represented both a boost and a risk for Perón, with her obvious power and intervention in a broad range of activities raising suspicions, fears, loathing and alarm within the military and other powerful sectors. As early as 1947, the British Embassy had noted that 'Perón's weakness of character and [...] the great influence of his wife' were key factors in the army's loathing of the first lady, while in 1950 the ambassador remarked that 'I imagine that she is more dangerous to the regime than he. By himself, he might manage to pursue a fairly sensible and resolute course.'[37] Debates (however clandestine) were rife as to whether Perón exploited his wife or whether she dominated him – the latter notion one that weakened his supposed 'masculine authority' and allowed Evita to be pilloried as 'masculine'. While many who knew them, including Father Benítez, rejected any suggestion of bad behaviour or disrespect between the presidential couple, the image of Perón as a 'wimp' dominated by his wife was a caricature that the anti-Peronists used to advantage.

Whatever the truth of this, Evita's activities in the public sphere went far beyond what was associated with women at the time, giving them a masculine edge despite the obviously maternal spin she placed on them. However controversial those activities were, her legacy from these years does include a greater acceptance of women in roles of social and political responsibility (albeit also creating a mould and an example for those activities which has yet to be fully broken). That legacy would survive, despite efforts to expunge Evita from history and despite the real (if unintended) difficulties that that force of nature would soon create for her husband.

CHAPTER 13

Mortality

O N 2 JANUARY 1950, Evita received a formal expression of gratitude
from Pope Pius XII for the Foundation's humanitarian assistance.
A week later, on 9 January, while participating in the opening of a new
office of the taxi drivers' union, she unexpectedly fainted. Present was the
education minister, Oscar Ivanissevich, who was also the personal physician to the president and his wife. Following her transfer to the presidential
residence, Ivanissevich proposed to carry out a more thorough examination, given that, as noted earlier, she had already suffered from pains,
swollen ankles and other symptoms for some time, despite her efforts to
conceal them. These had not become publicly known; as Borroni and Vacca
observed, her frequent bouts of ill health had previously been defined as
anaemia, angina, flu or exhaustion, and on this occasion the excessive summer heat was given as the reason for her collapse.[1] In this case, the media
published nothing about her condition for several days, and in the meantime Ivanissevich prevailed upon Perón to insist that she be hospitalised
three days later. The doctor subsequently issued a statement saying that
she had been operated on for 'acute appendicitis, without complications'.
However, Ivanissevich realised that her appendix was not the cause of her
pains, and at least suspected that the problem was an entirely different and
more dangerous one, supposedly recommending a hysterectomy.

On 13 January, the Sub-Secretariat of Information confirmed that
her health 'had not been encouraging' for some time, but that she had
insisted on carrying on with her work, and that her recent surgery would
now require her 'temporary withdrawal from her functions', although
'*Señora* Perón did not want to abandon, for a single instant, the attention

to thousands of problems, big and small, of the unions, the humble people who come to her seeking help. The insistence of General Perón himself became necessary.'[2]

When exactly Perón was informed that Evita might be suffering from the same cancer that killed his first wife is disputed, though at this stage he appears to have limited himself to encouraging her to rest, rather than insisting on a surgical intervention. Although Perón himself would later refer to the 'anaemia' she suffered from 1949 onwards, and there are suggestions that Ivanissevich told him of his suspicions in early 1950, other sources claim he was only informed in September 1951, after she had had her first full examination. At that point, he apparently acknowledged that he had guessed the truth, remarking that 'Eva represents something very important as wife, companion, friend, counsellor and a point of loyal support in the struggle I am engaged in'.[3]

The news of Evita's surgery prompted strong shows of sympathy and support in the press and in public demonstrations. Evita refused, however, to listen to Ivanissevich's urgings that she have further examinations and possibly surgery; indeed, she reportedly struck him in the face with her handbag and accused him of plotting to sideline her from politics. Ivanissevich would resign as education minister shortly thereafter, in May 1950, replaced by Armando Méndez San Martín, former director of social assistance within the Secretariat of Labour and director general of the Foundation. The doctor himself would later say in 1967 that 'she could have saved her life, if she had listened to me: her mother had the same disease and is still alive. Unconsciously, she committed suicide.'[4] This is possible, although even this diagnosis may be optimistic given the level of cancer treatment available at the time, and the fact that she was young and the cancer might have been expected to advance relatively rapidly – in particular if she had in fact been experiencing symptoms for a year or more when Ivanissevich examined her. In any case, her own temperament and the times she lived in were not on her side: unwilling to slow down and perhaps believing that she would overcome or that 'it could not happen to her', she also came from a generation that did not benefit from the most advanced of cancer treatments, as well as one for which the loss of a womb was a deep psychological blow for most women. Evita may perhaps still have harboured the hope of having a child with Perón, or she may have felt on some level that the loss of her capacity to be a mother, for someone seen symbolically as a mother figure by millions of Argentines, was impossible to contemplate.

Despite already persistent rumours concerning her health, Evita's will-power and histrionic skills would continue to carry her for some time. The Spanish doctor Pedro Ara, who would eventually embalm her emaciated body in July 1952, noted that he had occasion to stand near her on the balcony of the Casa Rosada during a speech during this period and that he had focused his attention on trying to discern whether the claims of severe anaemia were true. According to Ara, such a condition would cause her to weary and to suffer from shortness of breath, and force her to take rests during her speech. However, he noted that not only was she 'agile' and active both before and after, but that her speech was delivered with both great skill and energy:

> not only did she show no signs of fatigue, but with voice and gestures she begged the crowd not to interrupt. And the paragraphs kept following, ever more emphatic and violent [...] We can't doubt now that her anaemia was real. How did the *señora* overcome it? Where did such a fragile woman find the strength and breath for her stentorian speech?[5]

Nevertheless, at least some premonition that things were worse than they appeared was already present: many of the poems and other writings in 1950 by the group that formed her Peña Eva Perón contained ominous notes despite her apparent vigour. Fermín Chávez would write '*Señora*, so exquisite and illuminated, stay here with us', while Gregorio Santos Hernando referred to her as the '*señora*, among the angels, who keeps watch over us' and José María Castiñeira de Dios said 'in a prophecy that still seems inexplicable to me, "but your voice will not die, *Señora*".'[6]

Evita returned to the residence on 14 January following her operation, and was required to remain there for two weeks afterward, although this did not stop her from receiving a trade union delegation on the 25th and a visit from the racing driver Juan Manuel Fangio. She was forced to miss the official inauguration of the Working Women's Home in Avenida de Mayo on the 17th. Two weeks later she was back at her office, receiving union delegates, cabinet members and representatives of the PPF. In early February the presidential couple travelled by yacht to the city of San Lorenzo for one of the year-long ceremonies commemorating the 100th anniversary of General José de San Martín, the Liberator, who died on 17 August 1850. These ceremonies would require frequent travels across the country, interrupted only briefly by Ivanessivich's insistence that she rest, which halted her pre-election visits to the provinces for a few weeks in March. By the middle of the month her usual frenetic activity had restarted, as she justified her demented pace by insisting that her time was short to accomplish all she felt was her 'mission in life'. Whether this furious pace and impetuosity was due to the foreboding that she had only a short time to live, as some have claimed, or whether it reflected her youth – Evita was only 30 at the time – is an open question.

In those days alone, she opened the finals of the 'Evita youth championships', the national football tournament that brought thousands of children across the country physical training and medical attention; received several visiting delegations from the United States; presented the keys to over 400 houses built by the Foundation in the Saavedra neighbourhood of Buenos Aires (warning the new residents to take good care of them); and inaugurated the 'Rights of the Elderly Park' on lands confiscated from the Pereyra Iraola family in payment of back taxes. Perón himself would say 'I practically lost my wife. We saw each other occasionally and briefly, as if we lived in two different cities.'[7] From late March she visited Paraná, in Entre Ríos province, Rosario, San Juan, Tucumán, Jujuy and Catamarca, accompanied by her new secretary, Emma Nicolini, and inaugurated schools and other Foundation institutions in the latter three. On 11 July of that year, she finished working at the Foundation at 5.00 in the morning, a 'personal best'. In Rosario she delivered seven speeches in two days, maintaining this furious pace until October, when she was persuaded to rest for a few days in San Vicente. Throughout, she insisted that nothing was wrong with her, that she would not have surgery, and that she was too busy for medical treatment. 'I don't have time, treatments are for oligarchs, for people who don't work. My "*grasitas*" can't wait anymore, they've already waited too long.'[8]

Following a lunch with Evita in mid-1950, British ambassador John Balfour observed that 'all the symptoms are present of a fatal preoccupation', although he recognised that 'it is also true that Sra Perón has been largely responsible for making the welfare of the workers a foremost preoccupation of the state.' 'Thanks to her activities […] the status of the hitherto under-privileged masses in the community now appears to be such as to preclude a return to the laissez-faire attitude of earlier Argentine governments.' Those activities, however, continued to give rise to considerable misgivings in both Washington and the armed forces. Balfour quotes a contact acquainted with the presidential couple as remarking that Perón and Evita together 'were something, and apart they were nothing. You could see the change come over them when they met or separated.' The same source remarked that 'if the moment came when the General had to choose between the people and the Army, and chose the Army, he would remove her and she, for her part, would declare herself communist and lead an insurrection against him.'⁹ This is not credible on any level, given the fact that Evita's tremendous power was informal and non-institutional and still depended on Perón (for whom she still clearly felt great love and loyalty), despite the supposed weight of some of her backers and the 'Duarte group' composed of her siblings and their husbands – which also had influence but lacked weight in government except through her own power. However implausible, though, this was a perception that spelled a threat to vested interests already ill-disposed towards the intractable first lady.

In practice, it is difficult to construe Evita as a 'communist', as opposed to a 'revolutionary'; the latter description would appear more apposite. She herself would say 'I think I was born for the Revolution. I have always lived in freedom', although she admitted 'I like "disorder", as if disorder were my natural medium.'¹⁰ Even this set her apart from her husband and could have become a point of increasing friction had she lived; Perón was no revolutionary but an inherently somewhat conservative reformist who disliked disorder and believed that greater equality and a modicum of social reform were the most effective way of avoiding revolution. Moreover, as she herself said to the British ambassador on one occasion, 'I love a fight. If there were no fight I would have to invent one.'¹¹ That fighting quality, no doubt honed during a difficult youth in which little was given and everything was struggled for, stood her in good stead as a survivor and as a leader, but it did not make for harmonious social relations.

Although she described herself as not being a 'candle licker', Evita was unquestionably informed on all levels by a traditional Catholic culture, and her warnings against 'demagogic' communism that 'links the slavery of the workers to a super-production obtained through extremely low pay for workers' were as frequent as her warnings against 'the exploitation of capitalist imperialism'.¹² Father Hernán Benítez (himself a somewhat narcissistic personality who rarely missed an opportunity to point out his own influence) would note that the Foundation's installations all had their own chapel, at Evita's insistence, as well as a staff of religious workers under his authority as the Foundation's spiritual adviser. However, Evita's highly public form of dispensing social justice was anathema to the Catholic concept of performing charitable acts discreetly, while some of the aid organisations that 'competed' with the Foundation were under Church auspices – not only the defunct Sociedad de Beneficencia, but also Monsignor Miguel De Andrea's Federation of Catholic Working Women's Associations, founded in 1923, and his Working Women's Home in Buenos Aires. Moreover, her lower-class and unorthodox background were also anathema to much of the practising Catholic community, usually well-off, and distressed by an illegitimate, former actress of ill repute and with a dockworker's vocabulary. Whatever the dose of hypocrisy and double standards involved here, doubtless much of the criticism of Evita's divisive, clientelistic and exclusive takeover of 'social justice' was valid and justifiable, although the notion of her 'communism' was far-fetched.

By this time it was clear that Perón was the sole political figure in Argentina possibly more important than this unelected first lady with no official post, limited education and (until the 1951 elections made women's enfranchisement a reality for the first time) no vote. She was even more often in the public eye than her husband, making a constant round of visits, speeches, tours of the Foundation's achievements with illustrious visitors and travels up and down the country. Even as early as 1948, it was 'noticeable that in the mural propaganda at the moment Evita figures as the patroness, to the complete exclusion of Perón'.[13] Her role with the trade unions was greater than Perón's, now that he was a full-time president and she his delegate (or 'providence', as he described it), as was her contact with the *descamisado* support base. The labour minister, Ramón Freire, and the leader of the CGT, José Espejo, were both bland and subservient figures, easily overshadowed, which gave her even greater leadership over the union base. Moreover, she was on the superior council of the Peronist Party and would become one of the key figures at the Superior Peronist School founded in 1951 to train Peronist cadres, where among other things she taught the history of Peronism (relatively brief at the time, but one in which she had had a privileged position almost from its inception).

If further evidence were required, from this period party meetings and rallies now included the singing of 'Las muchachas peronistas' following the 'Marcha peronista'. And, with her brother as the president's personal secretary and her family ties within ministries and Congress (not to mention unshakeable Evita loyalists like communications minister Oscar

Nicolini, whose daughter Emma replaced Isabel Ernst as Evita's secretary, and Lower House leader Héctor Cámpora), she also had direct leverage over policy-making and the president's agenda, which she could easily monitor. The supposed clashes between the 'Duarte group' and the 'Perón group' (to a large degree made up of former military colleagues) were a factor in undermining Perón's influence in the army, the other initial pillar of his support, and the only one that remained outside Evita's direct influence and hostile to her presence. Other sectors such as the social elites were, by definition, not by and large Peronist and her influence there was minimal. With Mercante sidelined, there was no other figure but the president himself who, in theory at least, had greater authority.

As noted earlier, it remains remarkable that Perón had allowed her to assume so much power, possibly unwittingly to some degree, and unclear what his motivations were. Almost certainly he had no idea of the reach she would attain, and presumably he was aware that his own position still imposed some limitations – perhaps to some degree it was simply the case that, given their age difference, he was initially inclined to indulge his young wife. However, the fact that an indulged young woman was able to use her husband's position to extend her own power so far (and to control, through the Foundation, such vast resources) sat ill with the army and with many sectors of society – not exclusively the elites, and not exclusively without reason. Her power was vast and often used arbitrarily; according to one opposition leader, 'the totalitarian government put powers of coercion, violence and threat in the arbitrary and capricious hands of the wife of the president, who imposed "spontaneous" contributions on people, companies, capitalist institutions, workers, etc.'[14]

While, as noted earlier, many of those supposedly coerced contributions were not begrudged, either out of genuine enthusiasm or because the contributors anticipated some benefit in return, there is justice in these criticisms, however much the Foundation may have done with the money – not least given that, through the government's generosity to the Foundation, Evita also had control over the lands of the Pereyra Iraola family and huge back taxes from the Bemberg family, two oligarchic institutions where a strong degree of revenge might be suspected. In particular, the Bembergs were claimed to have circulated photos of a scantily clad Evita from her hungry theatrical days during her European visit, some of which came, not accidentally, into the Pope's hands shortly before her visit. Moreover, the loathing was mutual: her vindictiveness reportedly extended to having oligarchic women protesters against the government locked up with prosti-tutes. However justified many of the criticisms, though, it is difficult not to agree with Evita that she was an easier target for vitriol than her husband, by virtue of her gender, social class and lack of official position – 'they fire at me to avoid firing directly at Perón'.[15]

The year 1950 was not only the 'year of the Liberator', as announced on newspaper mastheads throughout the year, but also the year in which Peronist doctrine would come to be codified, a process in which Evita was also central. In addition to the international 'Third Position' already artic-ulated in 1947, at the time of Evita's European tour, and the 'organised community' launched in 1949 (which aimed to set out moral absolutes that would be marked out and imposed by a Peronist state), on 17 October 1950 the 'Twenty Truths of *Justicialismo*' (the distortion of 'social justice' that became the official title of the Peronist Party) were announced. While stating (somewhat inaccurately, as it would later prove), that 'for a Peronist there is nothing better than another Peronist', these also set forth, as if stressing Evita's part in the process, that 'the two arms of Peronism are social justice and social aid. With them we give the people an embrace of justice and love.'[16]

The Twenty Truths also stressed that '*Justicialismo* is a new phil-osophy of life, simple, practical, popular, profoundly Christian and pro-foundly human'.[17] This sort of statement, and the claim that *Justicialismo* was 'a doctrine whose object is the happiness of man within the society of mankind through the harmonising of material, spiritual, individual and collective forces',[18] suggest that Father Benítez's claims to influence over the presidential couple's thinking were not wholly exaggerated, and make it highly questionable that claims of Evita's 'communism' could have been taken seriously. Indeed, if anything, the Catholic Church's qualms about her appear to have stemmed more from this sort of co-opting of the Church's social doctrine, ostensibly for Peronist political purposes, rather than any real belief that she was atheist or Marxist. On the contrary, her social work won her plaudits from many Catholic authorities; by contrast, her tendency to use religious imagery and rhetoric that helped to 'bring the workers back to God' and, indeed, often cast Perón as a quasi-deity, were far more of an issue than any supposed communist sympathies. (Remarks such as 'Perón is the face of God in the darkness' were far more disturbing to the Church than any supposed embrace of foreign atheist beliefs on Evita's part.[19]) Moreover, if Perón was given somewhat divine status, the subliminal casting of Evita in the role of the Mother of God was difficult to disregard. The fact that Perón and Evita decided, at the last minute, to attend the closing session of the National Eucharistic Congress in Rosario on 29 October seemed to point to some effort to repair relations with the Church, and indeed the Pope's delegate then accompanied Evita to visit some of the Foundation's works, saying to *Democracia* before his departure that 'Señora Eva Perón's social work is extraordinary and I do not believe this can be denied'.[20]

Perhaps recognising Evita's increasingly fragile state of health, Perón also paid tribute on this 17 October to her outstanding contribution to the Peronist cause. Perón was not, as he himself recognised, especially effusive in his praise of others, but on this occasion he ended his speech by saying:

> So that the humble sons of this land have a permanent refuge in their pain and necessity, I have left my wife in my old and beloved Secretariat of Labour and Welfare, because I know she loves you as I do and maybe more than she loves me. My gratitude cannot omit to name this woman that you and I call by the same name: Evita. If I make my gratitude public today it's only because I know that you would not forgive me if I failed to do so.[21]

Thereafter, CGT leader José Espejo awarded her a necklace symbolising the Distinction of Recognition, a decoration invented by the unions in honour of Evita. Evita, the 'woman without tears', wept in public, in Perón's arms, for the first time in her life, describing it as 'one of the most intense emotions of my life. I will never forget this moment.'[22] Her speech then went on to detail very precisely the government's achievements in terms of social justice, most of which – the Children's City, the social housing, the temporary homes, the holiday hotels for workers – were in fact the work of the Foundation and of Evita herself.

The political significance of the year 1950 was marked not only by the illness of Evita and the anniversary of General San Martín, but also by two important and potentially clashing imperatives: the deterioration of the economic panorama and the looming presidential elections, in which Perón was no longer constitutionally banned from standing. In both of these imperatives, Evita had a crucial role to play. The economic deterioration from 1949 increased military dissatisfaction and impatience with

Evita in particular, but at the same time her strength with the trade unions made her key to government efforts to encourage greater output.

On the economic front, the government was in part a victim of its own success in Perón's strategy of boosting real wages and domestic consumption. In the first three years of Perón's government, real wages rose by an average of around a third, while gross domestic product expanded by a similar percentage and salaried workers rose to some 55 per cent of the workforce. With labour's share of gross domestic product rising and the average working week becoming shorter, consumption reached unprecedented levels as even working-class employees were able to increase their purchases of food, clothing, entertainments, leisure activities and consumer durables – notably radios, which became almost universal and offered an unparalleled channel for government propaganda, not least given Evita's experience and efficacy in the use of the 'ether'. Despite Evita's frequent exhortations to increase production (from April 1951 she would institute prizes for production records), output was lagging demand, with consequences for both scarcity-driven inflation and the trade balance, as greater domestic consumption of beef, wheat and other foodstuffs reduced the exportable surplus.

Moreover, the government's efforts to bring exports under central state control through the creation of the Institute for the Promotion of Trade (IAPI) had proved a disincentive for the agricultural sector (most of it dominated by anti-Peronist landed elites) to increase production, while the government's focus on developing industry (primarily import substitution through domestic production of consumer goods) had in any case reduced the resources directed to agriculture. Agricultural output was further damaged by drought in 1949 and again in 1951 and 1952, and export options were in any case limited by recovery in the United States and Europe, and the fact that Marshall Plan aid could not be used to purchase from Argentina.

At the same time, the government's early largesse in nationalising foreign-owned services such as railways and telecommunications was in part designed to flaunt Argentina's post-war wealth (the Central Bank's corridors were said to be clogged with gold bars), but those services required heavy investment and did little to generate new revenues, rapidly reducing gold reserves. In 1950 the British ambassador noted that 'it seems to me that policy in this country proceeds from a kind of drunkenness of the psyche',[23] which was perhaps a kind of 'drunkenness' of riches that appeared limitless. This also related to Perón's own calculation that the United States and Soviet Union would soon launch a third world war that would again place Argentina in the position of supplying food to the world. By 1949, reserves were down by more than half when compared with 1945, exports were declining and 'economic czar' Miguel Miranda had been dropped from the cabinet after failing to create the anticipated economic miracle.

Although workers' economic position remained largely better than a decade earlier, the worsening outlook and rising inflation led to concern and labour tensions; efforts by the Foundation to combat inflation both through its own subsidised stores and through consumer vigilance and denunciations of retailers raising their prices, which led to fines and closures, failed to contain the rise. In 1950 the government began to prepare a new, second Five-Year Plan (adducing that the first had been successfully completed a year early), a far more austere one than its 'drunken' predecessor. This in itself was an ominous sign coming into general elections.

Although labour disputes were already on the increase, the first serious challenge from the unions came from the railway workers of the Roca passenger line, who began a strike in late 1950 in support of demands for higher wages. This rapidly spread to the rest of the railway workers, and the Unión Ferroviaria declared a general strike on 7 January 1951, which was declared illegal by the government, with the support of the official CGT. This challenge came despite the longstanding close tie between the railway workers and the Peronist government, due in large part to Mercante's family connections to both railway unions, but also to the nationalisation of the railways in 1949. It also aroused Evita's wrath, leading her to accuse the union's leaders of treason, communism, infiltration and egoism. Certain of her weight with the workers themselves, she travelled extensively across the railway network, urging them to return to work on the grounds that they were providing grist to the opposition's mill and were selfishly forgetting all that Perón had done for them. The striking workers protested in vain that the action was not directed against her or the government, but rather in support of legitimate demands. The failure to lift the strike led to the resignation of the transport minister and the temporary militarisation of the railway services – and to Evita's first defeat in dealing with 'her' workers.

This was not a minor issue. Already ill, in pain and increasingly frustrated at the limitations of her own mortality, Evita could not but see the strike as a personal affront to herself and her husband. As Felipe Pigna correctly notes, she was fully convinced both of the undisputable superiority of Perón's 'New Argentina' and of her own personal influence over, and ability to interpret the desires of, the working class. However, these absolutes were called into question by labour disputes, and indeed by the rising militancy of an increasingly unionised workforce, becoming less willing to accept only what was given, regardless of the majority's sincere admiration for both Perón and Evita (the subject of genuine affection as well as admiration and respect). Her 'failure' also highlighted the limitations of her non-institutional authority: although her personal influence with the unions remained high, it was Perón who was able to end the strike by declaring it illegal and calling in the military (though in the end the wage demands were conceded).

It may hardly be surprising that her public discourse would become increasingly vehement, violent and aggressive; the more maternal tone of her earlier speeches largely disappeared in favour of the violently sectarian harangues for which she is more widely remembered. 'Whereas in private talks she gives an impression of engaging shyness and talks with a soft voice, her manner as a public speaker is hard and uncompromising and her eyes take on a beady look.'[24] These increasingly 'vindictive appeals to class hatred'[25] also did nothing to reassure either the Church or the armed forces, both of them with strong links to the wealthier classes as well as a vested interest in avoiding social disorder and class war. However, the increasingly frequent references to her willingness to die for her *descamisados* or to leave 'shreds of her life' on the road, and her invitation to the poor to use her body as a 'bridge' to pass over to a better Peronist future, referred less and less to an allegorical image and more and more to a painful reality.

Against this less than ideal panorama, it was determined that the presidential elections due for February 1952 should be brought forward to November 1951. Following the constitutional reform, there was no mystery about who would be the government's presidential candidate, but the vice-presidential post was more uncertain. The elderly Radical Hortensio Quijano, who had been Perón's running mate in 1946, was also suffering from cancer and had little desire to continue in office, while Mercante, long considered the obvious successor, had become increasingly distanced from the presidential couple. (Nevertheless, Perón would continue to float his name as a possible running mate, primarily to stave off the ambitions of others.) The sectoral nature of Perón's support base, with both military and union interests needing to be placated, made the choice of a vice-president difficult, given that it would almost certainly lead to frictions with the corporate interests not taken into account. From this point of view, Mercante would have been the obvious candidate – too obvious for Perón's liking, given the potential competition he still represented. Other potential political candidates such as provincial governors or Lower House leader Héctor Cámpora were also a risk given their own potential ambitions – or, in the case of Cámpora, were wholly identified with the 'Duarte group' that was anathema to the military.

In the midst of this quandary the name of Evita appeared, and with increasing strength. There is much debate as to whether Perón ever seriously considered this option, and there is every reason to think that he did not, given that he had nothing to gain and a great deal of military support to lose from his wife's candidacy. It is more likely that he allowed her name to remain in the mix in order to ward off other aspirants and avoid taking sides in the widening breach between his different pillars of support. (A similar tactic, in 1973, would lead to the designation of his third wife, María Estela 'Isabel' Martínez, as his running mate, making her the first woman president when he died in 1974.)

From Evita's point of view, as noted earlier, there are few obvious reasons why the largely irrelevant post of vice-president should have been attractive, given that she exercised far more power than any vice-president in the history of Latin America. However, it is difficult not to conclude that she did want it, and want it badly. This may have been because she felt (not unjustly) that she deserved the recognition of an elected post, and indeed of becoming the first woman to hold such a high-level position. Although she was not by any means the originator of the women's suffrage movement in Argentina, and the vote would likely have been granted at around the same time with or without her presence, Evita was widely seen as key to that process. Thanks to her influence and her tireless organisation of the PPF, 1951 would be not only the first time women voted, but the first time that women were elected to office. That she should not be one of them must have seemed unjust, although a congressional seat could in practice have been more constraining in its demands and therefore less attractive to a one-woman band like Evita.

Moreover, the post of first lady was traditionally even less visible or influential than that of vice-president, so from her point of view the lack of official power associated with the role was scarcely an obstacle, given her ability to give content and profile to a hitherto vacuous post – a considera-tion that must surely have increased the alarm of those sectors who were vehemently opposed to her candidacy. From her point of view also, the vice-presidency could have given her an institutional legitimacy that would count in favour of the unions and her *descamisados*, to counter the weight of the military. Most tellingly, had it not been for her own biologically deter-mined time limitations, the vice-presidency could realistically have been a stepping stone to the presidency after Perón, which would have made her the first woman president of any republic. This was a possibility that was truly horrifying to many, not least the military who could not tolerate the prospect of Evita as commander-in-chief.

Evita herself essentially launched the presidential campaign in February 1951, announcing that the 3,600 *unidades básicas* of the PPF sup-ported Perón's re-election: 'this will be their only political objective until it is attained'.[26] On 24 February a press release from the PPF, signed by Evita as its leader, stated that 'Peronist women want the glory that can never be renounced, that the first women's vote in Argentine history will be the one that raises Perón again to the presidency'.[27] At the same time, how-ever, Evita's newspaper *Democracia* observed that the women's party had not only implored Perón to accept the nomination, but had also expressed to him 'the vehement desire of all the workers that Señora Eva Perón be consecrated vice-president of the nation' – an expression of desire to which Perón made no response. Despite later contradictory versions that claim that Evita did not seek the vice-presidency, or allowed her name to be used only to flush out other over-ambitious would-be candidates, it is virtually impossible to imagine that she would have allowed 'her' women's party, vertically organised under a single leader, to put forward her name had she not been serious about pursuing the post.

Also in early 1951, another idea began to come to fruition that would both cement Evita's position in the Peronist firmament and create a new source of propaganda for the government. The possibility that Evita would write, or collaborate with, an autobiography had been mooted for some time, and around this time the project finally saw the light of day. Manuel Penella de Silva, a Spanish journalist, had been toying with the possibility of writing a biography of Eleanor Roosevelt, but the Argentine ambassador in Switzerland, Benito Llambí (the same who had organised and hosted Evita's visit to Switzerland in 1947), persuaded him to consider a different subject and brought him to Buenos Aires for an interview with Evita sometime in 1950. A first draft of her ghosted autobiography, which began life with the title *La pasión de mi vida* (The Passion of My Life) before finally becoming *La razón de mi vida* (The Reason for My Life), was handed to her in early 1951, reportedly prompting great emotion in Evita, who said that Penella had captured much of her life exactly as she remembered it. Penella himself was paid 50,000 pesos for the work (some 3,000 dollars at the time).

However, Perón was apparently less pleased with the draft, for whatever reason, and it slept the sleep of the just in a drawer for some time before being passed on to other hands, reportedly including technical affairs minister Raúl Mendé (a medical doctor who also attended Evita) and sub-secretary of information Raúl Apold. Perón himself may also have taken a hand, and Benítez is also said to have been involved. Mendé is said to have reworked much of the text, purportedly on the grounds that Penella's draft was written in overly 'Spanish' Spanish which sounded out of place in Argentina, although it has widely been supposed that it was substantially rewritten in order to deliver a message more in keeping with Perón's political necessities and aims than the original in which Evita participated. In April Evita read selections from the 'corrected' version to an august group including Prince Bernard of the Netherlands, who was visiting Buenos Aires to present Evita with the Grand Cross of the Orange Nassau Order – and, supposedly, to sell arms.

It is difficult to ascertain the extent to which *La razón de mi vida* as finally published did or did not coincide with Evita's thinking (the final version was published in late 1951, when she was too ill to attend the launch). Certainly there are sections that appear to express her feelings in a way in which she often did extemporaneously, and many elements (such as her claim to have 'lived in freedom') that ring true. Other elements, such as some rather one-dimensional reflections on feminism, may have been introduced for political convenience, but it cannot automatically be assumed that she would have disagreed with the final 'official' version. Both Mendé and Apold were propagandists for a movement of which Evita was perhaps the apex of propaganda and the generator of much of its content; moreover, Apold had written speeches for her, and there is no reason to assume that they were in fundamental disagreement. (At least when healthy, Evita was far too intelligent and strong-willed to have parroted prepared speeches with which she disagreed, although in her illness it is also perfectly possible that many elements were introduced without her consent.) Fermín Chávez at least is adamant that the revisions were made with her knowledge and consent and that the final bowdlerised version that was published had her approval.[28]

If the reason for assuming the book had been censored and modified is that it takes a disturbingly adoring tone when speaking of Perón (and a rather self-abasing one when speaking of the putative author), this is also in line with much of Evita's normal discourse and cannot be dismissed on this basis. However, the apparent manipulation of the book and of Evita's 'message' is yet another example of the extent to which others would constantly claim credit for having 'invented' her, and of the fact that her image and identity would be redrafted repeatedly over the years, either for the direct personal benefit of the person or group doing the redrafting, or in line with what the person or group wanted to believe she represented. Again, a strong and vibrant personality was on some level denied the possibility of being – and of expressing – herself as herself.

Apart from the question of authorship and whether *La razón de mi vida* truly represented Evita's own thoughts and feelings, however, the book would become another irritant for those already weary of ubiquitous Peronist propaganda. That propaganda, whether graphic, written or broadcast, stretched far beyond the pro-government media such as *Democracia* or the magazine *Mundo Peronista*, which individuals might choose to buy or not, and had become unavoidable. This was true in posters, which often depicted Perón and/or Evita (the latter often with a distinctly supernatural or angelic aspect), or an allegorical image of Argentina sheltering workers and *descamisados*, or brawny workmen or happy Peronist families in which the mother is in her comfortable home looking after her well-dressed children. All of these were illustrated in a monumental, square-jawed, overbearing graphic style widely associated with both the Nazi and Soviet regimes, which provided further grist to opponents of the government who denounced that Perón had slipped over the authoritarian edge into dictatorship.

Moreover, early learning readers for small children were full of phrases such as 'Evita loves me, I love my mother and Evita' or 'Mama and Papa love me, Perón and Evita love us' and references to 'the good fairy Evita' ('Mama, Evita and the teacher' were also defined as good fairies when the fairy dust was being distributed more widely). That such party propaganda should be part of the required primary school curriculum was widely resented for obvious reasons; that *La razón de mi vida* should be added to the curriculum made that resentment worse, although in practice many schools in the provinces in particular looked the other way if teachers refused to include it in their classes. This necessity for universal credit, for universal rather than simply majority support, was an oft-repeated and self-destructive obsession of the Peronist government: despite being genuinely popular, and achieving genuinely valuable advances in working conditions, wages, housing, health care and education, often it would insist on degrading those achievements through the constant reminder of who the benefactors were. The constant images and names of Perón, Evita and the Foundation imposed on schools, hospitals, homes, neighbourhoods and even provinces in the end did little more than debase the currency of the government's very real achievements, strengthening the position of the opposition and facilitating disparagement of its social programmes.

Needless to say, the looming presidential elections did nothing to reduce the barrage of propaganda – nor did Evita's putative candidacy for the vice-presidency. That candidacy received sometimes bizarre support from ordinary people determined to see her as Perón's running mate: the stunts undertaken for that purpose included a man who rolled a barrel all the way from Rosario to Buenos Aires (some 300 kilometres), two one-legged men who rode a bicycle for five days non-stop and a couple who walked along several hundred kilometres of roads wearing shirts that said 'Perón fulfils' and 'Evita dignifies'. For her own part, Evita maintained her feverish level of activity, which from March included teaching at the Superior Peronist School for future party leaders (six lectures later published as *Historia del Peronismo*), and in July included assuming the presidency of the newly constituted National Commission of the Peronist Women's Party. All this despite the fact that, according to Hernán Benítez, from June she began to suffer stabbing pains in her lower abdomen that gave the lie to her stalwartly repeated claims that there was nothing wrong with her, while according to the later testimony of two doctors who treated her she was having severe vaginal haemorrhages from August. Other versions suggest that the evidence was plain earlier, with her sister Erminda having shown an X-ray to a specialist as early as May which confirmed the cancer diagnosis.[29]

Evita herself remained busy with her normal functions, as well as political activities clearly aimed at launching a candidacy. In June it was announced that a plot to assassinate the president and his wife had been

uncovered, driven by a campaign from abroad and proposing to decapi-
tate the government and impose a campaign of terror in Argentina. Those
responsible purportedly included the US diplomat John Griffith (a claim
that harked back to 'Braden or Perón') and the Democratic Action Party
of Venezuela. Also in June, delegations from the province of Santiago del
Estero and from the Argentine naval federation brought hefty donations
and a folk song dedicated to Evita, received in the Casa Rosada. In July,
Congress approved an initiative of hers to convert the national territories
of La Pampa and Chaco into provinces – indeed, it went further, changing the name of La Pampa to Eva Perón and that of Chaco to Presidente
Perón. (The capital of Buenos Aires province, La Plata, would also briefly
be renamed as Eva Perón.) And on 9 July 1951, Independence Day, Evita
attended what would prove to be her last gala at the Teatro Colón. In the
run-up to the 22 August *Cabildo Abierto*, a range of union delegations visited Perón and Evita to ask them to accept the party's nominations, leaving
no doubt whatsoever that they were both more than aware of the plan and
did not reject it.

On 2 August the CGT adopted a resolution calling on Perón to accept
the presidential nomination, as well as reiterating the workers' 'vehement
desire' that Evita should be vice-president. A day later, representatives of
the PPF also proclaimed the Perón–Eva Perón ticket, beginning a series
of similar demonstrations and proclamations that would lead up to the
famous *Cabildo Abierto*, organised for 22 August. Both the CGT and the
PPF doubtless saw benefits in her rise to the vice-presidency, given her
closeness to and authority over both, which potentially would see their own
positions strengthened were her position in political life to be formalised.
Following these moves, on 6 August the Radical Party declared that its
own presidential ticket would be composed of Ricardo Balbín (a vociferous
opponent who had suffered both prison and exile) and Arturo Frondizi, a
more leftward-leaning Radical who represented a more nationalist faction
of the party.

Throughout these machinations Perón himself remained silent, at least
in public. As noted earlier, his feelings may have been coloured in part by
the knowledge that his wife was ill, or that she could represent a degree of
competition that no other political figure could – or indeed, that her candidacy brought him many perils and few benefits. Certainly the Church
was not in favour, nor were the elite institutions such as big business, the
Argentine Rural Society and other aristocratic bastions; however, none of

these institutions was of deep concern given the fact that they would not add or subtract votes one way or the other (and the violent split between Perón and the Church that came not long after Evita's death demonstrated the limited fear he had of making an enemy of the hierarchy). Moreover, some of these sectors might not have been displeased with an Evita candidacy, in the belief that it might have brought opposition to the government to a head and possibly even cost Perón the election.

However, the armed forces were a different matter. Here there was no question about the strength of animosity to Evita and any thought of her candidacy. According to the British Embassy, a source in the War Ministry had reported that on the very day of the *Cabildo Abierto* three generals close to Perón had told him in no uncertain terms that 'the Army would not stand for the Señora as vice-president'. While Perón apparently attempted to dissemble or to dismiss this position, a threat that there would be 'a move against the regime by seven regiments' purportedly sealed the deal. The same War Ministry source claimed that 48 out of 50 generals had stated 'emphatically that they did not support the lady's candidature'.[30] This adamant position is alluded to by many other sources, including Jorge Antonio, an eternal friend and (during his long exile) financial supporter of Perón, who noted that war minister Franklin Lucero had asked him to intercede with Perón to make him understand that the army was violently opposed to Evita's candidacy.[31] At the same time, a secret group was forming around General Eduardo Lonardi (who would eventually lead the coup against Perón four years later) with the intention of removing Perón and the 'Duarte group' from power; Lucero himself would promise Lonardi that Evita would desist from the candidacy.[32]

Against this backdrop, it is perhaps unsurprising that Perón appeared on the giant platform at the *Cabildo Abierto* unwilling to confirm his wife's candidacy. It is not clear what attitude he had expressed in private; some sources claim that he had always been adamant that a married couple could not stand for the presidency and vice-presidency and that Evita had been in agreement. However, others suggest that he had been far less clear than this about his intentions (which would not be surprising, as lack of clarity about his intentions was virtually Perón's default mode). This appears likely, given that events at the *Cabildo Abierto* suggest that Evita did not know how he intended her to proceed and that she was left – unusually for her – uncertain and doubtful as to what to do. Alternatively, her hesitation may have been a last-ditch effort to force Perón to accept an outcome that he was unable to permit, by demonstrating that she had the massive crowd (and the millions more they represented) on her side. In any case, the size and fervour of the rally appears to have taken all sides by surprise, and the carefully stage-managed event quickly eluded control even by the movement's supposedly all-powerful leaders.

Once the *Cabildo Abierto* had been called, planning had been meticulous and efficient, with buses and trains laid on for those wishing to come from the provinces for the event, entertainments provided and food and shelter organised. By the afternoon of the 22nd, all was in readiness at the site, in front of the Public Works Ministry on the corner of two majestic avenues, Belgrano and 9 de Julio. The official version of over a million people may be exaggerated, but contemporary film and photos of the event, however carefully edited, leave no doubt as to the huge magnitude of the crowd; even the estimate of the police and international media of 250,000 represented a vast number, many thousands of them from the PPF. A small aircraft flew overhead with a banner proclaiming 'Perón–Eva Perón', while the podium was dominated by a huge sign reading 'Perón–Eva Perón, the formula of the fatherland.'

Perón arrived on the stage at 5.30 pm, when the crowd had reached its maximum. Shortly afterward, José Espejo, the servile leader of the CGT, noted 'the absence of Eva Perón, who has won forever a place in the world, in history, in the love and veneration of the Argentine people [... T]his *Cabildo Abierto* cannot continue without the presence of Comrade Evita.'[33] Perón's own attempts to speak were drowned out by the roar of a crowd that had once come out only to see Perón, but which now came with a different purpose: that of seeing Evita become vice-president. Indeed, whatever the intentions of the organisers, there was no prospect of continuing otherwise, with the crowd's calls for Evita drowning out Espejo and even Perón himself (who can scarcely have been pleased, whatever his feelings about her candidacy).

Espejo disappeared and returned rapidly with Evita, presupposing that this move had been planned in advance. However, the Evita who took her place on the stage amid an overwhelming ovation was a nervous, tearful and doubtful one, who asked her husband what she should say. According to Vera Pichel, if she was expecting him to support her acceptance, she was to be disappointed: what he said instead was 'say yes without saying yes'.[34] Overcoming her weeping with difficulty, Evita attempted a non-specific speech in her usual vein, expressing her great emotion to find myself again with the *descamisados*, like on 17 October and all the dates when the people were present [...] Here, the people know what is going on, and they want General Perón to continue directing the destiny of the fatherland.[35]

However, here she was interrupted by shouts of 'with Evita, with Evita', and later 'Evita with Perón', making it virtually impossible for her to 'say yes without saying yes'.

Her constant efforts to turn her speech to the figure of Perón and his candidacy did nothing to halt the fevered interruptions, even as she reiterated her 'gratitude to the *descamisados* who on 17 October 1945 gave me life, light, soul and heart on giving me back the general'. 'They know well that before General Perón they lived in slavery and above all had lost hope for a better future. It was General Perón who dignified them, socially, morally and spiritually.'[36] She, too, was interrupted repeatedly by the crowd, shouting 'With Evita, with Evita, with Evita. Evita with Perón, Evita with Perón.' Both Perón and Evita appeared shocked on the stage, she with a look of anguish, Perón with a nervous and fixed smile. Evading the question of the vice-presidency, Evita continued to stress her desire only to accompany her husband and her people:

> I am nothing more than a woman of the Argentine people. I am nothing more than a *descamisada* of the Fatherland [...] I will always do what the people say. But I tell you, comrades, workers, that just as five years ago I said I preferred to be Evita rather than the wife of the president, if that Evita served to alleviate any pain in my country, today I say I prefer to be Evita, because being Evita I know that you will always carry me in your hearts.[37]

Only when she finished by saying that she was happy because 'I served my people and my general. I will always do what the people say' was there another ovation, as the crowd assumed that this implied acceptance, despite her insistence that she still 'preferred to be Evita' rather than vice-president.[38]

As remarkable as this exchange was, more astonishing things were to come. Perón himself, thus far the unquestioned leader and a highly charismatic speaker in his own right, got up to make his own speech, beginning with 'only strong and virtuous peoples are the masters of their destinies'.[39]

However, it rapidly became clear that he was losing his audience, and he was even interrupted by a shout from the crowd: 'Let Comrade Evita speak!' There seemed to be no way to end the event, now that the crowd had understood that Evita had not accepted the candidacy, and now that Evita had perhaps understood that her husband would not permit it despite (or possibly because of) the obvious adoration of the crowd and the strength of 'her people's' desire that she accept. Following this incredible conversation, remarkable even for a presidential couple whose dialogue with their supporters had always been a stock in trade, Evita asked for four days to consider a decision. 'No, no […] general strike!' was the response.

> Comrades, for the affection that unites us, I ask you, please, don't make me do what I do not want to do […] I ask you as a friend, as a comrade, to disperse […] Comrades, I am not giving up my place in the struggle, but only the honours.

'No!' came the inevitable reply. 'Comrades, I ask only one thing, when has Evita defrauded you? When has Evita not done what you wanted? I ask only one thing, wait until tomorrow.' 'No', they said, 'accept, accept, Evita'. Evita herself was heard to say 'they won't accept it', and Perón to demand in an undertone that the *Cabildo Abierto* be ended immediately.

Weeping again, she asked for a grace period until the following day, also rejected; uncertain, she appeared to accept before retreating and asking rhetorically 'do you think that if the post of vice-president were a duty and I were a solution I would not already have said yes?' Repeatedly asking tearfully that the crowd 'not make me do what I do not want to do' and asking them to disperse peacefully, she was unable to comply with Perón's demand that the rally be terminated, nor to avoid the remarkable fact that Perón had become seemingly irrelevant and ignored. Certainly Espejo did not read his leader well when he took the microphone and promised that no one would move from the spot until she decided, supposedly within two hours. The faces of both Perón and Evita make the crisis clear, both completely disconcerted, one enraged and one devastated. Finally, when she said 'I will do what the people want', the crowd dispersed; subsequent news reporting included only Perón and Espejo's speeches, boiling Evita's own part down to that single phrase.

With no certainty over what would come next, and Evita ill, wounded and suffering physically and emotionally, on the 28th the Peronist Party and the CGT officially nominated her for the vice-presidency, with the railway union La Fraternidad backing the ticket officially two days later. All of this was in vain when, on 31 August, Evita broadcast her 'irrevocable decision to renounce the honour that the workers and the people of my country wanted to confer upon me at the historic *Cabildo Abierto* of 22 August'.[40] From then on, for the remainder of her brief life, the honours and panegyrics over her sacrifice and 'renunciation' would increase even as her health deteriorated. The *Cabildo Abierto* was perhaps simultaneously the apogee and the twilight of her love affair with her people – genuinely felt on both sides – and her strength would rapidly diminish and leave her in the shadows even as her political and emotional hold rose higher. Sidelined by illness, her absence would become an increasing presence.

 CHAPTER 14

Immortality

AFTER SHE HAD held up to an astonishing degree throughout 1951, Evita's decline following her 'renunciation' was swift and irreversible. Whether this was because, as some felt, the frustration of her thwarted ambition to become vice-president devastated her ('our theory was that cancer appears when a desire is blocked […] Eva's blocked desire was to be vice-president of the Republic'[1]) or because the cancer had already advanced rapidly in her 32-year-old body ('she renounced the vice-presidency because she was ill, and she didn't want to undermine Perón's leadership'[2]), the widely hoped-for miraculous recovery did not occur.

The question of 'renunciation' and 'ambition' was one that plagued Peronists and anti-Peronists alike, although it left the Peronists with a more complicated conundrum. The opposition had always decried what it saw as Evita's overweening personal ambition, which many cited as the origin of her illness. By contrast, the Peronists were stout in their claim that she was not ambitious, beginning with Evita herself, who according to her own claims desired only to be little more than a footnote in the 'glorious chapter of history' that would be dedicated to Perón. At the *Cabildo Abierto*, one of the reasons she adduced for not wishing to accept the vice-presidency was that she did not want 'any worker of my fatherland to be left without arguments when the resentful ones, the mediocre ones who did not understand me, and do not understand me, think that everything I do is because of petty interests'.[3] Others, such as the Peronist legislator Rodolfo Decker, would consistently insist that she did not want the vice-presidency, given both that Perón was adamantly opposed to a married couple occupying the presidency and the vice-presidency, and that the job was 'too small' for someone who already had far more power than the post would confer.

Apart from the obvious fact that Evita did much to promote her own candidacy through the CGT and the Peronist Women's Party, and thus it is hardly credible that she had no such interest, these denials represent a contradiction: if she really did not want the post, then her 'renunciation' of it was not the sacrifice her supporters claimed. But this also begs the question of why her ambition should have been so unacceptable in her own sight and that of others. (As Marysa Navarro rightly notes, if Evita had had no ambition, she would scarcely have become such an historic and iconographic figure.[4]) For someone of her political activism, undoubted power and impressive trajectory, who had overseen if not originated the vote for women, organised a highly effective women's party and seen some of its activists become the first female members of Argentina's Congress, surely the ambition to hold an elected post was not outlandish. However, the fact that it was considered 'unfeminine' by both the opposition and the Peronists (and Evita herself) points not only to the traditionalist elements of Peronism that offset its more subversive characteristics, but to the fact that Evita herself may have felt that her image as the mother of the nation, already touched by her childlessness, would be somehow tarnished if she was seen to have ambitions other than the modest ones she had always claimed women should have for their home, hearth, family and fatherland.

Nor was Evita's renunciation sufficient to appease dissent in the military, already exacerbated by the increasingly inflammatory language she used as her health deteriorated. On 28 September an uprising led by General Benjamín Menéndez broke out against the government, quickly snuffed out after Perón declared a state of internal war; the rebels still had limited support and the CGT rallied rapidly, calling a general strike and turning out to provide a mass audience in the Plaza de Mayo for Perón's subsequent speech. Perón would dismiss the rebels as lackeys of 'communism and capitalism', although he was at pains to try to draw a line between them and the rest of the 'loyal' armed forces whom he still did not want to offend. Evita was not present on the balcony (rather, she was at home in bed, receiving a blood transfusion), nor was she told of the events until several hours after the uprising was over. Despite her state of health and her exhaustion, she insisted on making a radio broadcast to thank the *descamisados* for again defending her husband, and begging them, in tears, to pray that 'God will give me back the health I have lost, not for me, but for Perón and for you, my *descamisados*', so that she could 'soon be back in the struggle with you'.[5] Being back in the struggle was no mere euphemism for Evita: the following day she called several union leaders to her bedside, together with the army chief, General Humberto Sosa Molina, and ordered the purchase by the Foundation of 1,500 machine guns and 5,000 automatic pistols to be handed out to workers' militias in the event of another such uprising. (Perón, to whom the idea of armed workers' militias was anathema, would confiscate the weapons after her death and turned them over to the Gendarmería. Thus, as Vera Pichel commented, 'the last impulse of this great fighter, who wanted the people to have real protagonism in whatever way possible, was frustrated'.[6])

During the first half of October Evita remained bedridden in the presidential residence, with no sign of improvement; on the contrary, the stabbing pains in her abdomen were worsening. Although she was able to get up for a small celebration of Perón's birthday on the 8th, she was forced to miss the official launch of *La razón de mi vida* a week later. According to the ubiquitous Father Benítez, by this time Perón had been informed of her diagnosis, but it would appear that she had not and would not be told for some time to come. The secrecy that shrouded cancer at the time, born of fear, was not limited to Evita. Cancer was still a taboo subject, a 'dirty little secret' rather like adultery that people avoided mentioning, perhaps given the fact that treatment was still limited and the prognosis was more often than not desolate. Perhaps it was hoped that if you ignored it, it would go away, like an attention-seeking child. However, in Evita's case the secrecy seems to have been carried to an extreme, to the extent that she was not told even after major surgery in November 1951. This was despite an ever-multiplying team of doctors, many of them reportedly brought in by technical secretary Raúl Mendé and education minister Armando Méndez San Martín in a competitive bid to garner favour.[7]

Benítez would later claim that she found out by accident, near the end of her life, when one of the many women who had been praying outside the residence had a brief conversation with her and remarked bitterly how unjust it was that Evita should have cancer. According to Benítez, Evita rebuked him severely for lacking the courage to tell her sooner, telling him and Atilio Renzi 'you lie to me as if I were a coward. I know I'm in a pit and that no one can get me out.'[8] Perón also would say, whether accurately or for the benefit of posterity, that when he remonstrated that she should take care of her health, she told him 'I know I'm very sick and I know I won't be saved. But I think there are things more important than one's own life and if I didn't do them I would not feel I had fulfilled my destiny.'[9] However, is it really true that she did not know, even after having a major operation? Such a 'don't ask, don't tell' approach seems to be carrying denial to an extreme. In fact, her public speeches made it abundantly clear that she knew she was dying, even if on some level she seemed to deny the possibility in the belief that, because she was needed and millions of people would lose their protector, it might somehow not happen. However, Evita would not go gently into that good night.

Evita's first public appearance after the *Cabildo Abierto*, and her last at that annual event, was at the 17 October 1951 commemoration (an event which marked the first Argentine television broadcast), which would become a tribute (if not a eulogy) to her rather than to Perón and the *descamisados*. Somehow standing on the balcony through the singing of the national anthem and 'Los muchachos peronistas', often physically supported by Perón, Evita received a 'first class distinction' at the hands of CGT leader José Espejo, in recognition of her renunciation, before then being awarded the Great Peronist Medal (extraordinary grade) by her husband – the one and only time this medal was bestowed. Overcome with emotion, she remained in a long embrace with her husband; the 'woman without tears' took her place before the microphone but found herself unable to speak. Perón, who himself admitted that he was miserly with praise, launched into a speech in which he recognised that his wife was Peronism's 'soul and its example. For that reason, as leader of this Peronist movement, I make public my gratitude and my profound thanks to this incomparable woman of all times.' Enumerating her achievements in benefit of the unions and through the Foundation, and virtues such as her 'incomparable spirit' and 'her natural capacity for political leadership', he called her 'one of the greatest women in humanity', who had given 'this Peronist movement a new orientation, a mysticism and a capacity to achieve'.[10] He also singled out the Peronist Women's Party, 'the work of her intelligence and her creative spirit [...] an example of organisation'. 'Apart from all that, with her marvellous skill, she has taken care of my own back, entrusted to her intelligence and her loyalty.'[11] Overcome, Evita again buried herself in her husband's arms and wept.

'My dear *descamisados*', she said when she could finally speak,

> this is a day of many emotions for me [...] I could never miss this appointment with my people of every 17 October [...] I have a sacred debt with Perón and all of you [...]; I don't care if in order to pay it I have to leave shreds of my life on the way.

The emotional charge ran high, both in Evita and in her listeners. 'I have only one thing that has value, I have it in my heart, it burns my soul, it hurts my flesh and burns in my nerves. It is love for this people and for Perón.' However, love and death (her speech makes frequent references to her own death, however hypothetically, which suggests that the unspoken and unaccepted was nonetheless intuited by herself and her public) were not the only themes of the speech, which took on a violent and alarmist tone. 'I had to come to tell you that it is necessary to remain alert […] The danger has not passed […] The enemies work in the shadow of betrayal, and sometimes they hide behind a smile or an extended hand.' Thanking the *descamisados* again for coming out in support of Perón following the 28 September uprising, she warned that 'the enemies of the people, of Perón and the fatherland, have long known that Perón and Eva Perón were willing to die for this people. Now they also know that the people are willing to die for Perón.' She then asked them to swear to defend Perón unto death, calling on them to chant for a full minute 'my life for Perón' – a time span which was greatly exceeded. Recognising the fragility of her health, she repeated that she hoped to return to the struggle soon, but begged the crowd to take care of Perón if she could not do so. 'And to all the *descamisados* in the interior, I embrace them very very close to my heart and I want them to know how much I love them.'[12] And as the crowd chanted her name, again she burst into sobs and embraced her husband. The following day, usually called 'San Perón' and a workers' holiday to recover from the 17th, was declared 'Santa Evita' day.

Whether or not this type of political theatre is to the taste of all publics – and for some political cultures it doubtless sounds faintly risible if not ominous – there is no doubting the genuine emotion and sincerity on both sides. To see surviving footage and hear recordings of the speeches on this 17 October is deeply moving. The love, the commitment and the despair on both sides is evident, as the people gathered in the Plaza de Mayo were clearly aware that the woman before them would not be physically present for much longer. The grief and the sadness, and Evita's frantic concerns about what perils might come after her death, are palpable, as are her pain, frailty and exhaustion. She was physically diminished, but the energy and the voice, ever more harsh and urgent, had not been overcome.

Despite her continuing resistance to the prospect of an operation, on 3 November, only days before the presidential elections, a press release reported that Evita's doctors had decided that she required surgery and that she had therefore been admitted to the President Perón Polyclinic in the Greater Buenos Aires neighbourhood of Avellaneda, one of the ultra-modern hospitals constructed by the Foundation. She would, it said, be operated on by the distinguished surgeon Ricardo Finochietto, the head of the hospital, and her general state of health was 'good', raising optimism over the outcome of the operation. The reasons for the operation were not specified, nor was the press release accurate in many respects – not least its cheerful verdict on her overall health. The famed US cancer specialist George Pack was brought secretly from New York to carry out the operation, for which he was paid 10,000 dollars. Evita knew nothing of the 'Yankee' doctor who would operate on her, believing that Finochietto would be in charge and that the surgery related to an ulcer rather than a cancer, and Pack did not appear until after she had been anaesthetised. The operation was preceded by five days of radium treatment.

The operation took place on 5 November, not before she recorded a radio message to be broadcast two days before the 11 November elections, in which she warned darkly that to fail to vote for Perón was to 'betray the country'. The hospital was full of family, friends and functionaries, as well as a guard of honour by the nurses from the Foundation, and the streets outside crammed with well-wishers praying for her recovery. Reportedly, Pack would inform the family that he had removed even healthy tissue to ensure that no cancer was left and that 'Evita would be around for a while'. However, Perón himself would later write that, only weeks later, Pack was called to carry out a new biopsy and told him that she was gravely ill and incurable, with metastasis and little likelihood of living beyond March 1952 even with the best of care.

Still in hospital on election day, Evita was allowed to vote (for the first and only time) from her hospital bed. The anti-Peronist writer David Viñas, one of the electoral authorities charged with bringing the ballot box to her bedside, would later comment that although he was repulsed by the adulation around her, he was moved by the women outside praying who scrambled to touch or kiss the ballot box with her vote inside.[13] The women's vote was a key factor in augmenting Perón's majority: the ticket Perón–Quijano that had supplanted Perón–Eva Perón received 66 per cent of the vote. Although Evita had been unable to take part in Perón's campaign, much to her frustration, she can only have been well aware of the key role played by 'her' women in his impressive victory. More than half of his 4.6 million votes came from women.

On 14 November, an ambulance transported Evita back to the presidential residence, from which she would emerge only rarely in the remaining months before her death. Installed in a distant bedroom where her medical care would not disturb her husband, Evita virtually held court there over the next few months; although she never returned to the office in the Secretariat, the trade unionists, ministers and others came to her, keeping her informed about matters of politics and attempting the impossible to avoid informing her of the real state of her health. Her hairdresser Julio Alcaraz continued to arrive at 8.00 am to arrange her hair before she began to meet visiting delegations, and her manicurist Sara Gatti still came three times a week. The head of the presidential residence, her loyal Atilio Renzi, and old friend Oscar Nicolini spent time with her daily, as did her family and Perón. Juancito in particular spent much time with her; he had his own room in the residence and apparently curbed his playboy ways during his sister's illness to accompany her as much as his duties as Perón's secretary allowed.

On days when she felt a bit stronger, there were occasional outings with Perón and sometimes Renzi: on 2 December it was reported that they had a long drive around the city, repeated several days later, prompting spontaneous gatherings of well-wishers when they appeared. However, on 7 December she made a radio broadcast, which should have put paid to any hopes that she was recovering, saying that 'my life is no longer mine, now it belongs to all of you […] I can die peacefully, because every Peronist has taken as their own my own work of eternally protecting the Revolution.'[14] She managed to record a Christmas message, and to distribute gifts to a group of children who visited the residence; the Foundation distributed a total of 4 million toys that year, as well as 2 million packages of cider and fruit cake.

For Epiphany (6 January 1952), she again distributed gifts to children in the residence, urging them 'never to forget Perón', but her public activities were reduced to a minimum. Despite the official optimism that her surgery had been successful (Finochietto was awarded a special gold coin on 4 January, in Evita's presence, for his role in 'curing the greatest woman of our time and in history'[15]), by January the pains in her lower abdomen had returned and a biopsy demonstrated that the cancer was still in full force. Raúl Mendé, himself a doctor, reportedly suggested radiation, a therapy that was then in a primitive stage. The applications produced serious burns, generating even more pain and causing pieces of burnt skin to drop off (one of which was kept by her sister Blanca for some time). She was also given 20 doses of intravenous chemotherapy, another cancer treatment still in its infancy. Evita failed to appear at the opening of the Evita youth games on 2 February (though she attended the closing event a month later), but still managed to receive distinguished visitors – many of them foreign dignitaries bearing decorations – and friends, often after Perón had gone to bed. On 3 April she attended the funeral of Vice-President Hortensio Quijano, dead of cancer ahead of her.

Her final public speech came on May Day 1952, again from the balcony of the Casa Rosada before a multitude assembled by the CGT. Although it seemed impossible that she could do so, she went despite doctors' orders and the efforts of Perón and her family. In great pain and most probably aware that it would be her last chance to speak directly to her *descamisados*, it was the most violent speech of her career, as well as a remarkable effort from a woman whose physical energies were largely exhausted, although her emotional energies were not. Starting with her usual salute to and recognition of the *descamisados* and the 'historic plaza of the 17 October 1945', she quickly gathered momentum and rage. Again, the anger, despair and violence are vibrant in her hoarse voice. Ranting against the 'traitors within and without', she warned that

> I ask God not to allow those fools to raise a hand against Perón because woe betide that day! Woe betide that day! That day, my general, I will come out with the women of the people, I will come out with the *descamisados* of the fatherland, dead or alive, and leave no brick standing that is not Peronist [...] Let the traitors know that we will not come here to say 'present' to Perón, like on 28 September, but we will come to take justice into our own hands [...] Before I finish, comrades, I want to give you a message: be alert. The enemy lies in wait. The traitors within, who sell themselves for four coins, are also waiting to deal the blow at any time. But we are the people, and I know that if the people are alert we are invincible, because we are the fatherland itself.[16]

Afterwards she virtually collapsed and was carried indoors by Perón, who would note afterwards that 'only my breathing was audible. Eva's was imperceptible and fatigued. In my arms there was nothing more than a dead woman.'[17]

Six days later, on her 33rd birthday, Evita received visits from a number of political and union leaders and appeared in numerous photographs which show all too clearly that her weight was down to only 37 kilos. Renzi helped her stand upright on the terrace to wave to the well-wishers outside, while a parade of 130 taxi drivers drove round and round the residence honking their horns and shouting 'Happy birthday Evita!'. Also on that day, she was awarded her most grandiloquent title yet, 'Spiritual Leader of the Nation' – one which smacked of martyrdom and also proffered an offence to the Catholic Church, which not unnaturally considered itself to be the arbiter of things spiritual. By this time she had been moved to yet another bedroom, which had more of an aspect of a hospital room, and with an orthopaedic bed to help ease her pains from the cancer, the radiation burns and the long hours in bed. She would lie here much of the time, her poodle Canela with her, when she was unable to undertake any other activities. When she was somewhat better, she continued to demand constant reports of trade union doings and the activities of the Foundation. In a bid to try to raise her spirits, Renzi would try to 'adjust' the bathroom scale in order that she would not know how much weight she was losing.

None of this appears to have fooled Evita, who on 28 May said what was evidently a final farewell to the provincial governors, ending her brief speech to them with 'I leave you my heart of a friend and comrade'. Perhaps exercising her role as spiritual leader, and again hinting at the fire that was still within, she also told them:

> those who proclaim sweetness and love forget that Christ said 'I have come to bring fire to earth because I want it to burn more'. He gave us the example of fanaticism and that is why we must be fanatics of Perón unto death.[18]

It is unlikely that any of those present expected to see her alive again. Perón himself would recall that 'she was reduced to just skin, through which you could already see the white of her bones. Only her eyes seemed alive and eloquent. They lit on everything, interrogated everyone; sometimes they were serene, sometimes I thought they looked desperate.'[19]

However, her stubbornness and determination remained intact. Evita refused to be absent for Perón's second inauguration on 4 June, despite her weakness and pain, despite orders from the doctors and Perón himself, despite the cold weather. According to Raúl Apold, he was asked by Perón to deter her, but she became enraged and insisted that nothing would keep her in her bed that day except death. After receiving various injections of painkillers, she appeared robed in a full-length fur coat which helped to conceal a wire and plaster frame that allowed her to stand as the president's open car made its way to the Congress building. Later, at the Casa Rosada, she was forced to receive more painkillers but managed to stand throughout Perón's second swearing-in. However, no one who saw her could have been in any doubt that she had little time to live. Perón has often been accused of dragging her from her deathbed in order to exploit her pitiful presence at his inauguration, but it is entirely consonant with Evita's character that she would have refused to miss the moment of triumph – a triumph which owed so much to her, which she would never again have a chance to savour and which she felt entitled to share. However, her pale, emaciated, silent presence was her last public appearance alive, and she would not leave the residence again.

In these last weeks of her life, the tributes mounted, as did the efforts to bolster her spirits. Having already received every title and medal imaginable, on 16 June she was awarded the Order of the Liberator General San Martín, thanks to a law introduced by the ever-loyal Héctor Cámpora; the title came with a costly bejewelled necklace that she would have little opportunity to use. Days before her death, too, her former designer Paco Jamandreu received a late-night call from Perón, who told him tearfully that Evita was close to death and asked him to prepare a series of sketches of new clothes in order to make her believe that they were for a new wardrobe for a long trip they would take together. Perhaps the most ominous and least encouraging of these moves was the debate surrounding a monument to her, in itself a strong suggestion of mortality. However, Evita entered with some enthusiasm into the project, one that was anticipated to be the tallest such monument in the world and to house the mortal remains of a *descamisado* 'fallen during the events of 17 October' (there were none) and eventually of the presidential couple themselves. She saw a model of the proposed monument in December 1951 and suggested some changes, apparently along the lines of Napoleon's tomb. Congress approved the monumental project (never constructed) following a raft of speeches that competed grotesquely in their glorification of Evita, with the proviso that copies of the gigantic statue should be placed in every provincial capital. The speeches were typeset and bound and presented to Evita four days before her death.

Historically there has been some dispute over the behaviour and attitude of Perón himself with respect to Evita's illness, much of it informed by the prejudices of the 'pro-' and 'anti-' factions. While the latter were prone to claim that the president ignored his wife as much as possible and even refused to go into her sickroom without a mask over his face, less negative sources note that, having had a similar experience with the death of his first wife, Perón was deeply shaken and distressed by the impending loss of his second. If he may well have been somewhat less than demonstrative, as was his wont most of the time, some public expressions such as those of his 17 October 1951 speech and his attempts to distract her through a rushed set of designs for a travel wardrobe would suggest that he was far from indifferent, even if he found the circumstances emotionally difficult. Despite the fact that he was heavily occupied with the presidency and the fallout from the September 1951 coup attempt, he also began to work from home in the afternoons to be closer to her, and to visit her three times a day.

According to some claims that surfaced in 2011, his efforts to alleviate her intense suffering may have taken an unexpected and controversial course. That year, Daniel Nijensohn, an Argentine doctor based at Yale, claimed that Evita had been submitted to a lobotomy sometime around late May or early June, at the hands of neurosurgeons from the United States and Hungary, James Poppen and George Udvarhelyi. These claims, from several sources, may be supported by X-rays of her body that purportedly showed images of her skull consistent with a lobotomy. More recently, in 2015, Nijensohn went further, saying that the lobotomy was carried out not only to reduce her pain but to 'modify her personality', which, as noted, had become increasingly aggressive as her illness advanced.[20] According to this hypothesis, the decision may have been taken after she issued the order to arm worker militias after the September 1951 coup attempt.

The suggestion of a lobotomy has been hotly denied by many, including the nurse who attended Evita and Felipe Pigna, who defined the claim as an attempt to blacken the reputation of the Perón government; the president of the Juan Domingo Perón National Institute, Lorenzo Pepe, similarly denied the claim to the BBC on the grounds that Perón loved his wife and would never have been capable of such cruelty. However, many of these arguments against appear to lack substance. In the early 1950s a lobotomy was not seen as a barbaric notion, as it might be seen today, but as a real and 'modern' option for relieving severe pain in terminal patients or for modifying damaging behaviour. Thus, even had he authorised such a procedure, it would be wrong to accuse Perón of cruelty or lack of love on that basis; he would have done so from the perspective of 1952, not of the twenty-first century, and any worries about the possible effects on her personality or cognitive abilities would surely have been limited by the fact that she visibly had little time to live.

The claim that it could not have been done without becoming public knowledge is also questionable, given the censorship capacity of the government and the fact that many things about Evita's life remain outside public knowledge. (An anecdote cited by Borroni and Vacca, in which Evita fell into a coma on 18 July and was told on her unexpected awakening that her room was full of medical equipment because the doctors had removed a nerve to ease her pain, could be interpreted as a suggestion that at least the idea was not entirely unreal.[21]) In any case, if the lobotomy did take place, it sadly appears to have had little effect on the pain she suffered in her last weeks – nor indeed, on her personality or cognitive skills, which seem to have remained remarkably strong in her waning moments of strength and lucidity.

In these final weeks of her life, Evita is purported to have begun work on a second book, *Mi mensaje* (My Message), the existence and provenance of which remain in dispute. Part of this was her 'Supreme Will', which was read out on 17 October 1952 after her death, while the rest was supposedly an addendum to *La razón de mi vida*, in which, she says, 'I didn't manage to say all that I feel and think'.[22] Apart from her will, the remainder of the supposed text disappeared from view for decades, until it was auctioned in 1986 following the death of Jorge Garrido, formerly the chief notary under the Perón government. The historian Fermín Chávez authenticated the text, and others have also indicated that she was writing something in the weeks before her death. The long-serving Peronist politician Antonio Cafiero, who visited her several times before her death, indicated that on one occasion she showed him a number of sheets of paper which, he said, included strong language criticising the armed forces and the Church. He would also note that she maintained an active role in government, obliging him to withdraw a political appointment for someone she distrusted. However, he was unable, years later, to say with certainty whether the document that appeared was the same she had shown him in 1952. Of that document, there is one handwritten sheet and several typed pieces of paper with her name at the top and apparently initialled by her.

Her nurse, María Eugenia Alvarez, would also recall that Evita was dictating 'her memoirs so that her *descamisados* would know the truth', although she did not know the content.[23]

Chávez himself would insist that the document was genuine, arguing that Perón had decided to suppress everything apart from her will on the grounds that the strong antipathy to the armed forces and the Church would be damaging to his position. Moreover, according to Chávez, the document shows Evita in her true light as a revolutionary leader who represented competition rather than support for her husband. He also surmised that some of the violence of the language might be attributed to the pain she suffered in her last months, when he claims she said

> God is just […] I was a poor girl and suddenly I found Perón who gave me his love. God helped me to avoid taking another road […] Now God has the right to make me suffer a little […] but I would like to ask him for a vacation![24]

This does not, in itself, suggest a speaker who is anti-religion or atheist, although her anger against the Church doubtless had much less to do with God than with her view that the hierarchy had taken the side of the rich – 'I reproach them for having betrayed Christ'.[25] 'Some day, God will exact from them the precise cost of their betrayal.'[26]

For his part, Father Hernán Benítez was categorical that the work was a forgery, stating forcefully in an interview for the film *The Mystery of Eva Perón* that she had been pressed into producing a few paragraphs in her own hand to serve as a provenance and that in fact she knew nothing at all about the work. In point of fact, as in so many other areas, it is not difficult to see why different people wished to interpret Evita differently, and why her confessor would seek to repudiate any document that took such a critical view of Catholicism (even though his own view of the hierarchy was similarly harsh). In some respects the work does appear to have been written at a later date, after Evita's death, at a time when Perón's clash with the Church and his overthrow by the armed forces might have made it desirable to fabricate such warnings in Evita's voice. However, if it was written or dictated by her, it is easy to see why Perón would not have wanted it made public at a time when he was still trying to keep both 'the cross and the sword' onside.

In his introduction to the English translation of her supposed 'deathbed manuscript', Perón biographer Joseph Page notes rightly that Evita was too weak to have written or dictated an entire memoir, and that at least some of it must have been interposed by another source (in particular some classical allusions that she would certainly not have made). He also notes that the tone of the work is in line with many of her later speeches, although it went far beyond anything she ever said publicly in terms of open criticism of the military and Catholic hierarchy, and that it has some distinctly Marxist overtones that do not sound like her at all (albeit providing grist for the leftist guerrillas who would claim in the 1970s that she would have been one of them).

However, this does not presuppose that the document does not at least partially reflect Evita's dying thoughts or dictation. Her own speeches, and *La razón de mi vida*, were often written by others at least in large part, but this did not imply at all that she disagreed with what was expressed therein, and the speeches written for her by others became her own. Much of its extremism rings true: 'fanaticism turns life into a permanent and heroic process of dying; but it is the only way that life can defeat death'. 'I do not understand middle ground or moderation. I recognise only two words as the favoured daughters of my heart: hate and love. I never know when I hate or when I am loving.'[27] By contrast, as Page notes, the 'Supreme Will' read out following her death does not appear to be part of the same document and does not sound like a reflection of her character, essentially disinheriting her family and declaring Perón, in overblown praise that was excessive even in her terms, her only heir.

On 18 July Evita fell into what was expected to be a final coma, before astonishing the family gathered at her bedside by waking suddenly several hours later and getting out of bed, saying that she would die if she stayed there. Two days later Father Benítez officiated at an open-air mass at which Perón had asked him to prepare the public for Evita's death. She had already called him to her bedside and spoken with him at length, and according to him she was prepared, cognisant of her fate and facing it calmly. The staff at the residence hid all the radios during the mass, as Evita had expressed a wish to hear him speak, with Renzi claiming that her own radio was broken. Thousands of people prayed in the rain as Benítez spoke of her 'Christian heroism' and faith in the poor, calling her 'our sister and our mother in every workers' home'.[28] Not one to miss an opportunity, he also called her 'our martyr' and remarked that 'by choosing Eva Perón, [God] has also chosen us to be martyrs'. Eva Perón had brought about 'the miracle of having opened, through her pain, the doors of the church so that the workers would take refuge in the heart of Jesus Christ, redeemed from their communist atheism and anti-Christian nihilism'.[29]

Predictably, not all public reaction was so respectful or so grief-stricken – graffiti such as the phrase '*viva el cáncer*' and '*viva Perón viudo* [widower]'' would appear on walls around the city, including near the residence. However, even many who were not supporters were touched and moved by the decline and death of such a young and ubiquitous presence and by the outpouring of grief surrounding it. Thereafter there was little to do but wait, and the family, the government, the unions, the *descamisados* and the country as a whole appeared to be frozen, doing just that in a rainy, gloomy and chilly winter week.

According to Perón's own (questionable) later memories, on 25 July Evita called him to her bedside and, with great effort, thanked him for what he had done for her and begged him 'never to abandon the poor. They are the only ones who know how to be faithful.'[30] Other, similar farewells also took place. To Oscar Nicolini, she said 'I'm going. I know that. I pretend to live in a permanent stupor so they will think I don't know the end. It's my end in this world and in my fatherland. But not in the memory of my people.'[31] Other farewells had already been said; over several weeks Evita had distributed pieces of her jewellery and medallions to friends and assistants.

The following day, a dark and wet Saturday 26 July, Father Benítez gave Evita last rites and she again fell into a coma, surrounded by her husband, mother, siblings, and a few faithful friends like Nicolini, Renzi and Cámpora. At 3.00 pm it was announced that her health had deteriorated substantially, a description revised to 'very grave' by 8.00 pm that evening. At 8.25 pm she stopped breathing. An hour later, via radio, the Under-Secretariat of Information of the Presidency 'fulfilled the very painful obligation to inform the people of the Republic that at 20.25 Sra Eva Perón, the Spiritual Leader of the Nation, passed away'.[32] Her brother Juancito had an attack of hysteria and ran from the room shouting 'there is no God', with Erminda trying to comfort him. The others were more restrained, perhaps in some way relieved that the long agony and waiting were finally over. Outside, thousands prayed and wept in the rain. Without any order to do so, public places such as bars, restaurants and cinemas closed their doors on the news, and the city of Buenos Aires became suddenly, oddly quiet and deserted on a Saturday evening. Arguably even many of her opponents were stunned that she was suddenly, finally gone.

It was announced, appropriately, that Evita's body would lie in state at the Ministry ('Secretariat') of Labour and that everyone who wished would have the opportunity to pay their respects. However, a previous plan was already in action. According to Perón, Evita had wanted to be embalmed; whether this is true or not (and it would not be out of keeping with her desire for a permanent presence and place in history), it had been decided that Dr Pedro Ara, the cultural attaché at the Spanish Embassy and a famous anatomist and embalmer, would be charged with that task. Ara had already been called eight days earlier at the time of Evita's first coma but had gone away empty-handed, as it were; he was now called peremptorily to prepare the body for public view. He and his assistant worked through the night, before announcing at 7.30 the next morning that her body was now 'incorruptible'; he was followed by hairdresser Julio Alcaraz and manicurist Sara Gatti, who came to perform their duties for the last time. Gatti, according to her later memories, removed Evita's last nail varnish and replaced it with clear lacquer at her own request.

Later that morning, after representatives of the PPF had paid their respects, the body, dressed in a white tunic with the rosary given to her by the Pope and the Grand Peronist Medal on her chest, was taken from the Foundation to the Ministry of Labour in an ambulance, through streets already filling with floral tributes and queues of people waiting for their last glimpse of Evita. An estimated 65,000 people a day filed past the coffin. The CGT declared a three-day strike and the government national mourning, during which time no official activities would take place for two days. With Ara in almost constant attendance to monitor the condition of his 'patient', the lying in state continued until 9 August; Perón had promised it would continue as long as necessary, but Ara protested that he could not guarantee that the body would not begin to decompose if he could not begin the definitive work within two weeks. Similar altars and wakes were improvised across the country, causing the opposition to joke about 'wakes with branch offices'.

The opposition would also claim that the mourning was at least partially politically fomented, with public employees forced to wear mourning and those failing to do so at risk of losing their jobs. Evidence confirms that there is a degree of truth to this, but it does not explain the genuine outpouring of grief or the 35 blocks of people queuing up to see Evita (attended by soldiers and nurses from the Foundation when they fainted, and served with coffee and sandwiches to keep them on their feet). As usual, the Peronist machine – notably some functionaries who wanted extra points for effort – could not resist over-egging the pudding. Widespread and spontaneous grief was not enough; it had to be universal. That overweening desire to be universal rather than majoritarian would be a disagreeable and unnecessary obsession that gave fuel to the opposition's derision, lending an element of credibility to an otherwise unsustainable claim that Evita's funeral was no more than a carefully staged propaganda exercise.

On 9 August her coffin was taken to Congress for further masses and lying in state; that night, the CGT organised a parade of 600,000 torches that lit up the gloomy city centre. The following day, the coffin was taken to the CGT headquarters near the river, where the second floor was set aside for Ara to continue his work (which would continue for many months). Some 2 million people lined the route followed by the gun carriage on which her coffin was placed, drawn by 38 men chosen by the CGT and 10 women chosen by the Peronist Women's Party (Evita's influence over the CGT had apparently had a limited effect on its chauvinism), wearing white shirts and no jacket, as was the Peronist tradition. The cortege was also accompanied by a substantial military guard of honour, with cadets from all three forces participating, and all three forces also held ceremonies honouring Evita; one can only surmise what the feelings might have been on both sides. The city's florists had long since been stripped of their wares, with floral tributes piled up throughout the city centre, but flowers nevertheless rained down from balconies along the way. The choice of the CGT was disputed; according to some sources, it was Evita's choice, over the objections of Perón and Doña Juana. Given her affiliation with the Franciscan order, it had been widely assumed that she might be laid to rest in a Franciscan convent, but the project of immortality through embalming and a giant monument (the 'monument of popular gratitude') apparently won the day.

Evita's funeral, still by far the most monumental ever seen in Argentina and one of the largest in memory, was filmed by a Hollywood film crew for a documentary, *Y la Argentina detuvo su corazón* (And Argentina's Heart Stopped), which was released by the Secretariat of the Press and the Presidency of the Nation. The newsreel, which was justifiably defined as somewhat turgid Peronist propaganda, nonetheless gives a peerless record of what that funeral was like and the feelings of those who participated even in a small way as members of the interminable queues. The film refers to the event as heralding 'the dawn of a new religion', something that would indeed prove vexatious in Perón's deteriorating relationship with the Catholic Church. The sonorous voiceover, as the camera pans over the vast black-clothed crowds, states portentiously 'no one, even in the longest life, did as much as she did in the brief day of her passage. And the people know that. That is why the people are here.' A grandiloquent statement, but one that was not far removed from the truth.

CHAPTER 15

Life After Death

Es y será la guía de los trabajadores Argentinos y su legado iluminará por Siempre el camino de la justicia social.

    [*She is and will be the guide of the Argentine workers, and her legacy will illuminate forever the path of social justice.*]

(*From a plaque placed by the state workers' union on the tomb of Evita in 2002*)

T HE 'NECROLOGICAL BACCHANALE'[1] that followed Evita's death may have ended officially on 10 August, when Cardinal Copello said the final prayers over the body and the coffin was closed and transported solemnly to the CGT. However, this did not stop the outpouring of grief, the efforts to outdo others in honouring her memory or the long list of superlatives and glorifying titles heaped on her. Formal petitions were transmitted to the Vatican for her canonisation, including by the CGT – despite, as noted earlier, the fact that confessional trade unions were largely unknown in Argentina and the link between the unions and such formal Catholicism was limited. Indeed, while some of these expressions are those of popular religiosity, some were calculated by image-makers to make the link between Peronism and salvation, and others were used by priests such as Father Benítez who saw the opportunity to try to bring the working classes closer to the Church. Benítez himself would say that 'the CGT splendidly began the history of recovering the labouring world for Christ'.[2]

The petitions for canonisation, unsurprisingly, bore no fruit, in part given Evita's questionable past, her undoubted failure to renounce the riches of this world and the Church's close relations with the Argentine upper classes. However, given that the time since her death could be counted in hours and no post-mortem miracle could yet be attributed to her, the Vatican was left with a diplomatic and wholly reasonable excuse for its failure to declare her a saint. This did not stop others from doing so, calling her the 'martyr of labour', 'the guiding angel of the Fatherland', 'the standard-bearer of the suffering'. 'For us she was like a star of Bethlehem [...] And that Argentine woman, that important shrine for all those who suffer, burned up in her own fire. She died to save us. Like Christ.'[3] As hyperbolic as this language is, from Evita's own newspaper *Democracia*, it is nevertheless realistic to imagine that many of the beneficiaries of her largesse, her protection and her tireless efforts at the Foundation, most of them not regular churchgoers imbued with formal Catholic doctrine, might well have had reasons to believe that she deserved to be called a saint rather than a remarkable political leader.

With the funeral over and the need to return to some semblance of normality, life in Argentina began to go back to a more predictable rhythm, while Evita's corpse began its own peculiar half-life, attaining a longevity far greater than its owner did in this world. Ensconced on the second floor of the CGT building with Dr Ara, Evita's body, still covered in a white tunic, endured a long series of processes that at the end of a year would leave it impregnable and incorruptible. As Ara's eventual report in July 1953 would note, all of Evita's internal organs were intact and no tissues had been removed or wounds opened; the process had involved only two small incisions no longer visible after the embalming process was complete. Ara would spend many hours at the CGT with Evita every day, and her mother and sisters would often come to pray there, though other visitors were not permitted. Perón himself came once, after the embalming process was complete, expressing awe and perhaps some disquiet at the naturalness of his late wife, who appeared to him to be asleep and on the point of breathing. He would visit only twice more before departing for exile in 1955.

As the purported monument where Evita was to rest for all eternity had yet to be built (and never would be), Perón ordered that her body remain in the CGT for the time being, where Ara retained a key and maintained a steady guard over his 'creation'. Although there were no visitors beyond the family, on the 26th of every month a torch-lit march made its way to the CGT headquarters at 8.25 pm.

In the outside world, Argentina and the Perón government were no longer enjoying the glory of earlier years, although, as noted before, this was not entirely due to Evita's absence and much attributable to a changing international environment, a stagnant economy and stubborn inflation. The labour force's share of total income remained at historical highs, and real wages were still some 50 per cent above 1943 levels, but the wealth to be shared out was shrinking and, if it could not be made to expand, a general feeling that living standards were again declining was inevitable. While this trend pre-dated Evita's death, the loss of her charisma and communication skills may have helped to exacerbate public weariness with the downturn, and cemented the perception that the Peronist days of glory died with her.

In other respects, too, there was a perception that the government had lost the pulse of its loyalists. Perón promised, and initially attempted, to continue Evita's work at the Foundation, spending some afternoons there receiving innumerable petitions from endless queues of petitioners. However, he soon gave up the attempt, confiding that he could not stand it and could not understand how Evita had done so. In any case, apart from the fact that direct physical contact with a sea of pleading individuals was not his forte, and indeed provoked strong distaste in him, it was never practical to assume that the president of the nation would have the time to attend personally to thousands of individual requests for mattresses and sewing machines. Indeed, the fact that such a granular and personal task was beyond the possibilities of even a well-intentioned president was the reason cited by Evita for undertaking that role of 'bridge' between Perón and the people. With her death, that personal touch was irrevocably lost. Similarly, Evita had remained a spontaneous and fluid presence in a movement that had initially been improvisational and participatory but was now becoming increasingly structured and institutionalised. While this was part of an inevitable process and was not entirely connected with Evita's death, the government's declining dynamism also appeared linked (and, at least in part, was linked) to her departure.

The first 17 October after Evita's death, less than three months later, was marked by mourning crepe across the balcony of the Casa Rosada where she had so often been the focus of attention, and a recording of her violent 1 May speech was played to the crowd. Thereafter, Perón read out her 'Supreme Will', supposedly composed on her deathbed as part of the mysterious work 'My Message'. The actual document was contained in two separate and seemingly unconnected papers, one of which is only a few paragraphs long. The text read out on 17 October 1952, which may or may not be entirely authentic, was dated 29 June 1952 and begins with the 'Evitaesque' statement that

> I want to live eternally with Perón and with my people. This is my absolute and permanent desire and therefore my last will. Where Perón and my *descamisados* are, my heart will always be to love them with all the force of my life and all the fanaticism that burns my soul.

It goes on to repeat her conviction that she would remain with her husband and her people, asking them to continue to write to her at the Foundation as if she were still alive. As was her custom, the text enters into a virtual dialogue with the eventual listeners, calling on them to accompany Perón, 'my sun and my heaven', and reminding them that she would be with them on the road to victory against the oligarchy. She states that all her belongings, including royalties from her books, belong first to Perón and then to her people, proposing that they could be used to establish a permanent social aid fund, a source of grants for poor students and collateral for housing loans (although even the exaggerated claims of her enemies would not have suggested that her assets, ill-gotten or not, were so vast as to achieve all these things).

> While Perón lives, he can do what he wants with all my belongings [...] But after Perón, the only heir of my assets must be the people, and I ask the workers and the women of my people to demand by whatever means the fulfilment of this supreme will of my heart that loved them so much.[4]

Beyond the fact that this 'will' had no legal value, it reads far more as a political document than a private message or an actual testament, even for someone as public as Evita. As Joseph Page notes, the fact that it excludes her family is strange, and the overpowering panegyric in praise of Perón is unusually excessive even for Evita, although her impending death could explain this. It has been argued that, coming so shortly before her death, she was not able to resist a text imposed on her by another – most likely Perón. Her sisters Blanca and Erminda would claim the 'will' was a fake, whether for substantive reasons or because the family was left out. However, Evita was not notable for lacking resistance, even in extremis, and the version read out may have been selective but not forged. The emotional tone and the fanciful notion that her jewels and dresses could help untold thousands of people for years into the future are not out of keeping with her character or with the exalted mood on her in her last days. In any case, the question of a real and legally binding will was never resolved; her widower and her mother were legally entitled to half-shares in her estate, but in 1953 Doña Juana signed over her rights to Perón. In 1960 she would bring a lawsuit claiming to have signed under duress; the suit was only finalised after her death, when in 1972 a court decided the claim against Perón in favour of Evita's sisters Blanca and Erminda.

The reading of the 'will' did little to shift the negative course of the post-Evita era. By 1953, shortages of meat and the imposition of rationing, modest by European post-war standards but a scandal in a beef-addicted country like Argentina, created much disquiet, prompting an investigation by a military team into claims of speculation. That report concluded that some of Perón's close collaborators, though not the president himself, were using their position to engage in speculation, influence-peddling and other corrupt practices, leading Perón to promise publicly and violently in April 1953 that all those found guilty would be punished.

One of those named by the investigation was none other than the president's secretary and brother-in-law, Juancito Duarte. Juancito had always been seen as something of a chancer and sometimes on the margins of what was legitimate (although he was generally perceived as too intellectually limited to be a truly successful crooked businessman), as well as a playboy with a complicated romantic life involving several well-known actresses. However, his charm and his sister's protection had sustained him for some years, and their close relationship and her oversight probably also kept him on a somewhat more even keel emotionally and on a comparatively straight and narrow path; the loss of Evita also undermined his emotional, psychological and perhaps physical condition (he was widely rumoured to have syphilis). On 6 April, when Perón's speech made clear that he would not enjoy the president's protection any longer, Juancito resigned, and three days later he was dead with a gun in his hand and a bullet in his head. A purported suicide note expressed his loyalty and gratitude to Perón, saying that 'I came with Evita and I go with her, shouting Viva Perón!'

Rumour immediately took over as speculation grew that the death was not a suicide; an investigation by the military government that overthrew Perón would conclude that Duarte was murdered, that his death had not occurred where the body was found, and that the gun in his hand did not match the calibre of the bullet. If true, this would not be the first or last case in which an inconvenient figure in Argentine politics had been 'suicided', either by outright murder or by being coerced into killing themselves. Several statements would indicate that Raúl Apold had been involved and may even have wielded the gun, although Apold's career suggests a bully and a character assassin rather than a violent criminal.[5] Doña Juana, rightly or wrongly, was certainly convinced that her son did not commit suicide (purportedly on the grounds that he urged her to sign her share of Evita's estate to Perón in order to save him from death or exile), and would later blame Perón, however questionably, for the deaths of her two children. However, the post-1955 military authorities were anxious to discredit Perón, and many of their reports were no more above suspicion than statements by the Perón government. In practice, there were certainly those around Perón who would not have been above such methods of ridding the government of an embarrassing individual, especially one who knew where many figurative bodies were buried and could have proved more a danger than an embarrassment to many. However, here again, this possibility does not rule out suicide either, given Juancito's evident distress following his sister's death, a complicated love life and rumours of both ill health and large debts. What does seem highly unlikely is that Perón would have ordered his brother-in-law's death, a move that would have been out of character (although standing back and allowing 'providence' to resolve the problem would not). However, while this marked the apparent end of the influence of the 'Duarte clan', it did nothing to repair Perón's ragged relations with the military, still deteriorating despite the fact that the death of Evita had ostensibly removed one of its greatest irritants.

Days after Juancito's death, two bombs exploded during a speech by Perón outlining his anti-inflation plan, killing five. The response was sharp and violent, with Perón exhorting his supporters to respond; the headquarters of the Radical, Socialist and National Democratic Parties were attacked and burned, along with the Jockey Club and the offices of Socialist newspaper *La Vanguardia*, while a number of opposition members were imprisoned. This appeared to mark a shift towards greater authoritarianism, which had previously been more subtle but was now becoming more overt. This type of authoritarianism would become more of an issue the following year, when Perón began an ill-advised and seemingly pointless conflict with the Catholic Church – something that would play a role in his overthrow in 1955, if not the crucial one sometimes claimed.

Another source of tension with the Church was the Union de Estudiantes Secundarias (UES), a Peronist secondary school students' organisation designed to provide activities that potentially clashed with the extracurricular activities offered by church youth groups. More particularly, however, the issue at the heart of this conflict was Perón's own rumoured activities with the UES, which was claimed by the opposition to be no more than a means of procuring young girls for the president and his cronies. This story has been widely denied, although even Perón's open and public relations with the UES students, who used the president's residence for some activities, were considered at best undignified as he rode scooters around the grounds of the estate with them. Moreover, while many of the more lurid stories can be discarded, it was not possible to dismiss the existence of 14-year-old Nelly Rivas, who would become Perón's mistress until he fled Argentina in 1955. What many of these things point to, in fact, is an ageing president tired of the burdens of power and frustrated with the difficulties of a worsening economy after so many years in office.

In part due to the fact that political demonstrations were banned, Catholic marches began to attract strong support from non-religious quarters. Attendance at the Corpus Christi procession on 11 June 1955 far exceeded that at a rival government rally. Following the Mass, some 'Catholics' were reported to have burned an Argentine flag. Two days later, two bishops were expelled, prompting the Vatican to issue a sweeping excommunication apparently including Perón, although he was not named.

Five days later, the air force and navy attempted a coup, bombarding the Plaza de Mayo and the Casa Rosada. The CGT called unionists to come to the Plaza to defend the government, as it had done in 1945 – a futile gesture that led to at least 355 dead and 600 wounded as the air force indiscriminately bombed the people below. The army managed to restore order and Perón called for calm, but on the evening of 16 June mobs burned 12 churches in Buenos Aires and priests were attacked and arrested. Again, responsibility was disputed, although given the state of siege in force it is implausible that the perpetrators lacked government sanction. Although Perón thereafter sought to reduce tensions, making peace with the Church and overtures to the opposition, it was too late. Moreover, Perón himself could not keep up the attempt for long; on 31 August it was announced that he would resign, following which he improvised a violent speech to the crowds seeking to prevent his resignation, calling for violence to meet violence and promising that 'when one of ours falls, five of theirs will fall'.

The famous 'five for one' speech (the tone of which was in fact more like that of Evita than Perón) would prove the death knell for the government, forced out finally by a successful military coup on 22 September 1955. Perón would depart for a long and peripatetic exile, and he would be replaced first by General Eduardo Lonardi, who promised 'neither victors nor vanquished', and two months later by General Pedro Aramburu, a violent anti-Peronist who would take a very different position. His 'Liberating Revolution' would attempt to annihilate all traces of Perón, Evita and Peronism, intervening in the CGT, prohibiting newspapers from mentioning the names of the party or its founders (Perón would thereafter be referred to as the 'fugitive tyrant') and banning the Peronist march. Shockingly and uniquely for the time, a group of pro-Peronist officers who attempted an uprising in June 1956 were summarily executed, together with a group of workers not involved in the plan.

A key target for revenge was the Eva Perón Foundation. Although the late government had been absurdly thorough in putting the names and images of Perón and Evita on anything and everything to hand, the new regime was similarly thorough, tearing down anything bearing their names, images and associations (including the presidential residence). It became a crime for people to have photos of them in their homes, although many of the faithful disregarded this and continued to maintain their images. Most wastefully, that destruction ran to schools, hospitals and hostels constructed by the Foundation, including the halting of work on hospitals nearing completion. The trouble was taken to pick the embroidered initials 'FEP' out of the linens at Foundation hostels. However, the 'investigations' into the former first couple's nefarious doings, which produced lurid claims of malfeasance as well as legitimate accusations, failed to find evidence of theft from the Foundation, as had been widely expected; indeed, investigators noted that the Foundation had been spendthrift but not corrupt, and that the officers who intervened in it and took control of its assets were less scrupulous in their honesty than its original administrators. Inevitably, this storm of revenge did not have the desired effect of obliterating Perón and Evita; on the contrary, for many (especially the young), it had the effect of obliterating, or at least excusing, their worst defects while maintaining them as a constant presence and an ideal, icons of a better time of social justice and caring government.

In her sanctuary in the CGT, Evita was a key focus of this 'cleansing' obsession, and would soon begin a post-mortem peregrination that would last for two decades and encompass two continents. Three months after the coup, in December 1955 her body was taken from the CGT building by troops led by an intelligence officer, Colonel Carlos Moori Koenig, a virulent anti-Peronist who by all accounts became obsessed with the body to the detriment of his own mental health. The body, allegedly mutilated, urinated on and even subjected to sexual abuse, was eventually taken from Moori Koenig's care and hidden in the house of another officer, who purportedly became so concerned about Peronist attempts to retake it that he mistook his pregnant wife for an intruder and shot her dead. President Aramburu, a Catholic who did not shrink from ordering summary executions but who considered the cremation of a body to be a sin, ordered Evita's remains hidden in various places, including in a box labelled 'radio equipment'. This was stored in the office of an unsuspecting army officer, who received a nasty shock on opening it one day to check the contents. Eventually it would be left in an army truck in an unmarked box and moved from place to place for some six months. Everywhere it was left, flowers and candles mysteriously appeared around and under the truck, prompting hysteria and paranoia among military officers who somehow believed that 'that woman's' body had some supernatural destructive property. In fact, the lurid and widely discussed travails of Evita's body have little or nothing to do with Evita herself, and relatively little to do with the rank-and-file Peronists who still loved her. On the contrary, the destructive properties arose from the military's own hatred and paranoia, which apparently did not allow them to consider the relatively unsupernatural fact that some of their brothers in arms who knew where the body was (not) buried might be Peronist sympathisers (or at least individuals horrified at the despoiling of a corpse) who put candles and flowers there and alerted other sympathisers as to where Evita was hidden.

Determined that Evita's body should have a Christian burial, but not in a location that could become a shrine, Aramburu finally ordered its despatch to Europe, refusing to hand it over to Doña Juana on the theory that it would become a rallying point and a potential weapon. (Doña Juana and her remaining daughters were forced to go into exile in Chile.) Cautious to an extreme, Aramburu refused to be informed of its eventual disposal, in order to be able to say truthfully under duress, if necessary, that he did not know where Evita was. The information was placed in a sealed envelope to be opened only on Aramburu's death, and then left in the custody of his successors in the presidency. The body itself was sent to Milan, where it was buried under the name of María Maggi de Magistris, supposedly an Italian widow who had died in Argentina, and accompanied by an army officer posing as her brother. It would remain there until 1971, when it would again emerge as a political prize, precisely as Aramburu had feared.

Perón, meanwhile, passed through periods of exile in Paraguay, Nicaragua, Panama, Venezuela and the Dominican Republic before finally settling in Spain in 1960 (after being offered refuge in Cuba, where the Argentine revolutionary leader Ernesto 'Che' Guevara had convinced Fidel Castro that Perón was the leader of an Argentine brand of revolutionary socialism, despite Che's anti-Peronist origins – and the fact that if there was a leader of an Argentine brand of revolutionary socialism, it was Evita and not her cautious husband). During his travels he acquired a third wife, the dancer María Estela Martínez, known as Isabel, and a sinister secretary, José López Rega, a former police corporal who had once been on custody duty at the Secretariat of Labour. López Rega, known as Daniel, shared with Isabel a fascination with the esoteric and spiritism that would give him considerable power over her – and by extension, an increasingly elderly Perón, who in his lucid moments scoffed at 'Lopecito'. López Rega's hold over Isabel would become increasingly salient when, through an improbable set of circumstances, she became Perón's vice-president – the role denied to Evita – and then president on his death.

Both official repression and unofficial violence mounted following a new *coup d'état* in 1966. The largest of the Peronist guerrilla groups, the Montoneros, made themselves known in May 1970, when they kidnapped retired General Aramburu and subjected him to 'revolutionary justice' – that is, summary 'execution' following a 'popular trial' on charges that included the theft of Evita's body. The Montoneros subsequently adopted Evita as their standard-bearer, using the slogan '*si Evita viviera, sería montonera*' (if Evita were alive she would be a Montonero).

Hitherto Evita had largely been seen as 'la Señora', the defender of the poor and disenfranchised, but not altogether as a revolutionary, and the image was not necessarily one that sat well with an older generation of Peronists. However, not only her violent rhetoric but her absolute non-conformity with social and political norms and the freewheeling style with which she approached what needed to be done perhaps lent itself to this new interpretation – as did the fact that she and Perón had been banned for most of the lifetime of this new generation of activists. At the same time, many of the Montoneros came from a Catholic background (often former members of Catholic Action), and they tended to see Evita in quasi-religious rather than purely revolutionary terms; they had a penchant for martyrdom shared by both Catholicism and Peronism (in its enforced role as a resistance, opposition movement since 1955) and once referred to a dead guerrilla as 'the little Montonero virgin, daughter of Evita'.[6]

Not only did the Montoneros adopt Evita as their own, but a generation of young priests and Catholic activists also did so, although perhaps ironically they saw her primarily as a revolutionary rather than a quasi-religious figure. Citing her dictum that 'Peronism will be revolutionary or it will be nothing' and her overriding concern for the poor, the Third World Priests' movement in Argentina, notably the priests and catechists who worked in the shanty towns (*curas villeros*) recognised in Evita 'the prototype of a certain revolutionary militant: one who tenaciously executes the objectives of the revolution'[7], a reversion back to the image built around her in the early 1950s by Benítez and others as a bridge between the working classes and the Church, combined with the more revolutionary image adopted by the Montoneros.

In practice, the *curas villeros* discovered that most of their parishioners in the shanty towns were Peronists and admirers of Evita, and tended to take Peronism somewhat at its own valuation. They were aided in this by Perón's own writings from exile, far more revolutionary than his discourse when in power, and by the fact that, as already noted, Peronism had now become a movement of national resistance rather than power, with Evita a clear symbol of that resistance. This also helped to return Evita to her central role in Peronism, which Perón himself had been at some pains to downplay in the intervening years, never missing an opportunity to claim that she was his own 'creation' or 'invention'.

With the military government tottering, by 1971 General Alejandro Lanusse was negotiating more or less openly with Perón in a bid to stabilise an impossible situation and move towards open elections (in which Lanusse himself hoped to stand, but without grasping that Perón had similar ambitions). One of Lanusse's goodwill gestures in the course of those negotiations was the return of Evita. In September 1971 her coffin was removed from the Milan cemetery and transported to Madrid, where she was received by Perón, Isabel, López Rega and her surviving sisters Blanca and Erminda, with Dr Ara on hand to make necessary repairs. Thereafter, Evita was installed in the attic of the Perón residence to await developments.

In a bid to outfox Perón, Lanusse decreed in July 1972 that candidates for the 1973 elections must be resident in Argentina by 25 August 1972. While this was a challenge too far, Perón announced (via his current 'representative', one-time Lower House leader and Evita loyalist Héctor Cámpora) that he would return before the end of the year. He did so on 17 November, for the first time in 17 years, remaining less than a month – long enough to make a number of inflammatory statements and hold quasi-secret meetings with a range of political factions. With his candidacy barred, Perón designated the loyal Cámpora as the presidential candidate, and on 11 March 1973 Cámpora won nearly 50 per cent of the vote, to just over 21 per cent for Radical candidate Ricardo Balbín, bringing Peronism back to power for the first time since 1955.

Cámpora, who won on the dubious slogan of 'Cámpora to the presidency, Perón to power', was sworn in on 25 May. Although he was pressed into naming López Rega as social welfare minister (a post from which he would run a right-wing death squad, the Argentine Anti-Communist Alliance), Cámpora was to a large degree seen as over-sympathetic to the Peronist left, signing an amnesty for a number of political prisoners immediately on taking office. His good intentions would serve only to inflame violence between the movement's left and right, and to infuriate Perón, irate over the apparent growth of the left's influence in the government. It was announced that Perón would finally return to Argentina on 20 June 1973, a mythic event despite the fact that Evita remained in the Madrid attic.

Perón's return to Ezeiza airport would provide an opportunity for revenge by the Peronist right, slighted, as it believed, by the well-intentioned Cámpora. With an estimated 3 million people waiting near Ezeiza to see the leader, fighting broke out among left- and right-wing groups over control of the area near the platform where he would stand, apparently started by the well-armed right-wing shock troops. Neither the causes nor the final death toll were ever wholly clear, although estimates claim some 13 dead and 365 wounded, and many more tortured; Perón's aircraft eventually landed at Morón and the 'great event' evaporated. A few days later, Perón suffered a heart attack.

Despite (or because of) the signs that Perón was in deteriorating health, Cámpora obediently resigned the presidency on 13 July to pave the way for his return at the earliest possible moment. New elections were called for 23 September, won by a landslide by Perón, with Isabel as his running mate, to a large degree due to the hopes of a weary population that Perón would be able to end the violence that had been plaguing the country. However, his ill health, the intransigence of a range of actors and a tottering economic situation all militated against any stabilisation; if anything, right-wing attacks on left-wing activists were stepped up as Perón increasingly inveighed against the 'beardless youth' he had hitherto encouraged. After a pitched battle between left and right in the Plaza de Mayo at a May Day rally, the splits became unbridgeable. Perón died on 1 July 1974; his funeral, if less overwhelming than that of Evita, was nonetheless a sombre and massive event, as supporters and detractors alike contemplated the loss of a figure who had dominated politics for 30 years, and whose departure left a huge power vacuum at a time of apparently insurmountable strife.

With violence surging ever upwards and the hapless Isabel in the presidency (and López Rega effectively in power), the crisis deteriorated rapidly and politics again turned to the dead. In 1975 the Montoneros kidnapped Aramburu's body and announced that it would not be returned until Evita's body was brought back to Argentina. This Isabel later decided to do, as a last desperate throw of the dice as her presidency trembled and her order to the armed forces to 'annihilate subversion' brought the 'dirty war' to centre stage and the tactic of 'disappearances' to the forefront of counter-insurgency. Despite pressures from all sides, including her allies, Isabel refused to step down and call early elections, and sought to retain a measure of control by bringing Evita's body back (prompting the Montoneros to return that of Aramburu). Evita was again put on display in the chapel of the presidential residence in Olivos, next to the closed coffin of Perón (who had adamantly refused to be embalmed himself), but public interest in necrophilia appeared to have waned as the problems of the living became far more pressing than those of the dead.

The military junta that seized power on 24 March 1976 would be by far the bloodiest in Argentina's history, and its crackdown on subversion and all those suspected of even tangential relations with violence would lead to somewhere between 9,000 and 30,000 disappearances in its seven-year regime. Yet again, the dictatorship was faced with the intractable problem of what to do with the stubbornly indestructible body of Evita. Perhaps adopting a more pragmatic position than that of Aramburu (not least given the time that had elapsed), the junta determined that the body should be interred in the Duarte family tomb in La Recoleta cemetery, a bastion of the aristocracy where the Duartes in theory had no business being. A supposedly nuclear-proof metal vault was constructed below the above-ground tomb, and the body was finally laid to rest there, where it has remained to date.

Radical president Raúl Alfonsín's election in 1983 raised questions as to whether Peronism was a spent force following Perón's death, although the presidential elections in 1989 made clear that this was not the case. Marking the return of Peronism to the presidency for the first time since 1976, President Carlos Menem (1989–99) made little use of the symbolism surrounding Perón and Evita, which ran counter to his eventual neo-liberal policy. Having promised huge salary increases and a 'productive revolution' in his campaign, Menem would set about dismantling the Peronist legacy once in office, embarking on a programme of privatisations and embrace of foreign investors and US relations in particular, as well as the weakening of the trade unions and a sharp rise in both public debt and unemployment. For such a programme, the figures of Perón and Evita would have been inconvenient rather than enabling; Menem was also sharply criticised for allowing Alan Parker and Madonna to film part of *Evita* on the balcony of the Casa Rosada, considered by many (not just die-hard Peronists) to be virtually Evita's sacred territory.

However, while Evita was not a convenient emblem for Menem, she became again a symbol of rebellion against the neo-liberal, savage interpretation of capitalism under Menemism, and her name and face again graced social movements of the period, notably the '*piquetero*' protest movements of unemployed workers, the soup kitchens that opened for the poor and the community organisations in the shanty towns that tried to ensure a modicum of dignity and decent living among those who had lost hope amid rampant unemployment and the rise of drug trafficking that left many victims in its wake.

However, the new crisis that beset Argentina from 2001 arguably provided a new opportunity for Evita. After three years of recession and austerity, the government of Radical president Fernando de la Rúa collapsed amid violent protests and a state of siege in December 2001; his interim (Peronist) successors declared the largest sovereign default in history and devalued the currency, pegged at one-to-one with the dollar for a decade.

Amid the social crisis that followed, with poverty levels reaching over 50 per cent of the population, the image and name of Evita were widespread. The government itself, under interim president Eduardo Duhalde, spent the limited funds not earmarked for debt servicing on social programmes, including subsidies for unemployed heads of household in exchange for some public service. Many of those programmes operated under the auspices of Duhalde's wife, Hilda 'Chiche' Duarte, who during his governorship of Buenos Aires province had organised networks of women charged with surveying their neighbourhoods to identify necessities both personal, social and political. Her *'manzaneras'* were highly reminiscent of the *'censistas'* and *'delegadas'* that Evita had sent across the country to establish the women's party and to determine social needs at the neighbourhood level. Somewhat like those of the Eva Perón Foundation, these efforts were inadequately institutionalised and at best temporary measures, but proved effective to a degree in ameliorating short-term distress if not in establishing longer-term solutions.

Following the election of Peronist president Néstor Kirchner in 2003, Evita would return yet again to a more central symbolic role. Like Perón, Kirchner had a politically active and astute wife, Cristina Fernández de Kirchner, who during his term as governor of Santa Cruz province had become a provincial legislator, a member of the Lower House and a senator, before becoming senator for Buenos Aires province in 2005. Devoted to maintaining a glamorous personal style as well as a professional career, Cristina, as she would be known, lost few opportunities to draw parallels between herself and Evita, referring to her humble origins in a working-class family in La Plata (although, as a lawyer, she could hardly justify the sort of lofty disregard for intellectual and legal processes that Evita affected). Despite her own professional accomplishments, Cristina could also be interpreted as owing much of her political career to her husband – while he himself benefited from the presence of a charismatic and glamorous wife. As leftist student activists in the 1970s, both Kirchner and Cristina had been touched by the fervour surrounding Evita (although they were not involved in the more militant movements, despite later seeking to identify with the Montoneros), and Cristina in particular would prove far more 'Evitista' than 'Peronista'.

The governments of Kirchner and later Cristina (2007–15) took a number of initiatives that might have done honour to Evita, such as institutionalising a universal child allowance and other social benefits, as well as other initiatives that, while doing her less honour, fell within the sort of short-term, populist measures that characterised the Peronist movement both during and after Evita's lifetime. At the same time, no effort was spared to maintain the purported link between Evita and Cristina (who, according to some biographers, may also have been an illegitimate daughter). Two images of Evita, one smiling and one combative, with clenched fist, became *de rigeur* during Cristina's speeches, depending on the content of the speech. Her appearance on the 100-peso note made her almost ubiquitous.

In 2007, on winning the presidency to succeed her husband (whose role in essentially designating her as his successor and his continuing influence over her decision-making tended to belie the feminist triumph implied by her election victory), Cristina made reference to Evita in her inaugural speech, remarking that 'she perhaps deserved it more'.[8] It is questionable whether the presidency should be a matter of 'deserving' as opposed to other qualities and capabilities – and it is even more questionable that Evita would have fulfilled that role equitably and democratically. Nevertheless, in terms of effort, passion and her groundbreaking role, it is hard to argue with the suggestion that Evita 'perhaps deserved it more'.

 NOTES

Preface

1 J. Page in the introduction to E. Perón, *Evita: In My Own Words*, 43.

Introduction: The Personal is Political

1 Quoted in F. Pigna, *Evita, jirones de su vida*, 269.
2 L. Zanatta, *Eva Perón: una biografía política*, 2401 of 9276.
3 Quoted in F. Pigna, *Evita, jirones de su vida*, 271.
4 L. Zanatta, *Eva Perón: una biografía política*, 642.
5 G. Indij, *Perón Mediante: Gráfica peronista del periódo clásico*, 100–1.
6 J. M. Taylor, *Eva Perón: The Myths of a Woman*.

Chapter 1 Los Toldos

1 Quoted in S. Collier, *The Life, Music and Times of Carlos Gardel*, 33.
2 See, e.g., A. Dujovne Ortiz, *Eva Perón*, 10.
3 Interview with Raúl Suárez.
4 E. Perón, *La razón de mi vida*, 23.
5 Quoted in F. Pigna, *Evita, jirones de su vida*, 35.
6 *Ibid*, 147, 148.
7 E. Duarte, *Mi hermana Evita*, 22.
8 *Ibid*, 18.
9 E. Perón, *La razón de mi vida*, 15–16.
10 I. M. Cloppet, *Los orígenes de Juan Perón y Eva Duarte*, 296.
11 E. Duarte, *Mi hermana Evita*, 19.
12 *Ibid*, 20.

Chapter 2 Junín

1 www.junin.gov.ar
2 M. Sucarrat, *Vida sentimental de Eva Perón*, 18–19.

3   *Ibid*, 13; M. Navarro, *Evita*, 32; F. Pigna, *Evita, jirones de su vida*, 25.
4   Cited in M. Navarro, *Evita,* 35
5   M. Main, *Evita: The Woman with the Whip*, 20.
6   Arturo Jauretche, quoted in O. Borroni and R. Vacca, *La vida de Eva Perón*, 86–7.
7   Renata Coronado de Nuosi, quoted *ibid*, 28.
8   Irma Cabrera, quoted *ibid*, 315.
9   See, e.g., A. Dujovne Ortiz, *Eva Perón*, 29–30; M. Sucarrat, *Vida sentimental de Eva Perón*, 20–1.
10 V. Pichel, *Evita íntima*, 28–31.
11 J. Hedges, *Argentina: A Modern History*, 74.
12 Quoted in F. Pigna, *Evita, jirones de su vida*, 33.

Chapter 3 Buenos Aires

1   Quoted in J. Hedges, *Argentina: A Modern History*, xv.
2   See, e.g., J. Finkielman, *The Film Industry in Argentina*, 1.
3   See, e.g., O. Borroni and R. Vacca, *La vida de Eva Perón*, 49.
4   See, e.g., F. Pigna, *Evita, jirones de su vida*, 39.
5   Quoted in M. Sucarrat, *Vida sentimental de Eva Perón*, 82–3.
6   Quoted in F. Pigna, *Evita, jirones de su vida*, 42.
7   Quoted in *ibid*, 46.
8   M. Main, *The Woman with the Whip*, 40.
9   Quoted in O. Borroni and R. Vacca, *La vida de Eva Perón*, 90.
10 J. M. Bergoglio, *Biblia: diálogo vigente*, 316.
11 M. Carlson, *Feminismo!*, 179.
12 Quoted in M. Navarro, *Evita*, 86.
13 *Ibid*, 50.
14 Quoted in O. Borroni and R. Vacca, *La vida de Eva Perón*, 90.
15 M. Navarro, *Evita*, 53–4.
16 Quoted in F. Pigna, *Evita, jirones de su vida*, 53.
17 Testimonies of Eduardo del Castillo and Mauricio Rubinstein, in O. Borroni and R. Vacca, *La vida de Eva Perón*, 50, 49.
18 *Ibid*, 49.
19 See, e.g., V. Pichel, *Evita íntima*, 34–6.
20 Quoted in M. Sucarrat, *Vida sentimental de Eva Perón*, 67.
21 Quoted *ibid*, 83.
22 Quoted in F. Pigna, *Evita, jirones de su vida*, 54–5.
23 O. Borroni and R. Vacca, *La vida de Eva Perón*, 61.

Chapter 4 Radiolandia

1   *Radiolandia* was one of the biggest radio-related fan magazines of the day.
2   J. Finkielman, *The Film Industry in Argentina*, 106.
3   FO 118/755, 7 March 1947.

4   FO 118/786, 30 May 1950.
5   V. Pichel, *Evita íntima*, 46–7.
6   Quoted in F. Pigna, *Evita*, 61.
7   M. Sucarrat, *Vida sentimental de Eva Perón*, 88–90.
8   Quoted in O. Borroni and R. Vacca, *La vida de Eva Perón*, 64.
9   F. Pigna, *Evita*, 51.
10 The letter appears in M. Cichero, *Cartas peligrosas*, 25–7.
11 Quoted in N. Galasso, *Yo fui el confessor de Eva Perón*, 19.
12 V. Pichel, *Evita íntima*, 179.
13 *Ibid*, 50.
14 J. Hedges, *Argentina: A Modern History*, 58.
15 Domingo Mercante, quoted in F. Luna, *El 45*, 57.
16 *Antena*, June 1943, quoted in M. Navarro, *Evita*, 63.
17 Carmelo Santiago, quoted in O. Borroni and R. Vacca, *La vida de Eva Perón*, 87.
18 Quoted *ibid*, 90.
19 Quoted *ibid*, 64.

Chapter 5 Perón

1   See, e.g., H. Gambini, *Historia del peronismo*, 15.
2   See, e.g., J. Page, *Perón*; T. Eloy Martínez, *Las memorias del General*.
3   D. Kelly, *The Ruling Few*, 310.
4   Quoted in E. Pavón Pereira (ed.), *Diario secreto de Perón*, 18.
5   See E. Pavón Pereira, *Yo, Perón*.
6   See T. Eloy Martínez, *Las memorias del General*, 36.
7   See H. Vázquez-Rial, *Perón, tal vez la historia*, 106–27.
8   See A. Bellotta, *Las mujeres de Perón*, 42.
9   In *Las memorias del General*, p. 99, Eloy Martínez cites a statement by the sister of Aurelia Tizón to this effect, saying that medical tests indicated that Aurelia was physically able to have children, although she also states that Aurelia refused to submit Perón to similar tests, in order to spare him any possible embarrassment. Araceli Bellota (*Las mujeres de Perón*, 43–4) also claims that Perón suffered an accident in 1913 while performing gymnastics that produced 'a traumatic blow to the lower genital zone' that left him hospitalised for four days and could have affected his fertility.
10 E. Pavón Pereira (ed.), *Diario secreto de Perón*, 35.
11 A much fuller account of the incident appears in J. Page, *Perón*.
12 Quoted in A. Bellotta, *Las mujeres de Perón*, 47.
13 D. Kelly, *The Ruling Few*, 310.
14 P. Raccioppi, quoted in O. Borroni and R. Vacca, *La vida de Eva Perón*, 93.
15 See, e.g., C. Becker, *Domingo A. Mercante*, 1462 of 7451.
16 *Ibid*, 1472–84.
17 Quoted in E. Pavón Pereira (ed.), *Diario secreto de Perón*, 63.

Chapter 6 Political Earthquake

1 Quoted in E. Pavón Pereira (ed.), *Diario secreto de Perón*, 76.
2 Quoted in G. Varela, *Perón y Evita, Memoria íntima*, 527 of 638.
3 Quoted in E. Pavón Pereira (ed.), *Diario secreto de Perón*, 77.
4 *Ibid.*
5 Roberto Galán, quoted in A. Dujovne Ortiz, *Eva Perón*, 72–3.
6 Quoted in F. Pigna, *Evita, jirones de su vida*, 76; C. Becker, *Domingo A. Mercante*, 2067–127.
7 Quoted in E. Pavón Pereira (ed.), *Diario secreto de Perón*, 77.
8 A. Jauretche, quoted in O. Borroni and R. Vacca, *La vida de Eva Perón*, 85–6.
9 Quoted in V. Pichel, *Evita íntima*, 57.
10 R. Decker, *Arreando recuerdos*, 39.
11 Quoted in A. Bellotta, *Las mujeres de Perón*, 73.
12 Quoted in V. Pichel, *Evita íntima*, 59.
13 Quoted *ibid*, 59.
14 Quoted in N. Galasso, *Yo fui el confesor de Eva Perón*, 27.
15 *Ibid*, 50.
16 Quoted in F. Pigna, *Evita, jirones de su vida*, 85.
17 L. Zanatta, *Eva Perón, una biografía política*.
18 Quoted in E. Pavón Pereira (ed.), *Diario secreto de Perón*, 78.
19 *Ibid.*
20 *Ibid*, 77.
21 A. Jauretche, quoted in O. Borroni and R. Vacca, *La vida de Eva Perón*, 86.
22 *Ibid*, 85. This quotation has frequently been translated as 'girls who screw everybody', but this does not appear to be what the speaker was trying to convey, even though his tone is clearly derogatory. The slang word '*joder*' in Spanish is used in the sense of 'to screw' in Spain, but not in Argentina, where it is used in the sense of 'to annoy' or 'to bother'.
23 C. Becker, *Domingo A. Mercante*, 2200–20.
24 M. Navarro, *Evita*, 75–6.
25 Quoted in O. Borroni and R. Vacca, *La vida de Eva Perón*, 322.
26 M. Navarro, *Evita*, 77.
27 Quoted in F. Pigna, *Evita, jirones de su vida*, 91.
28 Quoted in O. Borroni and R. Vacca, *La vida de Eva Perón*, 75.
29 *Ibid*, 75.
30 Quoted in M. Navarro, *Evita*, 79.
31 Quoted *ibid*, 82.
32 Quoted in O. Borroni and R. Vacca, *La vida de Eva Perón*, 78.
33 *Ibid*, 80.

Chapter 7 Los Muchachos Peronistas

1 British Embassy, FO 118/755, 7 March 1947.
2 Quoted in H. Gambini, *Historia del peronismo*, 20.

3 Colonel Gerardo Demetro, quoted in O. Borroni and R. Vacca, *La vida de Eva Perón*, 114.

4 Irma Cabrera de Ferrari, quoted *ibid*, 222.

5 Gerardo Demetro, quoted *ibid*, 114–15.

6 *Buenos Aires Herald*, 20 September 1945.

7 D. Kelly, *The Ruling Few*, 307.

8 *Ibid*, 307.

9 S. Braden, *Diplomats and Demagogues*, 323, 331. The book itself leaves the over-riding impression that Mister Braden himself belonged to the latter category rather than the former.

10 M. Navarro, *Evita*, 100.

11 Quoted *ibid*, 102.

12 *The Times*, 10 October 1945.

13 E. Perón, *La razón de mi vida*, 37–8.

14 *Ibid*, 38.

15 Quoted in F. Pigna, *Evita, jirones de su vida*, 103.

16 Quoted *ibid*, 107.

17 D. Kelly, *The Ruling Few*, 309.

18 Quoted in M. Navarro, *Evita*, 110.

19 L. Monzalvo, *Testigo de la primera hora del peronismo*, 79.

20 J. D. Perón, *Diálogo entre Perón y las Fuerzas Armadas*, 26.

21 F. Luna, *El 45*, 513.

22 Quoted in O. Borroni and R. Vacca, *La vida de Eva Perón*, 111; V. Pichel, *Evita íntima*, 69–70.

23 *La Nación*, 27 July 1952.

24 Quoted in L. Monzalvo, *Testigo de la primera hora del peronismo*, 79.

25 See, e.g., C. Becker, *Domingo Mercante*, 3211 of 7451.

26 R. Decker, *Arreando recuerdos*, 50.

27 E. Perón, *La razón de mi vida*, 37.

28 *Ibid*, 41.

29 Quoted in V. Pichel, *Evita íntima*, 216.

Chapter 8 First Lady

1 See, e.g., V. Pichel, *Evita íntima*, 48.

2 N. Galasso, *Yo fui el confesor de Eva Perón*, 19.

3 O. Borroni and R. Vacca, *La vida de Eva Perón*, 130.

4 Adela Rodas, quoted in L. Lardone, *20.25, Quince mujeres hablan de Eva Perón*, 300, 330 of 2160.

5 Quoted in O. Borroni and R. Vacca, *La vida de Eva Perón*, 132–3.

6 L. Lagomarsino de Guardo, *Y ahora … hablo yo*, 87.

7 *Ibid*, 96, 94.

8 E. Perón, *La razón de mi vida*, 88.

9 Quoted in F. Chávez, *Eva Perón sin mitos*, 29.

10 L. Demitrópulos, *Eva Perón*, 83.
11 Quoted in M. B. Karush and O. Chamosa (eds), *The New Cultural History of Peronism*, 58.
12 British Embassy, FO 118/755, 23 June 1947
13 Quoted in V. Pichel, *Evita íntima*, 85.
14 Quoted *ibid*, 89.
15 Quoted *ibid*, 98.
16 Quoted in O. Borroni and R. Vacca, *La vida de Eva Perón*, 144.
17 *Ibid*, 144.
18 D. James, *Resistance and Integration: Peronism and the Argentine Working Class 1946–1976.*

Chapter 9 Europe

1 FO 118/755, 10 February 1947.
2 *Ibid*, 7 March 1947.
3 A. Dujovne Ortiz, *Eva Perón: A Biography*, 195–6.
4 L. Zanatta, *Eva Perón, una biografía política*, 796 of 9278.
5 FO 188/755, 7 March 1947.
6 *Ibid*, 8 May 1947; 19 May 1947.
7 *Ibid*, 120.
8 *Ibid*, 34–6.
9 *Ibid*, 119–20.
10 V. Pichel, *Evita íntima*, 115.
11 Quoted *ibid*, 116–17.
12 L. Lagomarsino de Guardo, *Y ahora … hablo yo*, 126.
13 *Ibid*, 127.
14 *Ibid*, 128–9.
15 Quoted in F. Pigna, *Evita, jirones de su vida*, 147.
16 Quoted in V. Pichel, *Evita íntima*, 121–2.
17 Quoted *ibid*, 112.
18 Quoted in F. Pigna, *Evita, jirones de su vida*, 151.
19 Quoted in V. Pichel, *Evita íntima*, 126.
20 Quoted in F. Pigna, *Evita, jirones de su vida*, 156.
21 Quoted in J. Page, *Perón*, 193.
22 Quoted in M. Navarro, *Evita*, 168.
23 Quoted in F. Pigna, *Evita, jirones de su vida*, 165.
24 *Buenos Aires Herald*, 29 June 1947.
25 See, e.g., F. Pigna, *Evita, jirones de su vida*, 161–2.
26 J. D. Perón, *Del poder al exilio*, 77. A somewhat different account appears on page 42.
27 *Buenos Aires Herald*, 28 June 1947.
28 US Department of State, Despatch from Vatican City, 1 July 1947, Microfilm 341, Reel 2:0311.
29 *Ibid*, Microfilm 312.

30 U. Goñi, *The Real Odessa*, 136. Skorzeny, who rescued Mussolini from arrest in 1943 and who was later acquitted of war crimes charges in 1947, would live in Argentina in the late 1940s, where he purportedly became Eva's bodyguard and even her lover. The latter point is not credible and appears to be part of the 'black myth' gossip machine, as well as perhaps a result of bragging by Skorzeny himself: the idea that Eva, who was claimed to have little interest in sex and who demonstrably adored her husband and his cause, would have spent time with lovers amid her frenetic activities as first lady and as Evita is not believable.

31 R. Rein, *Los muchachos peronistas judíos*, 13.

32 Quoted in J. Hedges, *Argentina: A Modern History*, 132.

33 L. Zanatta, *Eva Perón, una biografía política*, 2362 of 9278.

34 N. Galasso, *Yo fui el confesor de Eva Perón*, 38–9.

35 V. Pichel, *Evita íntima*, 136.

36 L. Zanatta, *Eva Perón, una biografía política*, 2401 of 9278.

37 Quoted in L. Lagomarsino de Guardo, *Y ahora … hablo yo*, 158.

38 U. Goñi, *The Real Odessa*, 137.

39 Quoted in L. Lagomarsino de Guardo, *Y ahora … hablo yo*, 165.

40 *Ibid*, 144.

41 *Ibid*, 150.

42 Quoted in O. Borroni and R. Vacca, *La vida de Eva Perón*, 201.

43 Quoted in N. Galasso, *Yo fui el confesor de Eva Perón*, 29.

Chapter 10 Enter Evita

1 Quoted in F. Pigna, *Evita, jirones de su vida*, 176.

2 M. Navarro, *Evita*, 206.

3 José Presta, quoted in O. Borroni and R. Vacca, *La vida de Eva Perón*, 141.

4 Quoted in F. Chávez, *Eva Perón sin mitos*, 132.

5 O. Borroni and R. Vacca, *La vida de Eva Perón*, 139; V. Pichel, *Evita íntima*, 174–5.

6 Quoted in F. Pigna, *Evita, jirones de su vida*, 180.

7 Raúl Salinas, quoted in O. Borroni and R. Vacca, *La vida de Eva Perón*, 145–6.

8 C. Becker, *Domingo Mercante*, 5016 of 7451.

9 Raúl Salinas, quoted in O. Borroni and R. Vacca, *La vida de Eva Perón*, 146.

10 *Ibid*, 1719 of 7451.

11 O. Borroni and R. Vacca, *La vida de Eva Perón*, 134

12 Quoted *ibid*, 146.

13 Fermín Arenas Luque, quoted *ibid*, 145.

Chapter 11 Las Muchachas Peronistas

1 Quoted in J. Hedges, *Argentina*, 169.

2 E. Sábato, *El otro rostro del peronismo*, 41–3.

3 British Embassy, FO 118/757, 11 September 1947.

4 Quoted in F. Pigna, *Evita, jirones de su vida*, 197.

5 María Teresa Morini, quoted in L. Lardone, *20.25, Quince mujeres hablan de Eva Perón*, 1661 of 2160.
6 British Embassy, FO 118/757, 11 September 1947.
7 British Embassy, FO 118/766, 14 January 1947.
8 British Embassy, FO 118/757, 25 August 1947.
9 *Ibid*, 11 September 1947.
10 Avilia Nieves Rodríguez de Bilbao, quoted in L. Lardone, *20.25, Quince mujeres hablan de Eva Perón*, 652 of 2160.
11 Berta Feiguin de Ferrari, quoted *ibid*, 828 of 2160.
12 María Teresa Morini, quoted *ibid*, 1710 of 2160.
13 Rosa Huespe de Morandini, quoted *ibid* 1920 of 2160.
14 Adela Rodas, quoted *ibid*, 340 of 2160.
15 Avilia Nieves Rodríguez de Bilbao, quoted *ibid*, 848 of 2160.
16 Idilia Palacín, quoted *ibid*, 1187, 1206 of 2160.
17 Speech of 17 January 1949, in E. Perón, *Discursos completos Tomo 1*, 109 of 6916.
18 E. Perón, *La razón de mi vida*, 202.
19 Speech of 17 January 1949, in E. Perón, *Discursos completos Tomo 1*, 122 of 6916.
20 Speech of 21 January 1949, in E. Perón, *Discursos completos Tomo 1*, 189 of 6916.
21 British Embassy, FO 118/757, 12 December 1947.
22 E. Perón, *Evita, su legado de puño y letra*, 121, 126.
23 Speech of 1 May 1949, in E. Perón, *Discursos completos Tomo 1*, 416 of 6916.
24 Quoted in N. Milanesio, *Cuando los trabajadores salieron de compras*, 140, 143, 202.
25 See, e.g., M. Zaida Lobato, et al., 'Working-Class Beauty Queens Under Peronism', in M. Karush and O. Chamosa (eds), *The New Cultural History of Peronism*, 171–208.
26 E. Elena, 'Peronism in "Good Taste"', in M. Karush and O. Chamosa (eds), *The New Cultural History of Peronism*, 209–38.
27 British Embassy, FO 118/766, 23 July 1948.
28 N. Milanesio, *Cuando los trabajadores salieron de compras*, 113, 124.
29 Speech of 5 January 1949, in E. Perón, *Discursos completos Tomo 1*, 48 of 6916.
30 *Ibid*, 10 January 1949, 66 of 6916.
31 *Ibid*, 90 of 6916.
32 See, e.g., E. Elena, *Dignifying Argentina*, 94, 48.
33 Quoted in F. Pigna, *Evita, jirones de su vida*, 203–4.
34 Quoted in M. Navarro, *Evita*, 220.
35 Speech of 21 January 1949, in E. Perón, *Discursos completos Tomo 1*, 154 of 6916.
36 Speech of 1 May 1949, in E. Perón, *Discursos completos Tomo 1*, 380 of 6916.
37 Quoted in C. Barry, *Evita Capitana*, 171.
38 Quoted in O. Borroni and R. Vacca, *La vida de Eva Perón*, 218.
39 A. C. Macri, *Mi biografía política*, 9.
40 E. Perón, *La razón de mi vida*, 277–8.
41 H. Castañeira, in Castañeira et al., *Legisladoras de Evita*, 34.
42 Avilia Nieves Rodríguez de Bilbao, quoted in L. Lardone, *20.25, Quince mujeres hablan de Eva Perón*, 652 of 2160.

43 Berta Feiguin de Ferrari, quoted *ibid*, 752 of 2160.
44 C. Becker, *Domingo Mercante*, 5764 of 7451.
45 British Embassy, FO 118/786, 29 May 1950.

Chapter 12 The Foundation

1 Quoted in, among other sources, V. Pichel, *Evita íntima*, 143.
2 E. Perón, *La razón de mi vida*, 165.
3 Decree 11.116, September 1946, quoted *ibid*, 144.
4 See, e.g., M. Navarro, *Evita*, 258.
5 E. Perón, *Discursos completos*, 134 of 6916.
6 See V. Pichel, *Evita íntima*, 161.
7 Quoted in A. Dujovne Ortiz, *Eva Perón*, 291.
8 Berta Feiguin de Ferrari, quoted in L. Lardone, *20.25, Quince mujeres hablan de Eva Perón*, 752 of 2130.
9 Susana Fiorito, quoted *ibid*, 2000 of 2130.
10 Alcira Villegas de Albornoz, quoted *ibid*, 521 of 2160.
11 Helvicia Scamara de Gianola, quoted *ibid*, 1005 of 2160.
12 Quoted in V. Pichel, *Evita íntima*, 145.
13 C. Barry, et al., *La Fundación Eva Perón*, 27.
14 Quoted *ibid*, 192.
15 Quoted *ibid*, 59.
16 Atilio Renzi, quoted in O. Borroni and R. Vacca, *La vida de Eva Perón*, 298.
17 Quoted in O. Borroni and R. Vacca, *La vida de Eva Perón*, 324.
18 Quoted *ibid*, 226.
19 E. Perón, *La razón de mi vida*, 169.
20 C. Barry, et al., *La Fundación Eva Perón*, 91.
21 Quoted in M. Navarro, *Evita*, 244.
22 Susana Fiorito, quoted in L. Lardone, *20.25, Quince mujeres hablan de Eva Perón*, 1981 of 2130.
23 Delia Maldonado, quoted in L. Demitrópulos, *Eva Perón*, 129.
24 F. Chávez, *Eva Perón sin mitos*, 158.
25 Quoted in. O. Borroni and R. Vacca, *La vida de Eva Perón*, 223.
26 V. Pichel, *Evita íntima*, 155.
27 Quoted in V. Pichel, *Evita íntima*, 181.
28 Quoted in E. Perón, *Discursos completos*, 109 of 6916
29 *Ibid*, 122 of 6916.
30 *Ibid*, 189 of 6916.
31 British Embassy, FO 118/786, 6 June 1950.
32 E. Perón, 23 August 1949, in *Discursos completos*, 1946 of 6916.
33 *Ibid*, 1982 of 6916.
34 *Ibid*, 2001 of 6916.
35 Quoted in V. Pichel, *Evita íntima*, 157.
36 Quoted in F. Chávez, *Eva Perón sin mitos*, 144.
37 British Embassy, FO 118/756, 29 August 1947; FO 118/786, 30 May 1950.

Chapter 13 Mortality

1 O. Borroni and R. Vacca, *La vida de Eva Perón*, 237.
2 Quoted *ibid*, 238.
3 Quoted in F. Pigna, *Evita, jirones de su vida*, 278–9.
4 Quoted *ibid*, 250.
5 P. Ara, *El caso Eva Perón*, 45.
6 Quoted in F. Chávez, *Eva Perón en la historia*, 7–9.
7 Quoted in M. Navarro, *Evita*, 269.
8 Quoted in F. Pigna, *Evita, jirones de su vida*, 252.
9 British Embassy, FO 118/786, 2 June 1950.
10 E. Perón, *La razón de mi vida*, xx.
11 British Embassy, FO 118/786, 2 June 1950.
12 E. Perón, 10 January 1949, in *Discursos completos II*, 78 of 6916.
13 British Embassy, FO 118/766, 14 January 1948.
14 Américo Ghioldi, quoted in V. Pichel, *Evita íntima*, 194.
15 Quoted *ibid*, 196.
16 Quoted *ibid*, 200.
17 Quoted in J. Hedges, *Argentina: A Modern History*, 130.
18 *Ibid*.
19 Quoted *ibid*, 131.
20 Quoted in V. Pichel, *Evita íntima*, 201.
21 Quoted *ibid*, 198.
22 Quoted *ibid*, 199.
23 British Embassy, FO 118/786, 30 May 1950.
24 *Ibid*, 2 June 1950.
25 *Ibid*.
26 Quoted in M. Navarro, *Evita*, 280.
27 Quoted in F. Pigna, *Evita, jirones de su vida*, 257.
28 F. Chávez, *Eva Perón sin mitos*, 172.
29 O. Borroni and R. Vacca, *La vida de Eva Perón*, 257.
30 British Embassy, FO 118/809, 20 September 1951.
31 F. Pigna, *Evita, jirones de su vida*, 262.
32 V. Pichel, *Evita íntima*, 206, 212.
33 Quoted in F. Pigna, *Evita, Jirones de su vida*, 266.
34 Quoted *ibid*, 215.
35 Quoted in O. Borroni and R. Vacca, *La vida de Eva Perón*, 261.
36 *Discurso de Eva Perón en el Cabildo Abierto del Justicialismo del 22 de agosto de 1951*, http://biblioteca.educ.ar.
37 *Ibid*.
38 Quoted *ibid*, 262.
39 Quoted *ibid*.
40 Quoted *ibid*, 264.

Chapter 14 Immortality

1 Susana Fiorito, quoted in L. Lardone, *20.25, Quince mujeres hablan de Eva Perón*, 1972 of 2160.
2 Alicia Villegas de Albornoz, quoted *ibid*, 502 of 2160.
3 Quoted in M. Navarro, *Evita*, 283.
4 *Ibid*, 289.
5 Quoted *ibid*, 290.
6 Quoted in V. Pichel, *Evita íntima*, 226.
7 See, e.g., N. Castro, *Los últimos días de Eva*.
8 Quoted in O. Borroni and R. Vacca, *La vida de Eva Perón*, 299.
9 Quoted in F. Pigna, *Evita, jirones de su vida*, 290.
10 Quoted *ibid*, 269–70.
11 Quoted in M. Navarro, *Evita*, 292.
12 Quoted in O. Borroni and R. Vacca, *La vida de Eva Perón*, 270–2.
13 Quoted *ibid*, 296.
14 Quoted in F. Pigna, *Evita, jirones de su vida*, 298.
15 Quoted in M. Navarro, *Evita*, 301.
16 Quoted in O. Borroni and R. Vacca, *La vida de Eva Perón*, 278–9.
17 Quoted in V. Pichel, *Evita íntima*, 252.
18 Quoted in O. Borroni and R. Vacca, *La vida de Eva Perón*, 281.
19 Quoted *ibid*, 291.
20 See, e.g., N. Castro, *Los últimos días de Eva*, 280–308.
21 Quoted in V. Pichel, *Evita íntima*, 258–9.
22 E. Perón, *Evita: In My Own Words*, 49.
23 M. E. Alvarez, *La enfermera de Evita*, 42.
24 F. Chávez, *Eva Perón sin mitos*, 192–3.
25 E. Perón, *Evita: In My Own Words*, 75.
26 *Ibid*, 79.
27 *Ibid*, 57, 66.
28 Quoted in M. Navarro, *Evita*, 311.
29 Quoted in O. Borroni and R. Vacca, *La vida de Eva Perón*, 292–3.
30 Quoted in M. Navarro, *Evita*, 311.
31 Quoted in O. Borroni and R. Vacca, *La vida de Eva Perón*, 294.
32 Quoted *ibid*, 316.

Chapter 15 Life After Death

1 J. Hedges, *Argentina: A Modern History*, 150.
2 H. Benítez, 'Eva Perón', *Revista de la Universidad de Buenos Aires*, July–September 1952, 20–1.
3 *Democracia*, 30 July 1952.
4 Quoted in O. Borroni and R. Vacca, *La vida de Eva Perón*, 285–6.

5 J. Camarasa, *La última noche de Juan Duarte*, 245–52.

6 Quoted in R. Gillespie, *Soldiers of Perón*, 118.

7 Movimiento de Sacerdotes para el Tercer Mundo – Mendoza, *Nuestra opción por el peronismo*, 80.

8 Quoted in A. Bellotta, *Eva y Cristina*, 11.

 # BIBLIOGRAPHY

Documents

Reports on the political situation in Argentina from the British Embassy, Buenos Aires, to the Foreign Office, 1944–1947, 1950–1951. Public Record Office, Kew, archives FO 118/728–749; FO 118/755–757; FO 118/766; FO 118/786; FO 118/809.

United States Department of State. Confidential Central Files on Argentina, 1945–1955. Microfilm Collection, London School of Economics, Microfilms 336, 337, 341, 342.

United States Department of State. 'Consultation Among the American Republics With Respect to the Argentine Situation'. Washington DC, February 1946.

Biographies

Barnes, J. *Evita: First Lady, A Biography of Eva Perón*. Grove Press, New York 1978.

Becker, C. *Domingo A. Mercante: A Democrat in the Shadow of Perón and Evita*. Kindle edition, 19 September 2005.

Bellotta, A. *Las mujeres de Perón*. Editorial Planeta, Buenos Aires 2005.

_____ *Eva y Cristina, La razón de sus vidas*. Editorial Vergara, Buenos Aires 2012.

Borroni, O. and Vacca, R. *La vida de Eva Perón. Tomo I – testimonios para su historia*. Editorial Galerna, Buenos Aires 1970.

Chávez, F. *Eva Perón sin mitos*. Editorial Fraterna, Buenos Aires 1990.

Collier, S. *The Life, Music, and Times of Carlos Gardel*. University of Pittsburgh Press, Pittsburgh, PA 1986.

Cowles, F. *Bloody Precedent: The Perón Story*. Frederick Muller, London 1952.

De Elía, T. and Quieroz, J. P. *Evita: An Intimate Portrait of Eva Perón*. Thames and Hudson, London 1997.

Demitrópulos, L. *Eva Perón*. Ediciones del Dock, Buenos Aires 2010.

Dujovne Ortiz, A. *Eva Perón: A Biography*. Warner Books, London 1997.

Foss, C. *Juan and Eva Perón*. Sutton Publishing, Stroud 2006.

Fraser, N. and Navarro, M. *Evita: The Real Lives of Eva Perón*. Andre Deutsch, London 1997.

Main, M. *Evita: The Woman with the Whip*. Corgi Books, London 1996.

Navarro Gerassi, M. *Evita*. Editorial Edhasa, Buenos Aires 2005.

Page, J. *Perón*. Random House, New York 1983.

Pigna, F. *Evita, jirones de su vida*. Editorial Planeta, Buenos Aires 2012.

Rein, R. *In the Shadow of Perón: Juan Atilio Bramuglia and the Second Line of Argentina's Populist Movement*. Stanford University Press, Stanford 2008.

Sucarrat, M. *Vida sentimental de Eva Perón*. Editorial Sudamericana, Buenos Aires 2006.

Taylor, J. M. *Eva Perón: The Myths of a Woman*. University of Chicago Press, Chicago 1979.

Vázquez Rial, H. *Perón: tal vez la historia*. Editorial El Ateneo, Buenos Aires 2005.

Zanatta, L. *Eva Perón: Una biografía política*. Kindle edition, 1 January 2012.

Books

Adamovsky, E. *Historia de la clase media argentina*. Editorial Planeta, Buenos Aires 2009.

Ara, P. *El caso Eva Perón*. CVS Ediciones, Madrid 1974.

Barreiro, H. *Juancito Sosa: el indio que cambió la historia*. Avellaneda Tehuelche, Buenos Aires, 2000.

Barry, C., Ramacciotti, K. and Valobra, A. (eds). *La Fundación Eva Perón y las mujeres; entre la provocación y la inclusión*. Editorial Biblos, Buenos Aires 2008.

_____ *Evita Capitana. El Partido Peronista Femenino 1949–1959*. Eduntref, Buenos Aires 2014.

Benedetti, H. A. (ed.). *Las mejores letras de tango*. Editorial Planeta, Buenos Aires 2003.

Benítez, H. 'Eva Perón', *Revista de la Universidad de Buenos Aires*, Vol. III (July–September 1952), 20–1.

_____ *La aristocracia frente a la revolución*. Copyright L. E. Benitez de Aldama, Buenos Aires 1953.

Bergoglio, J. M. *Biblia: diálogo vigente*. Editorial Planeta, Buenos Aires 2013.

Camarasa, J. *La enviada*. Editorial Planeta, Buenos Aires 1998.

_____ *La última noche de Juan Duarte*. Editorial Sudamericana, Buenos Aires 2003.

Carlson, M. *Feminismo! The Woman's Movement in Argentina from its Beginnings to Eva Perón*. Academy Chicago Publishers, Chicago 1988.

Castiñeiras, N. Fundación Eva Perón. *Desde sus inicios hasta la muerte de Evita*. Instituto Nacional de Investigaciones Históricas Eva Perón, Buenos Aires (undated).

_____ Fundación Eva Perón. *Sufragio femenino: algo más que un trámite legal*. Instituto Nacional de Investigaciones Históricas Eva Perón, Buenos Aires 2007.

Castro, N. *Los últimos días de Eva. Historia de un engaño*. Editorial Sudamericana, Buenos Aires 2014.

Cichero, M. *Cartas peligrosas*. Editorial Planeta, Buenos Aires 1992.

Cloppet, I. M. *Los orígenes de Juan Perón y Eva Duarte*. ALFAR Editora, Buenos Aires 2010.

Crassweller, R. *Perón and the Enigmas of Argentina*. W. W. Norton & Co., New York 1987.

Cromwell, J. *Hitler's Pope: The Secret History of Pius XII*. Viking Press, New York 1996.

Elena, E. *Dignifying Argentina: Peronism, Citizenship and Mass Consumption*. University of Pittsburgh Press, Pittsburgh, PA 2011.

Eloy Martínez, T. *Santa Evita*. Editorial Planeta, Buenos Aires 1995.

Ferioli, N. *La Fundación Eva Perón*. Centro Editor de América Latina, Buenos Aires 1990.

Finkielman, J. *The Film Industry in Argentina: An Illustrated Cultural History*. McFarland & Company, Jefferson, North Carolina 2004.

Gambini, H. *Historia del peronismo*. Editorial Planeta, Buenos Aires 1999.

Garbely, F. *El viaje del Arco Iris*. Editorial El Ateneo, Buenos Aires 2003.

Gillespie, R. *Soldiers of Perón: Argentina's Montoneros*. Oxford University Press, Oxford 1982.

Goñi, U. *The Real Odessa*. Granta Books, London 2003 (revised edn).

Hedges, J. *Argentina: A Modern History*. I.B.Tauris, London 2015.

Indij, G. *Perón Mediante: Mráfica peronista del periódo clásico*. La marca editadora, Buenos Aires 2006.

James, D. *Resistance and Integration: Peronism and the Argentine Working Class 1946–1976*. Cambridge University Press 1988.

Jauretche, A. *Política nacional y revisionismo histórico*. A. Peña Lillo Editor, Buenos Aires 1982 (6th edn).

Karush, M. B. and Chamosa, O. (eds). *The New Cultural History of Peronism*. Duke University Press, London 2010.

Luna, F. *El 45*. Editorial Sudamericana, Buenos Aires 1986.

_____ *Perón y su tiempo*. Editorial Sudamericana, Buenos Aires 1993 (2nd ed).

Mercado, S. *El inventor del peronismo*. Kindle edition, 16 April 2013.

_____ *El relato peronista*. Kindle edition, 1 August 2015.

Milanesio, N. *Cuando los trabajadores salieron de compras*. Siglo Veintiuno Editores, Buenos Aires 2014.

Movimiento de Sacerdotes para el Tercer Mundo – Mendoza. *Nuestra opción por el peronismo*. Buenos Aires 1975 (2nd edn).

Mugica, C. *Peronismo y cristianismo*. Editorial Merlin, Buenos Aires 1973.

Murmis, M. and Portantiero, J. C. *Estudio sobre los origenes del peronismo*. Siglo XXI, Buenos Aires 1971.

Perón, E. *Clases y escritos completos 1946–1952, Tomo III*. Editorial Megafón, Buenos Aires 1987.

Perón, J. *Peronist Doctrine*. Partido Peronista Consejo Superior Ejecutivo, Buenos Aires 1952.

_____ *La hora de los pueblos*. Editorial Norte, Buenos Aires 1968.

_____ *Diálogo entre Perón y las Fuerzas Armadas*. Editorial Jorge Mar, Buenos Aires 1973.

_____ *Libro Azul y Blanco*. Editorial Freeland, Buenos Aires 1973.

_____ *La comunidad organizada*. Editorial Pleamar, Buenos Aires 1975.

_____ *Política y estrategia: No ataco, critico*. Editorial Pleamar, Buenos Aires 1983.

_____ *Habla Perón*. Ediciones Realidad Política, Buenos Aires 1984.

_____ *Manual del Peronista*. Ediciones Los Coihues, Buenos Aires 1988.

_____ *Evita: In My Own Words*. The New Press, New York 1996.

_____ *Conducción política*. Editorial Megafón, Buenos Aires 1998.

_____ *Evita. Su legado de puño y letra 1946–1952*. Ediciones Fabro, Buenos Aires 2010.

_____ *Discursos completos, Tomos I y II*. Kindle edition, 12 September 2012.

_____ *Historia del Peronismo*. Ediciones Fabro, Buenos Aires 2012.

Pigna, F. *Los mitos de la historia argentina 3: De la ley Sáenz Peña a los albores del peronismo*. Editorial Planeta, Buenos Aires 2006.

_____ *Los mitos de la historia argentina 4: La Argentina peronista*. Editorial Planeta, Buenos Aires 2008.

_____ *Los mitos de la historia argentina 2: De San Martín a 'el granero del mundo'*, Editorial Planeta, Buenos Aires 2009 (3rd edn).

Plotkin, M. B. *Mañana es San Perón: A Cultural History of Perón's Argentina*. Kindle edition, 1 October 2002.

Poder Ejecutivo Nacional. *Libro Negro de la Segunda Tiranía*. Editorial Integración, Buenos Aires 1958.

Posse, A. *La pasión según Eva*. Editorial Planeta, Buenos Aires 2005.

Potash, R. (ed.). *The Army and Politics in Argentina 1928–1945 – Yrigoyen to Perón*. Stanford University Press, Stanford 1969.

_____ *The Army and Politics in Argentina 1945–1962 – Perón to Frondizi*. Athlone Press, London 1980.

_____ *Perón y el GOU*. Editorial Sudamericana, Buenos Aires 1984.

Rein, R. *Los muchachos peronistas judíos*. Editorial Sudamericana, Buenos Aires 2015.

Sampay, A. (ed.). *Las Constituciones de la Nación Argentina (1810–1972)*. Editorial Universitaria de Buenos Aires 1975.

Sirvén, P. *Perón y los medios de comunicación*. Kindle edition, 1 January 2012.

Turner, F. C. and Miguens, J. E. (eds). *Juan Perón and the Reshaping of Argentina*. University of Pittsburgh Press, Pittsburgh, PA 1983.

Memoirs

Alvarez, M. E. *La enfermera de Evita*. Instituto Nacional de Investigaciones Históricas Eva Perón, Buenos Aires 2010.

Braden, S. *Diplomats and Demagogues*. Arlington House, New York 1971.

Cafiero, A. *Mis diálogos con Evita*. Grupo Editor Altamira, Buenos Aires 2002.

Castañeira, H., Alvarez Seminario, M. and Chico de Arce, E. *Legisladoras de Evita*. Instituto Nacional de Investigaciones Históricas Eva Perón, Buenos Aires 2014.

Decker, R. *Arreando recuerdos*. Instituto Nacional de Investigaciones Históricas Eva Perón, Buenos Aires 2008.

Duarte, E. *Mi hermana Evita*. Ediciones Centro de Estudios Eva Perón, Buenos Aires 1972.

Eloy Martínez, T. *Las memorias del General*. Editorial Planeta, Buenos Aires 1996.

Galasso, N. *Yo fui el confesor de Eva Perón. Conversaciones con el Padre Hernán Benítez*. Homo Sapiens Ediciones, Buenos Aires 1999.

Kelly, Sir D. V. *The Ruling Few*. Hollis and Carter, London 1953 (4th ed.).

Lagomarsino de Guardo, L. *Y ahora … hablo yo*. Editorial Sudamericana, Buenos Aires 1996.

Lardone, L. *20.25. Quince mujeres hablan de Eva Perón*. Kindle edition, 1 July 2012.

Macri, A. C. *Mi biografía política*. Instituto Nacional de Investigaciones Históricas Eva Perón, Buenos Aires 2006.

Monzalvo, L. *Testigo de la primera hora del peronismo: memorias de un ferroviario*. Editorial Pleamar, Buenos Aires 1974.

Pavón Pereira, E. (ed). *Diario secreto de Perón*. Sudamericana-Planeta, Buenos Aires 1986.

——— *Yo, Perón*. Editorial Milsa, Buenos Aires 1993.

Perón, E. *La razón de mi vida*. Ediciones Peuser, Buenos Aires 1951.

Perón, J. D. *Yo, Juan Domingo Perón, Relato Autobiográfico*. (Torcuato Luca di Tena, Luis Calvo, Esteban Peicovich (eds). Editorial Planeta, Barcelona 1976.

——— *Del poder al exilio*. Ediciones Sntesis, Buenos Aires 1982.

——— *La fuerza es el derecho de las bestias*. Editorial Volver, Buenos Aires 1987.

Pichel, V. *Evita íntima*. Editorial Planeta, Buenos Aires 1993.

Reyes, C. *La farsa del peronismo*. Sudamericana-Planeta, Buenos Aires 1987.

Sabato, E. *El otro rostro del peronismo*. Imprenta López, Buenos Aires 1956 (2d ed).

Varela, G. *Perón y Evita, memoría íntima*. Kindle edition, 1 January 2014.

Interviews

Father Hernán Benítez, SJ, confessor to Eva Perón, rector of the University of Buenos Aires and spiritual adviser to the Eva Perón Foundation.

Dr Floreal Forni, sociologist, former member of *Acción Católica*.

Father Fernando Storni, SJ, director of Centro de Investigaciones y Acción Social, Buenos Aires.

Raúl Suárez, cousin of the Duarte family.

INDEX